Disarmament and Development

Disarmament and Development

A DESIGN FOR THE FUTURE?

STUART A. BREMER

*State University of New York
at Binghamton*

BARRY B. HUGHES

The University of Denver

PRENTICE HALL, *Englewood Cliffs, New Jersey 07632*

Library of Congress Cataloging-in-Publication Data

Bremer, Stuart A.
    Disarmament and development : a design for the future? / Stuart A.
Bremer, Barry B. Hughes.
        p.   cm.
    Includes bibliographical references.
    ISBN 0-13-215039-5
    1. Disarmament--Economic aspects. 2. Economic development.
3. Economic assistance. 4. International economic relations.
I. Hughes, Barry   II. Title.
HC79.D4B74 1990
338.9--dc20   89-38968
                                                   CIP

Editorial/production supervision and
  interior design: Carole R. Crouse
Cover design: Bruce Kenselaar
Manufacturing buyer: Bob Anderson

© 1990 by Prentice-Hall, Inc.
A Division of Simon & Schuster
Englewood Cliffs, New Jersey 07632

Printed in the United States of America

10 9 8 7 6 5 4 3 2 1

ISBN 0-13-215039-5

PRENTICE-HALL INTERNATIONAL (UK) LIMITED, *London*
PRENTICE-HALL OF AUSTRALIA PTY. LIMITED, *Sydney*
PRENTICE-HALL CANADA INC., *Toronto*
PRENTICE-HALL HISPANOAMERICANA, S.A., *Mexico*
PRENTICE-HALL OF INDIA PRIVATE LIMITED, *New Delhi*
PRENTICE-HALL OF JAPAN, INC., *Tokyo*
SIMON & SCHUSTER ASIA PTE. LTD., *Singapore*
EDITORA PRENTICE-HALL DO BRASIL, LTDA., *Rio de Janeiro*

To Karl W. Deutsch,
without whom there would be
no GLOBUS model

Contents

8

Global Momentum and Policy Leverage, 175

Appendix A: The Use of Simulation, 192

Appendix B: The GLOBUS Model, 214

References, 225

Index, 233

Preface

Among the most important issues on the international agenda in the last decade of the twentieth century are the continuing danger of devastating international conflict and the persistence of poverty over most of the globe. This book not only addresses both of these issues, it also examines possible linkages between them. The volume is by no means unique in recognizing the centrality of these issues or in considering their relationship. In fact, the United Nations convened an International Conference on the Relationship between Disarmament and Development in August and September 1987. Prestigious international commissions have studied the issues and presented their recommendations. Libraries abound with volumes calling for action on either or both issues.

This book stands apart from most of this discussion in two important ways. First, it subjects to scientific investigation a widespread and highly popular understanding of the relationship between the two issues and policies of arms control and foreign assistance. Second, it seeks to make that scientific investigation intelligible to a wide audience of students, policymakers, and interested citizens. It is simple to fall back on calls for international goodwill and action; it is more difficult to analyze systematically the possible consequences were specific actions taken. The issues are too complex and the dangers of false steps too high for us to rely on simple analyses or well-intentioned exhortations.

We bring two tools to this more systematic analysis. First, a review of the accumulated attention by a generation or more of scholars to aspects of each issue helps us assess the state of current knowledge. More specifically, it allows us to link the political debates about policy options to our knowledge of political and economic processes, both international and domestic.

Second, we bring to bear the first large-scale computer simulation of those same global political and economic processes. We do not burden the reader of this book with the technical details of GLOBUS or its use (that information is summarized in our appendixes and presented in great detail elsewhere). Instead, the model serves to structure an integrated, internally consistent analysis of the issues. And the fabric of the model once again carries much of the relevant knowledge accumulated by scientists.

The emphasis here on computer simulation and scientific analysis should not be read as implying that we feel this book can represent the last word on these issues or that it is clearly superior to prior or subsequent studies. We have jointly devoted nearly forty years to the development and use of computer simulations. That effort has impressed upon us the limitations of the approach and the fragility of conclusions based on it. Nonetheless, we believe that carefully specified, large-scale, and well-documented computer models have much to offer. That is especially true when one realizes that the normal policy analysis is based on compromises among, or a limited synthesis of, the mental models employed by individual analysts, each of which is frequently partial, internally inconsistent, and very poorly documented.

We owe debts to a large number of individuals and institutions. The most important is to the development team of the GLOBUS computer model. The social scientists on that team were Peter Brecke, Thomas Cusack, Wolf-Dieter Eberwein, Brian Pollins, Dale Smith, Stuart Bremer, and Barry Hughes. The primary computer scientists were Walter Gruhn and Peter Rindfuß. Many support staff members and assistants made the work possible. Among them we especially wish to thank Konstanza Prinzessin zu Löwenstein for administrative efforts.

The GLOBUS modeling project was part of the research initiated by Karl Deutsch when he became director of the International Institute for Comparative Social Research at the Wissenschaftszentrum Berlin (WZB) in 1976. It is for that action, and to express appreciation for the wider influence he has had on our professional lives, that we dedicate this book to him. Stuart Bremer served as team leader throughout the project and became leader of the GLOBUS Research Group in 1985.

Both model development and manuscript preparation took place at the Wissenschaftszentrum Berlin, which provided generous support over the entire period. The WZB was a nearly ideal environment in which to undertake large-scale, interdisciplinary research. Work on the book was also done at the Graduate School of International Studies, University of Denver.

Many individuals commented on early drafts of this book and on the papers that preceded it. We especially benefited from the advice of Harold Guetzkow and James Ray. We want to thank Harold Guetzkow additionally for the consistent support that he has provided to world modeling and the GLOBUS project, and for the personal support he has long given both of us.

The readers of this volume are being asked to undertake a serious study of important issues. Although we have attempted to make the analysis as straightforward as possible, study of it will not be simple. Thus, our last expression of appreciation is to those of you who have allocated your time to the effort.

Stuart A. Bremer
Barry B. Hughes

*Disarmament
and
Development*

A Divided World

CHAPTER 1

GLOBAL CLEAVAGES

Two major cleavages divide the world: the continuing conflict between the East and the West blocs, in which both groupings of nations devote large portions of their resources to preparing for a war that they hope will never occur and that they know they cannot win, and the large differences in wealth between the nations of the North and the South. The first of these is primarily political in nature but with economic implications; the second is usually seen as economic but always has an important political component as well.

Obviously, other cleavages divide the world. Oil producers and oil consumers regularly confront each other (in the market, if not in any specific international forum) on the issue of energy prices. The land-locked countries found common ground in opposition to the coastal states during the Law of the Sea negotiations. Moslem states sometimes share attitudes and positions that challenge non-Moslem states. And a wide variety of regional conflicts—especially the four-decade-old one surrounding the state of Israel, but including periodic clashes in all parts of the world (for example, India and Pakistan, Libya and Chad, Britain and Argentina, Vietnam and China)—frequently give rise to large-scale global divisions.

Very often, however, these lesser conflicts, especially the regional ones, spread globally along the two major "fault lines." And the primary

1

BOX 1-1   *Country Categorizations*

Some of the most basic terms in this volume, the country groupings created by global cleavages, are subject to alternative and ambiguous definitions. These are the meanings intended here and their relationship to other important categorizations.

West   The economically advanced and politically democratic countries of North America and Western Europe plus Japan, Australia, and New Zealand. Many, but not all, of these countries are members of the North Atlantic Treaty Organization (NATO) military alliance. **First World** is equivalent to West.

East   The communist countries, especially the Soviet Union and those of Eastern Europe. Since the deterioration of relationships between China and the Soviet Union, China is most often classified with the South. **Second World** is equivalent to East. Most of these countries are members of the Warsaw Treaty Organization (WTO) military alliance.

North   The economically more advanced countries of the world, both those with capitalist and those with communist economic/political systems. Most of these are in the northern part of the globe, although Australia and New Zealand are not. The category generally incorporates East and West.

South   The economically **less developed countries (LDCs)** of the world, most of which are in the southern part of the globe (although many, like Ethiopia and Honduras, are north of the equator). **Third World** is equivalent to South. Some identify an economically stagnant subgroup of the South as the **Fourth World.** Still another subgroup of the South are the **newly industrialized countries (NICs),** which include Taiwan, South Korea, Hong Kong, Singapore, Brazil, Mexico, Spain, Israel, and Yugoslavia.

divisions hold the greatest threat to global order. The East-West division, reinforced by enormous nuclear arsenals, actually threatens the survival of human life on the planet. The North-South conflict, and the struggles for independence that have characterized it during much of the post–World War II period, has cost a tremendous number of lives (for example, France and Algeria or Belgium and the Congo), while often interacting in complex ways with the East-West conflict (the United States and Vietnam, the Soviet Union and Afghanistan). It continues to pit the richest half of the world against the most populous.

The interaction of the two global conflict dimensions is, in fact, the focal point of this book. Before moving to the argument, however, we need to sketch the background and refresh memories concerning the cleavages.

THE EAST-WEST CONFLICT: PAST, PRESENT, AND FUTURE

The origins of the East-West conflict lie in the breakdown of the World War II coalition that defeated Germany, Italy, and Japan. The falling-out among the Allies, who had never been completely compatible, most notably between the United States and the Soviet Union, was a great disappointment to those who had anticipated a postwar global order of great power cooperation. For many others it was predictable. In fact as early as 1835, the French social observer Alexis de Tocqueville, in a famous passage, appeared to see the roots of the cold war:

> There are at the present time two great nations in the world, which started from different points, but seem to tend towards the same end. I allude to the Russians and the Americans. Both of them have grown up unnoticed; and while the attention of mankind was directed elsewhere, they have suddenly placed themselves in the front rank among the nations, and the world learned of their existence and their greatness at almost the same time. . . . Their starting point is different and their courses are not the same; yet each of them seems marked out by the will of heaven to sway the destinies of half the globe. (de Tocqueville 1945, vol. 1:452)

More modern political theory would also have predicted the splintering of the coalition. Grand coalitions, whether organized to defeat Napoleon in the early nineteenth century or Hitler in the twentieth, frequently dissolve when the conflict ends; when the opposing power has been neutralized, the members often fall to fighting among themselves.[1] Still others foresaw the opposition in the clash of ideologies. How, they wondered, could Western representative democracy and market economic systems ever coexist peacefully in the world with totalitarian communism? In the East, they wondered how democratic socialism could coexist with bourgeois democracy and imperialistic capitalism.

As early as 1946, when the Soviet forces missed their March timetable for withdrawal from Iran and the United States protested strongly, the tension between the two powers emerged openly. In 1947 Great Britain abandoned its historic role in Greece and Turkey, and the movement into that vacuum by the United States on the basis of the Truman Doctrine[2] reinforced the increasingly apparent bipolar structure of European military issues (Feis 1970).

[1] Riker (1962) elaborated this behavior as the minimum winning coalition principle. He explained the breakdown of grand coalitions and the establishment of groupings barely large enough to secure victory as rational behavior in the face of limited spoils and the desire to obtain the largest share possible.

[2] Speaking before Congress in March 1947, President Truman declared that the policy of the United States was to "support free people who are resisting subjection by armed minorities or outside pressures." The first funds allocated on the basis of this doctrine were provided to Greece and Turkey.

The East-West division took on a more formal structure with the creation of the North Atlantic Treaty Organization in 1949 and of the Warsaw Treaty Organization in 1955. The polarization became global as the alliance structures of the superpowers expanded into the Third World. After the capture of power by a communist government in China in 1949, a close working relationship developed between that country and the Soviet Union. During the 1952–1960 Eisenhower administration, the United States developed a chain of alliances around the world to give form to its containment policy. That policy grew out of the argument made by George F. Kennan in 1947 that the West should oppose any geographic expansion of Soviet influence and encourage modification of Soviet behavior.

The two superpowers seldom dared to confront each other militarily, and the few occasions in which they did, such as in Berlin and Cuba, represent the most severe crises of the postwar period. More often, the confrontation came through proxies. The West responded quickly to the invasion of South Korea by the communist North Korean government and the first major superpower proxy war was under way by 1950. The list of countries that subsequently fought on behalf of the superpowers, or whose civil wars served as their battlegrounds, has steadily lengthened and includes, among many others, Greece, Malaysia, Vietnam, Cuba, Angola, Ethiopia, Somalia, Libya, Lebanon, Nicaragua, Afghanistan.

By the middle of the 1950s, the world truly was divided into East and West. The rigidity and the extent of that division began to erode almost as soon as it was completed. In the East, Hungary and, less violently, Poland protested Soviet dominance in 1956; the split with China came in 1961. In the West, the 1955 Bandung conference of twenty-nine Asian and African states established a formally nonaligned grouping of states; in 1960 the French exploded their own nuclear bomb, and they withdrew from the integrated NATO command in 1966; the 1960s was a decade in which many African states gained independence from the European colonizers and in which the Latin American states continued to distance themselves from United States leadership. Nonetheless, the fundamental East-West division of the world remains pervasive, and in the North, it still structures most political-military relationships.

The dominant manifestation of the East-West division has always been and remains a military competition. The arms race has had both strategic (nuclear) and conventional components. On the strategic level, Russett (1983a) has divided it into four stages. The 1945–1952 period was one of *American nuclear monopoly*. Although the Soviets exploded their first atomic bomb in 1949, only four years after the Americans, it took some time before a credible operational capability emerged.

Between 1953 and 1957, the United States maintained *clear nuclear dominance.* It had a large stockpile of weapons, an intercontinental bomber force, and forward bases in Europe with which to threaten the Soviet Union. United States *predominance* extended further in time, from 1958 through 1966. Dominance and predominance made possible the United States strategy of massive retaliation—the threat to use full nuclear retaliation in response to even conventional transgressions by the U.S.S.R. While the Americans could with some credibility threaten a nuclear first strike in retaliation for conventional military action by the Soviets, the U.S.S.R. lacked sufficient capability to make equally believable first-strike threats. The aborted attempt to install missiles in Cuba during 1962 illustrated the importance the Soviets placed on remedying this imbalance. By 1967, a decade after the launching of Sputnik, the Soviets could no longer be considered second-class in nuclear capabilities. The period since 1967 has been one of *essential equivalence.* While in the early 1980s the United States retained a 20- to 30-percent advantage in warhead numbers and a less easily measured advantage in accuracy of delivery vehicles and security of them, the Soviets had captured as much as a 50-percent advantage in total nuclear megatonnage.[3] Although Russett did not make the distinction, the period since 1980 can usefully be separated from that of the 1970s because the Soviet Union now has at least *parity,* given its advantage in megatonnage and the near equality in warheads (see Figure 1-1).

Although they require a highly advanced technology to acquire, strategic forces are remarkably inexpensive power. By many estimates, the superpowers spend only about 10 percent of their defense budget on nuclear weaponry, while that weaponry is what truly makes them superpowers.[4] For instance, China has armed forces about the size of the U.S.S.R.'s and nearly twice that of the American forces; yet, it falls short of superpower status because it lacks a comparable nuclear ca-

---

[3] At the end of 1987, one study calculated the Soviet megatonnage to be 110 percent greater than United States levels (or the United States to be 52 percent behind the Soviets). Adjusting for size of warheads, the advantage drops to 67 percent. See the *Bulletin of Atomic Scientists* (January/February 1988:56). Putting aside the balance of megatonnage, even the comparison of warhead numbers is complex and uncertain. Because of the high level of secrecy surrounding the warhead count, a standard approach is to base the estimate on the number of launchers deployed, assuming the maximum number of warheads allowed by treaty. Should the counting rules proposed in the Strategic Arms Reduction Talks (START) replace those of the Strategic Arms Limitation Talks (SALT), the current warhead counts for the United States and the U.S.S.R. would move to 9,789 and 10,595, respectively, eliminating the apparent United States superiority of Figure 1-1 (IISS 1988:230–232).

[4] In 1985, the United States spent $31 billion on strategic forces from a total defense budget of $305 billion (Collins 1985:295). Portions of other budgetary categories, such as research and development, almost certainly augment that strategic spending somewhat.

pability. Even more than the acquisition of nuclear weapons itself, the requirement of sophisticated and secure delivery vehicles has restricted access to the superpower club.[5] The advances by China, Israel, Brazil, and others in missile technology are thus fundamentally important.

East-West conventional forces have been more nearly balanced throughout the post–World War II era. In the European "theater," the Warsaw Pact has maintained superiority. In 1987 it was estimated that the Warsaw Pact tank force outnumbered NATO forces by more than 2 to 1 and that their interceptor/fighter advantage was nearly 3 to 1 (IISS 1987:231). Balances on many other weapons systems are comparable. The East has also held a consistent manpower advantage in Europe, about 20 percent on the Central Front (Belgium, Luxembourg, the Netherlands, the two Germanys, Poland, and Czechoslovakia) and 5 percent overall. There are some reasons to believe, however, that the

FIGURE 1–1   American and Soviet Intercontinental Warhead Delivery Capability. *Source:* Holdren 1986:47; IISS 1987:225.

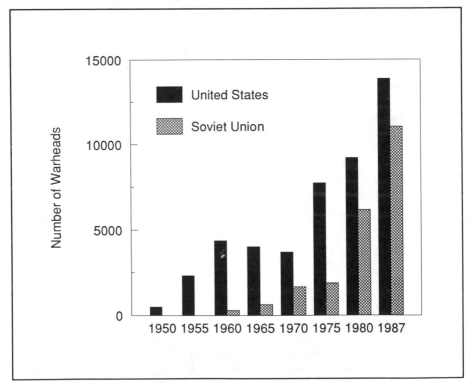

[5] In 1987 China had a total of 6 ICBMs, while the superpowers each possessed 1,000 or more. In addition, it did have 60 IRBMs and 2 nuclear missile-launching submarines with a total of 24 missiles (IISS 1987:145).

overall conventional balance is closer than those figures indicate. The technological lead is held by the West on most systems. And according to estimates of the U.S. Arms Control and Disarmament Agency, the total defense expenditures of NATO countries exceeded those of Warsaw Pact countries in 1984 by about 10 percent (ACDA 1987:2–4).

Historically, arms control efforts have fallen into a number of categories. Periodically, highly idealistic calls for general and complete disarmament echo even from the highest levels. It was proclaimed as a world goal by a unanimous vote of the United Nations General Assembly in 1960. Soviet arms control negotiators have frequently called for it. A variation was proposed by Woodrow Wilson at the end of World War I as his Point Four—namely, that arms be reduced to the lowest point consistent with domestic safety.

Most arms control negotiations, and all successful agreements, fall into partial or limited approach categories. For instance, qualitative limitations attempt to restrict or eliminate specific weapon types. A 1925 Geneva Protocol banned the use of biological and chemical weapons. An updated U.N. Convention in 1972 carried the long title Prohibition of the Development, Production, and Stockpiling of Bacteriological (Biological) and Toxin Weapons and Their Destruction. In 1987 the United States and the Soviet Union signed a treaty to eliminate intermediate nuclear forces, the first time in the cold-war era that a bilateral agreement was reached for the destruction of an entire class of weapons.

Quantitative approaches have a long history as well. In 1922 the Washington Naval Conference resulted in an agreement restricting the construction of battleships and aircraft carriers for ten years to the following ratios: U.S., 5; U.K., 5; Japan, 3; France, 1.67; Italy, 1.67. The 1972 Strategic Arms Limitations Talks (SALT I) resulted in an agreement that obligated the United States and the Soviets to restrict development of antiballistic missile (ABM) defense systems to two sites. The SALT I agreement also provided five-year interim limits on the number of strategic launchers. The 1979 SALT II treaty (never ratified by the United States but observed for many years by both parties) placed upper limits of 2,250 on the total numbers of delivery vehicles, namely ICBMs, SLBMs, heavy bombers, and ASBMs.

Another frequently proposed approach involves budgetary limitations. Russia proposed a five-year freeze in defense spending at the 1899 Hague Conference; Germany rejected it because their spending levels were lower. In 1963–1965 the United States and the U.S.S.R. discussed reciprocal reductions in defense spending. In 1973 Foreign Minister Gromyko proposed 10 percent cuts by both sides before the United Nations.

Interestingly, the defense budgets of both the United States and the Soviet Union did decline after 1952–1953, at the end of the Korean War (Russett 1983a:10). Moreover, even after the completion of the demobilization, the budgets of the two superpowers continued to decrease as a percentage of GNP into the early 1960s. In the case of the United States, where the decline was considerably more pronounced, the defense budget dropped from 10.1 percent of GNP in 1958 to 7.2 percent in 1965 (a nearly 30 percent reduction in seven years), at which point the Vietnam War began to reverse the erosion of spending (Collins 1985:300).

To date, East-West arms control efforts have focused almost exclusively on strategic weapons. The 1963 Partial Nuclear Test Ban Treaty prohibited nuclear explosions in the atmosphere, in outer space, and under water. The 1968 Nuclear Nonproliferation Treaty sought to prevent the acquisition of nuclear weapons by nonnuclear states. SALT I and SALT II were mentioned earlier, as was the 1987 agreement on Intermediate Nuclear Forces. The continuing Strategic Arms Reduction Talks (START) may result in a 50 percent reduction in the nuclear arsenals of the two superpowers.

Again, the large expenditures are on conventional weapons and forces. Potentially important steps toward agreements affecting conventional balances were taken by means of the 1975 Conference on Security and Cooperation in Europe (CSCE) and the 1984 Conference on Confidence and Security Building Measures and Disarmament in Europe (CDE). The Final Act of the CSCE (also known as the Helsinki Accords) obliged both sides to provide advance notice and international observation of large military exercises. The 1986 Stockholm agreement extended that obligation, including a clause permitting signatories to carry out inspections on territory of the other when violations are suspected.

Almost simultaneously with the beginning of the CSCE, Mutual and Balanced Force Reduction (MBFR) discussions began over conventional forces in Europe. Although these have yet to produce any agreements, the Soviets have conceded the need for asymmetrical reductions (Brown 1988:120). Both sides have a desire to make progress in the conventional arena because of the high cost of those forces; support for conventional forces in Europe costs the United States as much as $170 billion annually.

The future of East-West relations and the probability of significant arms control agreements is impossible to predict. Those relations depend on systemic developments and on factors internal to the two superpowers.

The systemic or global context is perhaps the easier to assess. Both the United States and the Soviet Union have been affected by the rising role of Japan and other Pacific Basin countries in the global economy and by the economic resurgence of an increasingly united Europe. Leaders of the superpowers have repeatedly tied the superior economic performance of Japan in part to its lesser defense burden. The declining primacy of the United States in the world economy no longer occupies the attention of only a relatively small number of academics, but instead captures that of a mass American audience. The diffusion of interest in the issue has awakened a wide-ranging discussion of policy options that might retard, if not reverse, the decline. Reductions in defense spending figure prominently in proposals. The popularity of Paul Kennedy's work (1988) on the rise and fall of great powers derives in part from the already existing acceptance of his thesis linking the decline of empire to overextension in defense.[6]

The nature of the internal reactions to the changing external environment is more difficult to assess. The willingness to reconsider long-standing negotiation positions exhibited by General Secretary Gorbachev illustrates the importance, and the essential unpredictability, of internal factors. He significantly altered Soviet positions on verification of arms control agreements, a sticky point that had long held up negotiations. Buttressing his individual role has been the weakness of the Soviet economy in recent years and widespread societal recognition of the need for external technology and economic restructuring. In the United States, the change of leadership from Reagan to Bush could have equally substantial consequences for the East-West relationship. The consistently large trade deficits of the 1980s have elicited societal demands for reconsideration of the American world role. That reassessment could conceivably lead to either military retrenchment or military intransigence; in reaction against the Reagan administration's defense buildup, reductions in arms spending seem more probable.

Returning briefly to the systemic context, the economic rise on the heels of Japan of a number of formerly "underdeveloped" countries, especially Taiwan and South Korea but also Brazil, Mexico, and perhaps even the People's Republic of China, has contributed greatly to the self-evaluations being undertaken by the superpowers. The relationship of East-West and North-South issues has thus become even more complex. It is to the North-South division of the globe that we now turn.

THE NORTH-SOUTH GAP: PAST, PRESENT, AND FUTURE

The relationship between North and South globally has still not been completely severed from its deep colonial roots. The historic core of the North, a small number of West European countries, engaged in two major waves of imperialism (the first beginning in the fifteenth century and the second at the end of the nineteenth century), which brought

---

[6] See earlier, more academic developments of the theme in Modelski (1978) and Gilpin (1981).

almost the whole of the globe under their control.[7] The loss of imperial territories by Germany and the Ottoman Empire at the end of World War I initiated a decline of colonialism. The disintegration of the British, Spanish, French, Belgian, and Portuguese empires during the last half of the twentieth century has eliminated nearly all direct political-military control by Northern states over Southern ones.

The emergence from the ruins of World War II of two fundamentally anti-imperialist powers, the United States and the Soviet Union, greatly accelerated the decline.[8] The emergence in the 1950s of the nonaligned-country group assisted less developed countries (LDCs) in seeking independence by balancing the East and the West in their cold war.

Although political-military issues remain important in the North-South relationship, and the Southern opposition to any vestige of direct military intervention is understandably intense, the focal point of the North-South conflict has shifted to an economic agenda. Debates now rage more often over the nature of the economic relationship between North and South. The countries of the Organization of Economic Cooperation and Development (OECD) constitute the Northwest of the globe—that is, the market-oriented, economically developed states. They generally portray the existence of more developed countries as a nearly unalloyed benefit for the South—as a source of technology and a market for goods. These countries, led by the United States, established global economic institutions at the end of World War II that were aimed at facilitating extensive growth in trade around the world. The General Agreement on Tariffs and Trade (GATT) has provided a framework within which successive rounds of negotiation have dramatically lowered tariff barriers to trade. Similarly, the countries of the West established the International Monetary Fund (IMF) to support trade through stable currencies and monetary transaction patterns.

Other perspectives, extensive in the South and reinforced by the socialist states of the Northeast, present a variety of arguments portraying the North-South relationship as a neocolonial one in which economic dominance has replaced political-military control and in which trade is often a mechanism to maintain that dominance. Raul Prebisch, a United

---

[7] McNeill (1982) presents a useful analysis of how advances in European military technology and organizational technology allowed that to occur.

[8] There are, of course, many arguments that both superpowers have been fundamentally imperialist. The case against the United States is made by Williams (1959), Horowitz (1971), Kolko (1972), Magdoff (1969), and others. The continental empire building of both countries attests to that historic bent, and their global economic and military roles still provide bases for such characterization. Nonetheless, both played active roles in the political self-determination movements of the postwar decades, with the United States even opposing its own allies on occasion (as during the Suez invasion by France and Britain in 1956).

Nations economist from Argentina, argued that North-South trade un-
equally benefits the South because the prices of Southern export goods
(largely agricultural commodities and raw materials) are in long-term
decline relative to the prices of goods (mostly manufactures) that the
LDCs import.[9] This trend toward adverse terms of trade calls into
question the beneficial implications for the South of increasing trade
with the North. At the least, it suggests the desirability of compensation
to the South—for instance preferential access to Northern markets while
simultaneously allowing Southern states to protect their "infant industries."

Another line of argument has focused on the unquestionable instability in prices of primary goods relative to prices of manufactures
and the difficulties that instability poses for economic development. The
oft-proposed suggestion for international action to stabilize commodity
prices follows logically. Still another argument suggests that Southern
debt is both result and instrument of economic dominance by the North.
That argument in turn leads naturally to calls for debt relief and
concessional flows of capital.

The OECD countries have resisted both the interpretations and
the policy recommendations. Their reaction has, in turn, reinforced
more radical views that have called into question the full gamut of
economic relationships with the capitalist North. The East generally
encourages such critical Southern views.

The South's perception of its relationship with the North has taken
on institutional form. In 1964 the United Nations Conference on Trade
and Development (UNCTAD), under the leadership of Raul Prebisch,
held its first meeting to challenge the global economic institutions and
policies of the North (especially GATT and the IMF). A formal coalition
of Third World countries came into being at the United Nations in
1965 as the Group of 77 (now comprising nearly 130 states). UNCTAD
has met regularly since 1964, and the Group of 77 is an important
U.N. caucus. In these and other groupings and forums, the South has
gradually elaborated its political economic program.

We should emphasize that the South, while we discuss it as a whole
here, is far from being a homogeneous grouping of countries. Among
important divisions is the one between the Third and the Fourth Worlds—
that is, those LDCs that are growing quite rapidly and those that have
made little progress in GDP (Gross Domestic Product) per capita. Another important cleavage separates the oil-producing countries of OPEC

---

[9] This argument, like the Northern claim of the mutual benefits from trade, is
difficult to assess empirically. Pollins (1987) examined the Prebisch thesis using the GLO-
BUS model and found some supporting evidence. See the competing portrayals of historic
changes in the terms of trade presented in Hughes (1985a:96–98).

from the nonoil LDCs. After the oil price increases of 1973, it appeared likely that the division would become a significant political fault line within the South. Surprisingly, that has not happened. In the Conference on International Economic Cooperation (CIEC) of 1975–1977, for example, the oil and the nonoil states of the South presented a generally united front.

Rises in commodity prices in the early 1970s and the success of the Organization of Petroleum Exporting Countries (OPEC) in greatly raising export revenues led many in the LDCs to hope and expect that the global North-South balance of power was shifting. The subsequent dramatic drop in commodity prices during the early 1980s, and the evaporation of the global capital flows that were based on the recycling of petrodollars, not only dashed those hopes but also led to a period of significant economic retrenchment in much of the Third World, especially in Latin America. Latin American GDP per capita was 6.5 percent lower in 1986 than in 1980 (IDB 1987:2).

In the spring of 1974, near the peak of Southern optimism, the United Nations accepted the LDC-sponsored Declaration and Action Program on a New International Economic Order (NIEO). That declaration consolidated many of the earlier proposals or demands of the South in its economic relationship with the North. These include the establishment of UNCTAD's proposed Integrated Program for Commodities with a Common Fund, which would stabilize and support commodity prices; the liberalization of the Generalized System of Preferences (GSP), which allows selected goods open access to Northern markets while maintaining some protection of Southern markets; better terms on loans from the IMF and the linkage of some IMF activities more clearly to development assistance; and attainment by the OECD countries of earlier UNCTAD foreign aid targets—namely, 0.7 percent of GNP as development assistance (Blake and Walters 1987:194).

In general, however, the NIEO remains a declaration, not an action program. Little has been done in implementing its elements. Some steps have been made toward satisfying the demands of the South. For instance, limited preferential access is allowed to OECD markets while those countries tolerate exceptions to the GATT principle of reciprocal openness of Southern markets. The International Bank for Reconstruction and Development (IBRD or World Bank) and the IMF both have some lending facilities that offer below-market rates. And a number of countries—for instance, the Scandinavian states—come close to or actually exceed the 0.7 percent aid target.

Nonetheless, the economic gap between the North and the South remains substantial. That gap is a remarkably recent phenomenon. Paul Bairoch estimated that in 1800 the per capita GNP (1960 prices) in West Europe was $213; another source places the level in the Third

World at the same time at $200 (Braudel 1979:534). The industrial revolution in Europe was beginning at that time and the gap widened steadily thereafter.

In the post–World War II period, the gap either has continued to widen or has stabilized, depending on the perspective and the statistical measures of the observer. Figure 1-2 provides the data for two perspectives. The first focuses on the absolute income gap. In 1960 the difference in per capita income between North and South was just over $4,000. By 1985 that had grown to over $9,000. That would certainly appear to indicate widening of the North-South gap. On the other hand, the ratio of per capita incomes between the two worlds has fluctuated around 13 to 1 over the entire twenty-five-year period. Since the ratio as well as the gap clearly grew sharply between 1800 and 1960, the stabilization of the ratio could be interpreted as signaling the end of the gap's widening and even as the precursor of its narrowing.

Still a third perspective focuses less on the economy and more on the satisfaction of basic human needs in the North and the South. The most fundamental human desire may well be greater longevity. Figure 1-3 shows that the North-South gap in life expectancy has been closing quite rapidly. Whereas in 1960, the average global Northerner lived twenty-two years longer than the average global Southerner (a ratio of 1.47 in life expectancy), the differential in 1985 had declined to fourteen years (a ratio of 1.24). In this perspective, the North-South gap is already narrowing.

THINGS TO COME (IN THIS WORK)

Tremendous volumes of scholarly writing, incredible amounts of policymakers' time, and scarcely believable levels of public finance are directed toward identifying and implementing policies that promise to bridge the two global cleavages. The most important policy focus of all this activity in relation to the East-West conflict is arms control. Proposals range across the various categories of strategic and conventional arms limitations that were outlined earlier. Through most of the 1980s, as a result of renewed intensity in the cold war, optimism concerning progress on arms control fell to low levels. But just as agreement on the SALT II treaty encouraged a revitalization of optimism at the end of the 1970s (before it was dashed by the Soviet invasion of Afghanistan), the signing of the Intermediate Nuclear Forces treaty and the continuing START negotiations are giving rise at the end of the 1980s to new hope for arms control. And there is a basis for belief that East-West arms spending may decline. United States arms spending since World War II has been cyclical. The first peak was in 1953, when defense spending took 13.5

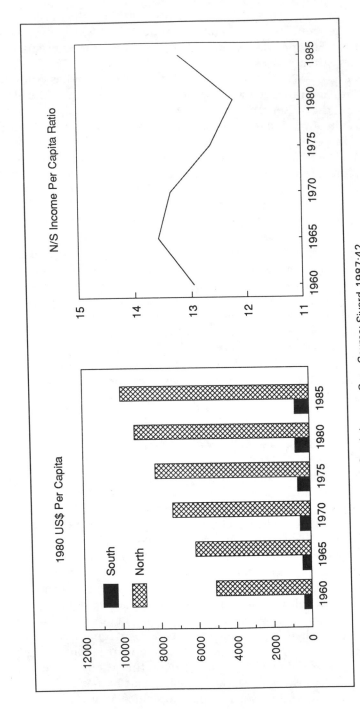

FIGURE 1–2 Absolute and Relative North-South Income Gap. *Source:* Sivard 1987:42.

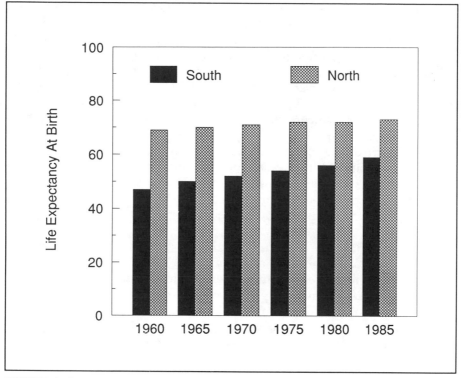

FIGURE 1–3   North-South Gap in Life Expectancy. *Source:* Hansen 1982:175; Sivard 1987:47.

percent of the GNP. The second was in 1968 at 9.0 percent of the GNP (Collins 1985:300). The third may well have been in 1985 at 6.9 percent (IISS 1987:300).[10] Soviet spending has grown with much more regularity but may be poised for decline under the new leadership and its economic restructuring.[11] This study will consider the implications were there to be significant reductions of spending in both the East and the West.

The failure to close the gap between North and South and the conflict to which that has contributed remain sources of frustration not only to those in the South but also to those in the North who are sympathetic to the plight of that region. The rapid economic recovery of Western Europe at the end of World War II, with the assistance

[10] The troughs were 4.2 percent in 1948, 7.2 percent in 1965, and 4.6 percent in 1979.

[11] China reported in 1987 that it had completed a 25 percent reduction in military manpower, a policy tied to its economic reforms.

from the United States in the form of the Marshall Plan,[12] encouraged many in the North to believe that similarly rapid growth could be achieved in the South and to believe that foreign aid could significantly accelerate growth. Although the shift in focus of the World Bank from Western European recovery to Southern development and the rise of foreign assistance programs across the OECD countries was in part an extension of the cold war into the South, a tremendous amount of attention and very sincere efforts have been devoted in the North to the encouragement of economic growth. Foreign aid programs, a fundamental part of the Northern effort to assist the South, have suffered from "donor fatigue" as a result of the frustration over results. Nonetheless, foreign aid remains one of the few instruments available to Northern governments in their efforts to help narrow the gap.[13] This study will analyze the potential impact of significantly increased foreign assistance.

We undertake here, then, an extensive analysis of the expectations for arms control and foreign assistance and of their potential as policy instruments. This differs from earlier studies in two important ways. First, this book simultaneously analyzes two dimensions of conflict and both policy tools. It looks carefully at their interactions. Second, the analysis relies upon a computer simulation of global politics and economics that facilitates the examination of secondary and tertiary consequences of a wide variety of policies.

Most policy analysis in these areas compartmentalizes the issues, narrows the focus to either political or economic aspects, and considers relatively brief time horizons (often no longer than the tenure of national chief executives). Much analysis is done from the perspective of an individual country. The brief overview in this chapter should make clear that these issues are interactive, interdisciplinary, long term, and global. The approach to analysis should, if possible, be tailored to the nature of the issues.

In this study, we rely on a world model called GLOBUS, a computer simulation of global political and economic processes. (Appendix A defines the terminology of modeling and simulation and explains the relationships among theory, formal models, and simulations.) Although the use of global models for policy analysis is in its infancy, the development of world models now builds upon the effort of a decade and

---

[12] Officially, the Marshall Plan was the European Recovery Program, through which the United States provided $15 billion in loans and grants to rebuild war-ravaged Europe during the period between 1948 and 1952.

[13] Obviously, trade preferences, commodity stabilization agreements, and encouragement of private capital flows are potentially very important instruments. Northern governments have exhibited only lukewarm support for the first, general antipathy for the second, and, with the debt crisis of the 1980s, absolute paralysis on the third.

a half. In each of the approximately ten principal world model projects (for reviews, see Ward and Guetzkow 1979; Hughes 1980 and 1985a; and Meadows et al. 1980; Siegmann 1987), painstaking care was taken to build upon the strengths and remedy the weaknesses of earlier efforts. So, too, in GLOBUS.

Since GLOBUS may not be well known to all or even many readers, a short description of the model is given in Appendix B. Here we will only note a few characteristics that make GLOBUS unique among world models. Two are especially important. First, it represents the world as a system of nations rather than as a global whole or a set of regional groups. The twenty-five countries of GLOBUS represent 75 percent of the world's population, 80 percent of gross world product, and 85 percent of global military expenditures. They also account for 67 percent of world exports and 68 percent of international hostility.[14] The twenty-five countries include seven economically advanced Western, five OPEC, four Eastern European, and nine developing nations.[15] National governments are the dominant actors within countries and in the international system; thus, countries constitute a logical basis upon which to build a global model. Second, the interest areas of GLOBUS are predominantly political and economic, as opposed to the biological and physical environment interests that were so important in earlier world models. This focus stemmed from the conviction of those who developed the model that most of the globe's pressing problems over the next half-century will be caused by maldistribution arising from particular policies rather than by insufficient production capabilities caused by exhausting the limits of our physical resources.

The GLOBUS model is viewed not as a "crystal ball" capable of forecasting the future but as a laboratory in which experiments about

[14] International hostility is measured by an index that gives values to individual hostile acts and then sums them. Appendix A includes a brief discussion of such data and indices.

[15] The twenty-five GLOBUS nations are:

WEST	EAST	SOUTH	OPEC
Canada	Czechoslovakia	Argentina	Indonesia
France	East Germany	Brazil	Iran
Italy	Poland	China	Nigeria
Japan	Soviet Union	Egypt	Saudi Arabia
United Kingdom		India	Venezuela
United States		Mexico	
West Germany		Pakistan	
		South Africa	
		Turkey	

the future can be carried out. That is, the results of a model run are not seen as constituting a prediction of what inevitably is to be but as the outcome of a very complex experiment that, we hope, tells us something about just how much control we have over that future. In this work, we use GLOBUS in precisely that way. After we have laid out the basic argument under consideration in this volume, we will then report on a series of experiments conducted using GLOBUS that test certain conclusions said to follow from this model. In much the same way as a chemist adds one ingredient to a compound and then stops to analyze the effects before adding another, we will implement different governmental policies in the realm of disarmament and development and observe their possible effects, before considering the impact of additional policy changes. In that way, we can approximate the laboratory method of scientific inquiry. Of course, the quality of the knowledge gained from any laboratory experiment is vitally dependent upon how well the relevant real-world conditions have been approximated in the laboratory.

A Design for Peace and Prosperity

DISARMAMENT AND DEVELOPMENT: THE ARGUMENT

Two prestigious commissions have studied the North-South and East-West cleavages in the decade of the 1980s. The first, headed by Willy Brandt (1980 and 1983), put forward a variety of recommendations as to how the disparity in wealth between the more developed and the less developed nations might be reduced. Almost all the recommendations entail some transfer of resources from the North to the South, and in the commission's view, an important precondition for making those resources available was ending the global arms race.

> The world's military spending dwarfs any spending on development. Total military expenditures are approaching $450 billion a year, of which over half is spent by the Soviet Union and the United States, while annual spending on official development aid is only $20 billion. If only a fraction of the money, manpower and research presently devoted to military uses were diverted to development, the future prospects of the Third World would look entirely different. (Brandt 1980:117)

The Palme Commission focused on the global security problem and suggested measures that could reduce the level of tension and militarization in the future. Arms reduction was a key component of those measures, and one of the arguments supporting it was that arms reduction would free substantial resources that could facilitate development.

> A doctrine of common security must replace the present expedient of deterrence through armaments. International peace must rest on a commitment to joint survival rather than a threat of mutual destruction. . . . The economic and social costs of military competition constitute strong reasons for countries to seek disarmament. The costs of military spending are especially onerous in the difficult economic circumstances of the 1980s. (Palme 1982:139)

It is not only prestigious commissions that have made such arguments linking reductions in arms spending with improved international relations and accelerated economic development (United Nations 1985:143–155). In 1955 France proposed an international fund for development and mutual assistance to be financed by funds released in arms reduction. In 1956 the Soviet Union proposed a special U.N. fund for development assistance, also to be financed by decreases in arms expenditure. Brazil did the same in 1964, and in 1973 the U.N. General Assembly actually passed a resolution calling for 10 percent reductions in arms spending, with released funds to be used for development. This is only a sampling of such proposals over the years. Several U.N. studies have argued that the arms race aggravates difficulties in development, pollution, and availability of raw materials, as well as contributing to other economic and social problems (U.N. 1985:147).

Implicit in these arguments and proposals is a theory of the relationships among military spending, international relations, economic development, and political stability. The theory looks fundamentally like that portrayed in Figure 2-1.

There are six important propositions in this theory:

1. Reductions in arms spending will improve economic performance in the North.
2. Reductions in arms spending will improve East-West relations and decrease the threat of war.
3. Reductions in arms spending will facilitate increases in development assistance.
4. Increased foreign aid will improve economic performance in the South.
5. Improved economic performance in the South will increase domestic political stability there.
6. Improved economic performance in the South will produce better North-South relations.

These six propositions touch on some of the most important questions facing the international political economy. All are cast as lawlike statements, but we recognize that some are more dependent upon

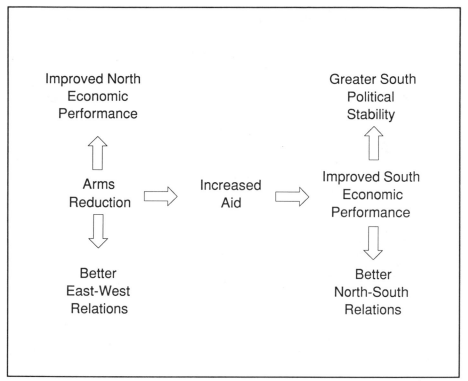

FIGURE 2–1   The Disarmament-Development Argument

"political will" than others. The third, for example, is predominantly a matter of political will, for there can be little debate that the United States, the Soviet Union, and their principal allies could, if they so agreed, divert the savings from any arms reductions undertaken to development assistance. The experience of the Marshall Plan and the relatively high proportions of GDP provided as aid by Scandinavian countries and by Arab oil exporters demonstrate feasibility, given the political will.

The other relationships are not simply a matter of political will. Not everyone agrees that reductions in arms spending would either improve economic performance or improve international relations. Because such outcomes hinge on the reactions of complex markets and large numbers of economic actors in the one case, and on the long-term dynamics of interstate relations in the other, those who are able to reduce arms spending may not be in a position to guarantee the economic or political outcomes that the arguments foresee. Nor does everyone agree that additional receipts of foreign aid will lead to improved economic performance in the South, which would, in turn, bring about better North-South relations and greater political stability in the South.

Taken together, these propositions constitute what might be called an Idealist/Internationalist (I/I) view of the world, and, as we shall see in the rest of the chapter, there are many with different political and ideological orientations who dispute the validity of the propositions. Nor do we mean to suggest that members of the Brandt and Palme commissions uniformly accept all propositions. We do argue, however, that these propositions often coexist in the belief systems of a substantial number of those who study and write about the two cleavages. Consider also this argument from the RIO (Reshaping the International Order) report:

> On the basis of first calculations, the group reported that a 20 per cent general reduction in military expenditures could contribute not only to the satisfaction of urgent economic needs of both developed and developing countries, but also to the reduction of the economic disparities between the two groups if development assistance was raised globally in the same proportion or slightly more. (Thorsson 1976:302)

In order to go beyond a purely ideological debate, we endeavor in this book to bring to bear the analytic power of a global political-economic computer simulation, GLOBUS, to assess this theory. In the following chapters, we examine each of the theory's five controversial propositions in turn. Additionally we raise, in the last chapter, a consideration of how much impact policies such as arms control and increased aid have relative to the forces of change and continuity at work in the global system. In other words, we wish to know not only the direction of policy impact and the magnitude of it but also the significance of it in comparison with the momentum of world developments. Before turning to the analysis, however, it is important to outline the political debates over the propositions and to review prior empirical analyses that have been undertaken with respect to them.

CRITIQUE AND EVALUATION
OF THE ARGUMENT

The literature can be divided into predominantly political-ideological and predominantly empirical-analytical categories, although most of the more polemical literature makes at least passing references to evidence and most of the more scientific literature is sensitive to (and, many would say, guided by) the highly normative (value-laden) nature of the questions it addresses.

The political-ideological literature can be usefully further divided by ideological viewpoint. The two cleavages cross over political-military and economic areas and draw the attention of those with two competing ideological (some would say world-view or paradigmatic) perspectives. One set of perspectives focuses predominantly on the political-military issues. The two dominant world views in this area are the *realist* or power politics view and the more *idealist* view emphasizing the possibility and desirability of cooperation among countries. Among many other differences in these perspectives, the realist is more likely to emphasize security through strength of the individual country or its alliance system, whereas the idealist looks more to multilateral agreements to resolve outstanding issues and to international organizations to facilitate international cooperation. The realist perspective is more often constant sum, arguing that one country's gain is another country's loss; the idealist emphasizes the possibility of mutual gain. American foreign policy has alternated between these perspectives. Woodrow Wilson was one of the best-known idealists, and Jimmy Carter, with his emphasis on human rights, generally also falls into this category. Like Harry Truman and Dean Acheson, the Richard Nixon and Henry Kissinger team was unabashedly realist. The Brandt and Palme commissions, and many others studying arms control issues, are basically idealist.

The second set of ideological perspectives focuses predominantly on the economic issues.[1] What we here call the *conservative* view em-

BOX 2–1   *Game Theory Concepts*

Concepts from game theory help explain the world views and will also appear in several subsequent discussions. Game theorists represent the interaction of individuals (or countries) in terms of standard patterns called games.

Constant sum   A type of game in which the gains of one party equal the losses of another. This type of interaction is often also called **win-lose** or **zero sum.** Territorial disputes tend to be constant-sum games—for example, the repeated transfer between Germany and France of the Alsace-Lorraine region after several wars.

Positive sum   A type of game in which the gains of one party do not come at the expense of other parties; in fact, the gains of one party may be dependent on gains by other parties. This is also known as **nonzero-sum** or **win-win** interaction. For example, the technological advances in the United States, Japan, and Europe and technological transfers among them build on each other and collectively contribute to improved living standards in all three areas.

[1] These categories are comparable to those of Blake and Walters (1987) and of Hughes (1985a and 1985c).

phasizes the beneficial workings of the free market, absent of intervention from governments. This perspective maintains a strong distinction between international politics and international economics. It holds in large part to a positive-sum view of the economic world, in which economic gain can accrue to many countries simultaneously and in large part because of their interaction. In the academic literature on political economy, it is quite common to refer to the conservative position as "classical liberal." We have endeavored to stay with labels more easily recognized in contemporary political discourse. In sharp contrast, the *radical* view, with roots in Marxism, argues that economics and politics cannot be separated and that international economics drives international politics just as domestic economics shapes domestic politics. In this perspective, the economic and the political power of the North reinforce each other in their dealings with the South. The perspective is more often constant sum, arguing that the economic gain of any class or region of the world frequently comes at the expense of other classes or regions. The *internationalist* position is an intermediate view that normally recognizes a relationship between international economics and politics but holds that political and economic cooperation can benefit all parties. We earlier characterized the reports of the Brandt and Palme commissions as internationalist. This position might also be labeled (modern) *liberal*.

The scientific literature can be further classified by methodological approach. Case studies, statistical analyses (cross-sectional and longitudinal), and formal models serve well as major methodological categories. Most of the literature reviewed here falls into the statistical category. Cross-sectional analyses consider the covariation between two variables (such as arms spending and conflict levels) across a set of countries at a single point in time. Longitudinal analyses look at the covariation for a single country over time. Both statistical approaches have strengths and weaknesses. The weaknesses are significant enough that scientific analysis seldom provides the incontrovertible results that would be needed to resolve the political-ideological debates. The primary weaknesses of both are that (1) the direction of causality between variables cannot be proven (although looking at the temporal sequencing of changes between variables in a longitudinal design is suggestive) and (2) the possibility of covariation caused by some unexamined third variable is always possible. In spite of these weaknesses, the scientific literature often builds a strong case in support of or contradicting propositions like those of the Idealist/ Internationalist world view.

Some readers will have difficulty understanding the scientific terminology that is needed to review scientific literature. The preceding paragraph illustrated that terminology. A special appendix following this chapter (see p. 54) defines and explains this language for such readers. Please consider turning to that appendix before proceeding further with this discussion. You may wish to use it for reference in any case.

In the remainder of this introduction, we will summarize the literature pertaining to the five controversial relationships identified earlier: arms reduction and economic performance, arms spending and international relations, foreign aid and economic performance, economic performance and domestic political stability, and economic performance and North-South relations.

Arms Reductions and Economic Performance

POLITICAL-IDEOLOGICAL LITERATURE

Whereas ideological or world-view categories prove very useful in distinguishing expectations for the impact of reductions in defense spending and the effectiveness of increased foreign aid (to be treated later), they contribute surprisingly little to an understanding of positions on the economic consequences of reductions in military spending. The argument that military spending contributes positively to economic growth (at least in capitalist countries) garners support and opposition from across the political spectrum. Many conservatives favor increased military spending and emphasize the technological spinoffs of advanced military technology. They even sometimes preempt the Keynesian arguments of liberals who admit the value of military spending as a means of increasing aggregate demand. That admission by liberals is often grudging or embarrassed, since many would prefer that demand be increased by nonmilitary spending. In fact, modern liberals or internationalists tend to emphasize the guns-butter trade-off, and they are perhaps least likely of those holding various ideological positions to actually argue that there is anything special about military spending that boosts economic performance. Radicals often point to the necessity (not just opportunity) for capitalist countries to use military spending to absorb surplus production that would otherwise result in significant overproduction crises for the economy (Baran and Sweezy 1968).[2] In addition, radicals draw attention to the fact that military spending provides the state, and those who control it, with the means to maintain control domestically and to extend it abroad.

The fairly widespread ideological acceptance of functional arguments on behalf of military spending helps explain the extensive appeal

---

[2] For development of the argument concerning support for military spending from multiple viewpoints, see Mosley 1985:1–2.

BOX 2–2 *Domestic Economic Concepts*

This section and several subsequent discussions assume knowledge of some terminology concerning the domestic economy. Many of the terms center on the impact of governmental spending on economic performance.

Keynesian economics In the analysis of downturns in economic activity, John Maynard Keynes (1883–1946) emphasized the importance of maintaining demand upon the productive capacity of the economy to compensate for the tendency in capitalism for oversaving, which leads to inadequate consumption and investment. He supported an active role of government in maintaining demand.

Aggregate demand The sum of private consumption, government consumption, investment, and exports (net of imports), all of which place demands upon the productive capacity of an economy.

Countercyclical spending Increased government spending during an economic downturn with the aim of increasing aggregate demand and boosting economic performance.

Crowding out A shorthand term for trade-offs among aggregate demand or expenditure categories of an economy. For instance, it is often said that government spending on defense or social programs crowds out spending on investment. When the economy is producing at full capacity, increased government spending may not add to demand but, rather, compete with existing demand.

Fiscal policy The use of government taxation and spending as instruments to maintain levels of aggregate demand so as to stimulate an economy when it is weak and to dampen the economy when demand is so strong as to threaten inflation.

Guns-butter trade-off Government spending on defense (guns) and social programs (butter) compete for the same limited government budget and thus restrict each other. This is similar to crowding out and may, in fact, interact with it when government seeks to simultaneously increase defense and social spending.

Laissez-faire An economic doctrine that opposes most government regulation or management of the economy and that supports unrestricted domestic and international commerce.

of the argument made in the satirical *Report from Iron Mountain* (Lewin 1967:36–37):[3]

> Far from constituting a "wasteful" drain on the economy, war spending, considered pragmatically, has been a consistently positive factor in the rise of gross national product and of individual productivity.

[3] See also the critique by many individuals with quite different positions in Boulding (1970).

Although such arguments may find support across an ideological spectrum, they also generate heated opposition. One of the more eloquent rebuttals was delivered by Dwight Eisenhower, general and Republican president:

> Every gun that is made, every warship launched, every rocket fired signifies, in the final sense, a theft from those who hunger and are not fed, those who are cold and are not clothed. This world in arms is not spending money alone. It is spending the sweat of its laborers, the genius of its scientists, the hopes of its children. (Cited in Russett 1983a:48–49)

Although it is almost impossible to make the economic case against military spending more emotionally forceful than Eisenhower did, it is modern liberals or internationalists who have devoted the most effort to refuting positive linkages and who have directly confronted the Keynesian-based supportive arguments. For instance, the Palme Commission (1982:173) concluded that

> . . . the economic problems of the 1970s and the early 1980s make the waste of human effort even more intolerable. The presumed economic benefits of military spending are a dangerous illusion. Increased military spending would make our economic problems worse, not better. Military expenditure is likely to create less employment than other forms of public expenditure, with greater risks for inflation and for future economic growth.

EMPIRICAL ANALYSES

Data-based studies of the linkage between military spending and economic growth recognize the same basic positive and negative arguments as do the political debates. On the positive side, technological spinoffs of military research and development and demand-increasing effects dominate. On the negative side, critics stress the trade-offs between military consumption and other consumption (either public or private) and the possibility that military spending might crowd out investment or create supply bottlenecks and thus slow growth.

In reality, most studies of the linkage between the two variables focus on the impact of *greater* military spending on the economy. Use of such studies to generalize about the implications of *reductions* in expenditure assumes a reversibility in the relationship that is not justified. It may be, for instance, that changes in spending, whether increases or decreases, have costs in terms of structural change (including underutilized capital and labor in some sectors of the economy that cannot easily be shifted to other sectors). Such costs could conceivably outweigh benefits of either increased or decreased spending, at least in the short- and the midterm. Nonetheless, we are obliged in the review of literature to largely ignore the difficulties of generalizing from the economic impact of increases in arms spending to that of decreases in arms spending (because the literature ignores the issue of reversibility). When we turn to our own empirical analysis, the modeling methodology employed can capture both similarities and differences in the economic impacts of spending increases and decreases.

Case studies. Case studies have the advantage of allowing detailed examination of a larger number of variables than can generally be considered in statistical analyses. They have the disadvantage of being unable to control for changes in such variables in any systematic way.

Some case studies are little more than political advocacies. For instance, in 1950 the National Security Council of the United States government undertook an examination (NSC-68) of the relationship between military spending and economic performance before, during, and after World War II. The authors somewhat tentatively concluded that the impact of spending was often beneficial, as could be further increases:

> From the point of view of the economy as a whole, the program might not result in a real decrease in the standard of living, for the economic effects of the program might be to increase the gross national product by more than the amount being absorbed for additional military and foreign assistance purposes. One of the most significant lessons of our World War II experience was that the American economy, when it operates at a level approaching full efficiency, can provide enormous resources for purposes other than civilian consumption while simultaneously providing a high standard of living. (Cited in Mosley 1985:8)

Clayton (1970) collected materials and data to allow an assessment of the economic costs and benefits of the cold war and the Vietnam War. In a brief consideration of the consequences of disarmament, he emphasized that the impact would fall on a small handful of industries with considerable geographic concentration and with relatively little conversion flexibility, thus leaving some capital and labor unemployed. Mosley (1985) presented short sketches of the macroeconomic performance of the United States economy during the demobilizations following World War II and the Korean and Vietnam conflicts. The sketches indicated that each transition period was marred by slow growth or a recession, although brief in each instance. Mosley attributed the downturns primarily to inadequate planning or to deliberate use of reduced military spending for fiscal restraint and anti-inflationary policies, or to both.

Several case studies have focused on the implications of arms spending for Soviet economic performance. Becker (1981, 1982, 1983) has actively studied the issue and concluded that

More elaborate approaches to measurement of the burden support each other in the expectable demonstration of a primary tradeoff between defense and investment, with inevitable, lagged effect on aggregate growth. Effects on consumption depend on government resource allocation policy. (Becker 1981:20)

Interestingly, many in the United States have suggested that such a defense burden on the Soviet economy could be used as a weapon by forcing the Soviets to undertake increased spending. Such logic seems to incorporate an implicit assumption that the United States is less susceptible to such economic penalties. Perhaps the basis for the asymmetry of argument lies in the fact that the United States economy is twice the size of that of the U.S.S.R., but it sometimes seems that in the heat of politics, the "Keynesian" assumption of a beneficial or neutral defense impact on the United States economy is made simultaneously with the "burden" assumption for the Soviet economy.

The debate over guns and butter trade-offs or complementaries has been extended in case studies to the Third World as well. Some of the early modernization literature argued through case studies that the military could serve as a significant force in development. The military's introduction of modern technology and modern management methods, as well as discipline and merit-based personnel review, may influence similar innovations in the broader society (Pye 1964). More recently, this argument has drawn much criticism (Kaldor 1986).

Statistical analyses.   Some cross-sectional analyses have been undertaken relating defense burden to economic growth.[4] For instance, Russett (1983a:49) has noted that

It is easy to point to the much lower military expenditures of Germany and Japan (3.2 and 0.9 percent, respectively, in 1979) than the United States (5.2 percent) and their substantially higher growth rates over a long time period.

Cross-sectional analysis of fifteen industrial countries has been undertaken by Smith (1977), who found a quite strong inverse relationship between military spending and investment as a percentage of GDP. Interestingly, this study proceeds from a Marxist perspective but empirically rejects the common Marxist argument that military spending is used in capitalist countries to offset underconsumption and stagnation.

But the weaknesses of cross-sectional analysis, particularly the possibility that additional variables explain the relationship, are well known.

---

[4] Mosley (1985) provides an excellent review of literature on the impact of defense spending. A briefer but more comprehensive review is that of Chan (1987).

It could be argued, for instance, that it is because the United States is the largest and leading Western economic power that it spends the most on defense (Olson and Zeckhauser 1966) and that other countries, as technological followers, can exceed United States productivity and growth gains by simply copying its technology (Freeman et al. 1982). Thus, the leading role of the United States could explain both higher spending and slower growth; the apparent causal relationship between higher military spending in the United States and slower growth would be spurious (false).

Although they have their own methodological weaknesses, a large portion of statistical analyses in this area are either longitudinal or combinations of cross-sectional and longitudinal. For instance, Smith (1980) followed his 1977 cross-sectional analysis with a combined cross-sectional, longitudinal analysis for fourteen OECD countries, which also found a negative relationship between military spending and investment. Russett (1970) undertook one of the best-known longitudinal analyses, focusing on the United States. He used regression analysis to determine the cost of military spending to other categories of expenditure and concluded that a dollar directed to defense reduced other spending as follows:

> 42 cents from personal consumption, 29 cents from fixed capital formation, 10 cents from exports, 5 cents from federal government civilian programs and 13 cents from state and local governments' activities. (1970:141)

Caputo (1975) contradicted part of this finding in a four-country longitudinal study of Australia, Sweden, the United Kingdom, and the United States over the 1950–1970 period. He found that military spending is positively associated with health spending (although negatively associated with education spending) and concluded that an inverse relationship between military spending and welfare cannot be supported. It is disappointing that he did not use his extensive data base to examine the broader economic consequences of military spending. In a more recent multivariate analysis of the United States, Russett (1982) criticized the Caputo study but failed to find the trade-off between military spending and other federal spending that he expected.

The longitudinal studies have their own methodological weaknesses. As Chan (1987:30) points out, it is impossible to know whether the apparent positive correlation he found between arms spending and economic growth for the Mediterranean countries of Greece, Turkey, Portugal, Spain, and Italy reflects a benefit from arms spending or the tendency for it to rise when economic growth is stronger.

Nincic and Cusack (1979) turned the question on its head and asked whether drops in private consumption and investment (as a measure of economic weakness) lead to increases in (countercyclical) military spending in the United States. In reaction to a clear methodological weakness of most other longitudinal analyses, they also studied time-lagged effects. They found that military spending does in fact appear to be so used. They went on to briefly consider whether the military spending actually increases employment. Although concluding that it does provide jobs, they emphasized studies that indicate that civilian spending creates them more efficiently.

A substantial statistical literature has arisen focusing on developing countries. Benoit (1973) analyzed forty-four countries over the 1950–1965 period in perhaps the best-known study. He combined longitudinal, cross-sectional, and some case studies in this approach. Overall, he concluded that the relationship between military spending and growth is probably positive, although he refused to state that it had been proven (see Ball 1983 for a critique of Benoit). The bulk of the literature since Benoit's famous study contradicts his conclusion (see, for example, Deger and Smith 1983).

Model-based analyses   Chan (1985), after an excellent review of the almost bewildering complexity of findings on this proposition, concluded that

> We have probably reached a point of diminishing returns in relying on aggregate cross-national studies to inform us about the economic impact of defense spending. . . . As some analysts have already noted, the search for universal patterns applicable to all places and times is likely to be disappointing. . . . Dynamic modeling—more suitable for the developed countries with available reliable data—is necessary for identifying the multiple direct and indirect causal paths, for determining the lagged influences and feedback loops, and for experimenting with "what if" questions. (Chan 1985:433–434)

There have been very few attempts to formally model the relationship between military spending and economic performance. Nobel Prize–winning economist Wassily Leontief has been involved in studies that have done so over a period of twenty years.[5] In a 1965 analysis, he and coauthors used his input-output modeling approach to consider the impact on the United States and on major regions within it of a shift of military spending to civilian expenditure. Although regions responded quite differently to such a shift, there was no net impact on the country as a whole.

More recent work by Leontief and coauthors has extended the relatively static and partial analysis of the earlier studies, most recently

[5] For an overview of these efforts, see Leontief and Duchin 1983:11.

undertaking a thirty-year analysis using the fifteen-region World Model constructed for the United Nations. With this model, Leontief and Duchin (1983:41–43) found that a large reduction in military spending by all regions (25 percent in 1990 and 40 percent by 2000), coupled with a shift of the expenditure to other uses, increases GDP by less than 5 percent in most regions of the world. The increase is slightly greater in the Soviet Union and Eastern Europe than in North America or Western Europe. The GDPs of oil producers are slightly damaged by the shift.

Leontief and Duchin also considered the reversibility issue by examining the consequences of a doubling of military spending as a portion of GDP. This does reduce GDP in all developed regions. The Soviet decline of more than 8 percent is the largest of developed regions.

In contrast to the Leontief model-based conclusion that reduced military spending boosts economic performance in both the East and the West, Allan and Luterbacher (1983:297) find with their SIMPEST model that an 8 percent reduction in defense expenditure by the United States lowers its GNP by 4 percent. A comparable reduction by the Soviet Union has no impact on its economy because of a shift from defense to consumption that maintains aggregate demand in this seemingly Keynesian economic model.

Becker (1983:28–33) reviewed three computer model-based studies of the implications for the Soviet economy of higher military expenditures. All, including the well-known SOVMOD, suggested important trade-offs between military spending and both consumption and investment.

Overall, the evidence is somewhat mixed but suggests that a reduction in defense spending most likely would have a positive impact on the economic growth of those countries undertaking it. That benefit might be greater after the initial costs of some economic restructuring are paid. To the degree that the conclusion of Chan and others about differential impact of defense spending on different countries is correct, the multiple-country model-based analysis used in this study may be able to capture such differentiation.

Arms Spending and International Relations

POLITICAL-IDEOLOGICAL LITERATURE

As with most serious questions about peace and war, there are two identifiable and contradictory positions with respect to the impact of arms on international relations. One school, often called idealists, tends to see the accumulation of arms as a clear danger to world peace. Their maxim might be "he who lives by the sword, dies by the sword," and their contention is that the very existence of large military establishments makes their use more likely (Noel-Baker 1958). Some argue that the militarization of a society, which involves extensive planning and preparation for a war that may occur at any minute, legitimates and encourages international violence while reducing the willingness to negotiate and compromise (Wallensteen et al. 1985). Still others assert that the risks of accidental war increase as arsenals increase in size and conclude that lower armaments levels would, therefore, promote peace.

On the other side, we find those who take as their maxim "if you seek peace, prepare for war" and contend that the threat of force is fundamentally a stabilizing factor in international relations. Often called realists, these observers argue that in a world without central authority, the ultimate guarantee of survival is force and, since the threat of force deters the use of force, the accumulation of arms is a regrettable but necessary outcome of maintaining peace. According to this view, the greater the size and destructive power of armaments, the lower the probability that they will be used and the greater the likelihood that other means of conflict resolution will be employed. This type of thinking is to be found in military establishments everywhere, be they located in the East or the West, the North or the South.

The proposition that arms reduction will lead to better East-West relations would certainly be accepted by most idealists and rejected by many realists, particularly the harder of the hard-liners to be found in the latter school. The former would see the lowering of arms expenditures as leading to lessened East-West tension and opening the way for more East-West cooperation. The latter group would argue that reducing arms poses great risks because of the likely disturbance of delicately balanced mutually deterrent forces and the introduction of compliance as an important issue in East-West affairs. Hence, for a variety of reasons, arms reduction per se cannot be expected to improve East-West relations and may actually make them worse.

There are other political-ideological positions, with adherents who cannot be characterized as either realist or idealist and who would normally view as irrelevant debates about whether bilateral decreases in arms spending ameliorate or intensify international conflict. Among these are beliefs that some states are peaceful and others warlike and that the level of international conflict depends on which parties hold superiority in forces.[6] This position can be found on both sides of the cold war. For instance, from the Eastern perspective comes this argument:

---

[6] Kenneth Waltz (1959) has characterized these as "second" image views. The first image sees war inherent in human nature and in individuals; the second image sees it in the nature of individual states; the third image explains war in terms of the international system (as realists do).

NEOREALISTS

World socialism's successes in economic, scientific, and cultural development; in the unity of the countries of the socialist community, growing
ever stronger, the downfall of colonialism, and the emergence of new
independent nations; in the unprecedented growth of the international
working class and communist movement and the new upswing of the peace
movement, have strengthened the position of the forces championing peace,
international cooperation, and the freedom and independence of peoples.
The forces of imperialism, reaction, and war have been irreversibly weakened. (Lebedev 1976:xi–xii)

EMPIRICAL ANALYSES

When we look for evidence as to which of these views is better
supported by empirical results, we find relatively little of a systematic
nature that bears directly on the proposition. Disarmament is not something that has been frequently tried; hence, it is difficult to assess its
"track record" in history. For that reason, then, most of the available
evidence pertains to the question of whether arms *increases* lead to war
rather than whether arms *decreases* lead to peace.

Case studies   Analysts of the two world wars have extracted clear
but contradictory lessons from each with respect to the relationship
between arms accumulation and the likelihood of war. The existence
of an arms race between the major powers in the prewar years was
often cited as one of the principal causes of World War I. That gave
impetus to a variety of measures immediately following the war to control
armaments and reduce the military burden. However, scholars examining
World War II have concluded that the failure to arm sufficiently by
some major actors (such as France, the United Kingdom, and the United
States) contributed to the outbreak of the war, since they were not able
to deter other nations (notably Germany and Japan). That may explain
why in the years following that war we have observed an unprecedented
military expansion by virtually all nations. Thus, case studies have tended
to show that arms both cause and prevent wars.

Paul Kennedy undertook a historical analysis of a substantial number
of arms races between 1850 and 1945. His conclusion was that

> If historians have a message for contemporary strategists and, more im-
> portantly, for today's politicians, it is precisely that: that despite some
> evidence to the contrary, the upward spiral is not inevitable even if it may
> be likely; and that the race need not end in an Armageddon. But it takes
> political willpower, percipience, a certain freedom from dogma, an ability
> to see other viewpoints and to make some allowance for them, in order
> to turn the spiral downwards and to reduce the arms-race. It is those
> *political* features which are nearly always in short supply, compared to the

ample stocks of weapons that nations usually find it more comforting to possess, both in the past, and at this very moment. (1983:176–177)

Statistical analyses   Until quite recently, very little systematic statistical analysis had been done on the question of whether the accumulation of arms per se promotes peace or war. To a great extent, that was due to the lack of relevant data. Comparable longitudinal data on defense spending for more than a few nations have only recently become available, thanks principally to the laborious efforts of the Correlates of War project (see, for example, Singer 1979 and 1980).

The relatively small number of statistical studies can be divided roughly into those that focus on the relationship between the *level* of defense spending and the propensity for national conflict (leading easily to a cross-sectional design), those that focus on the *systemic distribution* of defense spending and related capabilities, and those that emphasize the importance of *changes* in spending (longitudinal arms race studies). In the first category, Rummel (1963) found that defense expenditures, relative to population, government expenditures, and GNP, correlate significantly with international violence. Weede (1970), in a fifty-nine-country cross-sectional study, found a similar relationship.

Such cross-sectional analyses investigate the level of military spending of states and its relationship to the propensity for conflict. Are states that spend higher amounts on defense more often involved in conflict? The studies suggest that to be the case. A more complicated issue, however, is how the distribution of spending within the global system and changes in that distribution interact with the propensity for conflict. Some studies have theorized about such patterns.[7] The theories have been more discussed than tested, but there are a few empirical analyses that relate to our interest—namely whether changes in military spending could, through changes in the distribution of system capabilities, affect the propensity for conflict.

Choucri and North (1975), Ashley (1980), and Smith (1987b) all find that how one nation acts toward another diplomatically is conditioned by their relative military capabilities, but the direction and magnitude of this effect varies significantly across pairs of nations. From these studies, one would conclude that a *balanced* reduction in arms should not strongly affect relations between those participating in the reduction program but may significantly alter relations between participants and nonparticipants, since their relative military positions would change.

---

[7] See Bueno de Mesquita (1980) for a review of theories surrounding power transition, status inconsistency, and related concepts.

Substantial arms reductions by a subset of the world's nations might lead to changes in the hierarchy of military capability, and, according to some evidence, that could lead to changes in international behavior. Bremer (1980) examined war involvements between 1816 and 1965, and Eberwein (1982) looked at involvement in serious disputes between 1900 and 1976; both found that the higher a nation's rank on the military capability dimension, the greater its frequency of participation in those forms of conflict. Again, these findings relate to relative capability (rank rather than difference), so they do not tell us whether arms reduction per se necessarily leads to more or less conflictual international relations.

The third category of study focuses directly on changes in arms spending and capabilities and more specifically on arms races. Studies in this category generally ignore levels and distribution of expenditures, just as others ignore changes and rates of change. Although a large literature on individual arms races is of relevance here (as noted earlier in the discussion of case studies), most insightful are statistical analyses of arms races. Wallace (1979) examined the question of whether the existence of an arms race between major powers increased the probability of war between them, given the occurrence of a serious dispute, and concluded that the answer was affirmative for the period 1816–1965. Smith (1982:73) concluded after her study of thirty-two arms races that "most but not all arms racing eventually ends in war." In a later study, Wallace (1982) compared the "arms races promote war" and "preparedness promotes peace" hypotheses with respect to ninety-nine cases of conflict involving major powers. His conclusion was this:

> When two powers engage in acts of force or threats of violence against one another, we must assume their relationship is characterized by considerable tension. Yet, in only 3 of 71 cases did such acts lead to war when not preceded by an arms race. Conversely, when an arms race *did* precede a significant threat or act of violence, war was avoided only 5 out of 28 times. It is difficult, therefore, to avoid the conclusion that, over the 150 years from Waterloo to Vietnam, arms races are a danger to the peace of the international system. (Wallace 1982:49)

Wallace's findings were questioned by Weede (see Weede 1980 and Wallace 1980). Diehl's (1983) larger study of the relationship between arms races and the outbreak of war criticizes the methodological approach and contradicts the conclusions of Wallace, finding little evidence for the relationship of arms races and war. Specifically, Diehl codes arms races involving more than two states (such as that preceding World War I) as a single race, in contrast to the Wallace rule that each dyad (pair) of states is coded separately (World War I is thus preceded for Wallace by six arms races). Diehl concludes that "almost 80% of militarized disputes that were directly preceded by an arms race did not escalate to war" (Diehl 1983:168). Thus, according to current empirical analyses, the answer to the question of whether arms races promote war depends upon how one defines arms races and their outcomes.

Model analyses   Surprisingly, the voluminous Richardsonian literature[8] containing formal analyses of arms races has little direct relevance to the question of how arms spending affects international relations. These models focus almost exclusively on how levels of arms spending in two countries affect each other and have little or nothing to say about how that spending affects their diplomatic relations. There are, however, a very few models that are relevant to our discussion. Using a mathematical model of nuclear war initiation, Intriligator and Brito (1984) demonstrated that the likelihood of war may increase or decrease as a result of arms reduction, depending upon a variety of factors. Mayer (1986) questioned some aspects of their conclusion, but their reply (Intriligator and Brito 1986) seems convincing that arms reduction can, under some conditions, increase the incentives for initiating war.

Two simulation studies stemming from the GLOBUS project are more directly relevant to the question at hand. Cusack (1984) experimented with alternative options in Western defense policy and found that lower defense expenditures by the West led to relatively more cooperative and less hostile East-West relations. Smith (1987b) examined the long-term impact of a Reagan-like hard-line policy of the United States toward the Soviet Union, which included a policy of significant increases in American military capability, and found that this action, together with the resultant arms race, led to relatively less cooperative and more hostile East-West relations. In both Cusack's and Smith's scenarios, the policy of arms decrease or increase was initiated by members of the West bloc. In our scenario, we will examine a coordinated program of arms reduction in both the West and the East blocs.

On the whole, the empirical evidence is ambiguous as to whether arms reduction should improve East-West relations or not. It is an especially complex issue because it can be fully analyzed only in the systemic context of a large number of states. The change in levels of military expenditure by one state will potentially affect the international behavior of many other states, which in turn influence each other and

---

[8] Lewis Fry Richardson (1881–1953) was a British physicist and psychologist who laid many of the foundations for modern mathematical approaches to weather forecasting. A pacifist, he also collected and analyzed data on war, developing the first mathematical models of arms races. His work has been the basis for two generations of subsequent arms race modeling. Efforts with roots in his approach have come to be called Richardsonian.

the initiating state. It is an "*n*-body" (where *n* stands for any number greater than 2) as opposed to a "2-body" issue. Political scientists, like physicists, have struggled with the dramatically increased complexity of any analysis that focuses on more than two units. The multicountry model, GLOBUS, upon which we rely here should help us cut through this complexity in a way that statistical analyses cannot easily do.

Foreign Aid and Economic Performance

POLITICAL-IDEOLOGICAL LITERATURE

Any evaluation of proposals for increases in foreign aid occurs within the context of a highly politicized debate about the effectiveness of foreign assistance. At least three ideological positions can be identified: conservative, internationalist (modern liberal), and radical.[9]

The conservative position is that aid encourages the growth of unproductive and inefficient state structures in recipient countries. Not only do these bureaucracies waste the aid itself, they also develop patterns of interference in the economy that cause additional and longer-term economic damage. Thus, besides normally rejecting any claims for assistance based on historic compensation for colonial damage or based on moral and ethical grounds, the conservative position generally also argues aid to be counterproductive for recipient states.

> But not only is foreign aid potentially not required for development, it is, in actual fact, much more likely to obstruct it than to promote it. . . . Most importantly, aid increases the money, patronage and power of the recipient governments, and thereby their grip over the rest of society. (Bauer and Yamey 1984:294–295)

The internationalist world view often accepts a moral or humanitarian case for increased transfers from the North to the South. It also claims a mutual interest by rich and poor in such aid. The poor will benefit through direct reduction of poverty and hunger and through accelerated economic growth. The rich will benefit through the economic opportunities offered in a growing global South—for instance, through assured access to raw materials. In the words of the Brandt Commission report:

> The most urgent need is for the programme of large-scale transfer of funds from North to South to be stepped up substantially from year to

---

[9] These categories are comparable to those of Blake and Walters 1987 and of Hughes 1985a and 1985c. It is quite common in academic literature on political economy to refer to the conservative position as "classical liberal."

year during the final two decades of this century. Such an effort effectively directed towards the solution of the major problems discussed in this Report will benefit the South and turn back the rising tide of world poverty; it would also provide important benefits to the North. (1980:237)

Like other world views, the radical position incorporates variation and richness across a broad literature and is inevitably somewhat caricatured by a brief summary. There are some parallels between the conservative and the radical arguments. Radicals, too, argue that aid distorts political-economic structures of recipient countries, and therefore they often reach the conclusion that it does more harm than good (for example, Weissman 1975). The distortions radicals perceive lie largely in the socioeconomic divisions created by imperialism and reinforced by aid, such as dual economies (characterized by having distinct and largely separate traditional and modern components). Whereas conservatives argue that aid encourages statism and socialism, radicals perceive major aid donors, especially the World Bank and the IMF, as tools of the core capitalist states, often encouraging authoritarian governments that, in turn, conceal failures to be socially responsive behind laissez-faire philosophy. Prescriptively, unless significant global structural changes occur and alter the patterns of control of the economic system by advanced capitalist countries, radicals argue that self-reliance by LDCs (individually or collectively) may be superior to existing or even increased aid flows.

Most of these radical themes are to be found in the concluding chapter of Hayter and Watson (1985), who state:

> There is no possibility that the World Bank and the IMF will support policies that are not at least compatible with the perceived interests of the ruling class in the major capitalist powers which finance them. (p. 249)
>
> There is much to be gained in any case from a policy of greater self-reliance, a policy of using the resources of the country, especially its land, primarily to meet the basic needs of its people, and of reducing reliance on international trade and dependence on foreign products and skills. (pp. 253–254)
>
> Hard though it may be to establish a precise balance of the advantages and disadvantages of aid to right-wing governments from the point of view of the poor, there is no doubt that such advantages as may "trickle down" to the poor in those countries are very slight, and that they may well be outweighed by the disadvantages of bolstering oppressive governments and the luxury consumption of elites. (p. 259)

EMPIRICAL ANALYSES

Clearly, some points of disagreement appear open to empirical investigation, and considerable work has been done on the economic (and broader) impact of foreign aid. The studies of the effectiveness of foreign aid generally fall into our three methodological categories: case studies, statistical analyses, and model use.[10]

Case studies   The World Bank routinely analyzes individual projects and has reported that 94 percent of projects completed and evaluated in the 1970s met or exceeded a 10 percent rate of return (Marsden and Roe 1983). These case studies of projects can be and often are questioned because of the fungibility (substitutability) of development investment. That is, such project aid might be directed at high-return projects that would have been undertaken in any case, while the funds that aid displaces from these projects are then directed into lower-return projects or even redirected toward consumption. Kindleberger and Herrick graphically illustrate the point:

> One example deals with a low-income country that wanted to rebuild an ornate opera house. It applied for an aid loan to do so. The loan was refused on grounds that the opera house was not a development-oriented expenditure. The country had also been planning, as part of its development program, to build a dam with hydroelectric generators. It recognized an opening in the situation and returned to the potential lender, asking this time for a loan to build a dam. The lender, correctly identifying this as developmental infrastructure, granted the loan. Whereupon the country built both dam and opera house. (1977:301–302)

Marsden and Roe explicitly considered and rejected the argument that aid funds so displace other external private capital, but they did not address the argument that such funds could supplant domestic public or private investment. Analyses of entire countries (like Krueger's study of Korea, 1979) overcome the "big picture" problem, but they are often inconclusive because there is no control case (in which no aid is received) against which to compare the aid-receipt case.

Statistical analyses   The second methodological approach in this area, which attempts to address the control problem, is statistical, primarily of a cross-sectional nature. A number of analyses were undertaken in the early 1970s using this methodology. Griffin and Enos found an inverse relationship between aid and growth and argued that

> If anything, aid may have retarded development by leading to lower domestic savings, by distorting the composition of investment and thereby raising the capital-output ratio, by frustrating the emergence of an indigenous entrepreneurial class, and by inhibiting institutional reforms. (1970:326)

[10] A very useful review of the literature, which does not use these methodological categories as an organizing device but which discusses literature in each category, is Mikesell (1983).

Weisskopf (1972) seconded the argument about domestic savings in another cross-sectional analysis.

These statistical analyses, while identifying an important question, have significant weaknesses. Most fundamentally, higher foreign assistance could be associated with lower domestic savings for reasons other than the implied causality of higher aid leading to lower savings. Cross-sectionally, the result could arise from the reverse direction of causality—namely, that states with low savings rates attract a larger portion of internationally available foreign assistance. Longitudinally, a slowing of growth (because of emergencies such as earthquakes or droughts or because of crises such as reduced prices for export goods) could lead to both lower savings and higher aid in certain periods for individual countries.

One of the most recent large-scale studies of the effectiveness of foreign aid was commissioned by the eighteen governments of the Development Committee of the World Bank and the IMF (Cassen and Associates 1986; see also Development Committee 1986). The authors of the study did an extensive review of the literature and concluded that "inter-country statistical analyses do not show anything conclusive—positive or negative—about the impact of aid on growth" (Cassen 1986:33).

One of the central arguments of the Cassen study, and an important one for the analysis here, is that the impact of aid depends heavily upon the broader policy context. For instance, one underpinning of the statistical studies' conclusion that aid negatively affects domestic savings is the argument that states reduce taxes in the face of aid, effectively substituting aid for tax revenues. The reduction in taxes increases disposable household income, which is channeled almost entirely to consumption. That behavior by government need not necessarily be invariant across countries or political leaders.

Model-based studies A third methodological approach to analysis of the effectiveness of aid utilizes formal theory, in some cases imbedded in mathematical or computer models. The statistical analyses of the early 1970s reviewed in the preceding section were, in fact, reacting against what some saw to be an inappropriate treatment of aid through the use of two-gap models (see, for example, the two-gap analysis of aid to Greece by Adelman and Chenery 1966). Two-gap models posit that one of two restrictions exists on LDC economic growth: (1) savings, of which a shortage (or gap between demand and availability) can restrict investment, or (2) imports, especially raw materials or industrial goods needed to allow growth in domestic production. Foreign aid can contribute to growth by increasing savings or allowing payment for imports, depending on which of the gaps is currently binding. When investigating the savings gap, analysts using two-gap models treat foreign resources as additive to domestic savings and thus as direct increments to investment. It was this treatment that the statistical studies argued to be inappropriate. Naturally, one of the principal advantages of using a model—namely, the formalization of theory—can be lost if the specification (equation and parameter structure) is theoretically or empirically unsound.

The statistical analysis (reacting against the two-gap models) of the relationship between savings and investment led Dacy (1975) to undertake a dynamic model analysis of aid effectiveness also focusing on this linkage. Dacy argued that aid can improve growth but that with reasonable assumptions about reductions in savings and about difficulties in reversing savings decline, a subsequent withdrawal of aid might well leave an economy on a lower growth path than it would have been without aid.

An important modeling treatment is that of Leontief and Duchin (1983), who devoted one chapter of their analysis of reduced military spending to a consideration of the impact on LDCs should that reduction be channeled to foreign aid. They found that GDPs of recipient countries are very positively affected by the aid—in African countries in particular. Consumption increases somewhat more than GDP, but not a great deal faster. This result reveals perhaps a weakness of this particular model-based analysis: Because no financial representation exists, analysis of the possible aid-savings trade-off noted in many studies cannot reasonably be examined.[11] The Leontief model and the interpretation Leontief and Duchin offer of its results have much in common with the earlier two-gap analysis. In addition to the considerable increment aid provides for investment, the authors stress the importance aid has in relieving balance-of-payments constraints on imports.

Just as those pursuing statistical analyses reacted against the assumptions in the two-gap model concerning savings and investment, other scholars have challenged the trade analysis of the two-gap models—namely, the assumption that aid could finance an increment of imports comparable to the aid received. One such challenge comes from another model. An open-economy disequilibrium model analysis by Wijnbergen (1986) emphasizes the tendency for aid inflows to lead to appreciation of the real exchange rate and a decline in exports. Such a decline in export earnings would both offset the aid inflow and reduce domestic economic activity (the production of exports), thereby reducing the welfare effects of aid. The GLOBUS model does not make the simplified assumptions about either savings or import effects of aid that are found

---

[11] In a related analysis, Duchin (1983:551–552) argues that the aid will have a significant impact on recipients only in combination with structural change (although it is not clear from the analysis why that conclusion is reached).

in the two-gap models. It therefore may be able to shed light on some of the controversies.

Again, it is difficult to draw from the literature any strong conclusion concerning the validity of the proposition. Whereas statistical studies generally contradict the argument that increased aid would improve Southern economic performance, the model-based studies more often support the proposition.

Southern Economic Performance and Political Stability

POLITICAL-IDEOLOGICAL LITERATURE

The belief that economic development in the South contributes to greater political stability in Southern countries is an important part of the Idealist/Internationalist argument in support of foreign aid. Again the Brandt Commission illustrated the pattern of thought:

> So far we have referred only to economic interests which are shared by North and South. Yet they also share strong political interests in the proposals we put forward.
> Those political interests are based on the fact that development—widely shared development—is a condition for national and international stability. . . . While many causes underlie conflict and instability, failure of development often provides the conditions in which they can originate and flourish. (1983:35)

The I/I argument often has two components: that economic advance satisfies pressures from the poorest in society who would otherwise potentially translate dissatisfaction into political unrest and that economic progress will facilitate the creation of a large and stable middle class. The second component also often links economic development to the creation of more democratic political structures. (See especially Lipset 1959; also Cnudde and Neubauer 1969; and the review by Huntington 1985:258–261.)

Concern with the linkage between economic failures and political instability is widespread. Writing on behalf of the Overseas Development Council's regular reports on United States–Third World relationships, Hansen argued that

> . . . it is understandable why most observers assign a significant probability to a continuation of—if not an increase in—political instability in the world's developing countries in the 1980s. [Social mobilization leads] to the creation of expectations which the process of economic development in these same countries has considerable difficulty in meeting. Given economic growth projections for most of the developing countries in the

troubled period of the early to mid-1980s at a minimum, the difficulties would seem to be growing in magnitude every year. (Hansen 1982:27)

Although Hansen thus sketched a linkage between economic factors and political instability, he did so in a manner that moved him away from a simplistic idealist argument. Namely, he argued that political instability is inevitable in LDCs in the near future because development itself causes instability.

> [Instability] is an integral part of the processes of (a) "modernization," "development," or whatever label we choose to give the processes of industrialization, urbanization, education, and (global) communication generally incorporated under these labels, and (b) the processes of regional state-system formation. Therefore the one absolutely null policy option is to eliminate the instability. It must be lived with. (Hansen 1982:28)

One of the earliest developments of the argument that growth *causes* instability was that of Mancur Olson (1971). He began by reviewing statements of scholars and practitioners in support of the Idealist/ Internationalist thesis linking foreign aid, economic development, and political stability. He quoted Eugene Black, who, when he was president of the World Bank, stated: "Economic development is one of the keys to stability and peace in the world." Similarly, he cited a report from Richard Nixon to President Eisenhower claiming that it is "conditions of want and instability on which communism breeds." Eisenhower himself characterized foreign aid as "an investment in peace and orderly political evolution toward a democratic world" (Olson 1971:215).

Olson went on to present his own argument that economic change leads to the rise in class status of some and the fall of others, and that this breaking of old class ties threatens the social order. Although Olson did not use the expression, part of his argument is one of "status discrepancy" and focuses on the tensions created by a gap between status ascribed to individuals in the old order and their actual status in the evolving new order. Olson, who like Hansen was interested in the policy implications for the United States of this analysis, concluded that

> If, when these nations reach the takeoff stage, the United States then gives them vast amounts of aid and makes the transition to a modern economy even more abrupt and disruptive than it would otherwise be, this will surely stimulate political and social instability.
> If, on the other hand, the United States gives a great deal of emphasis to *preparing* the poorest countries to survive the storm and stress of delayed industrialization and attempts to build a basis for steady and sustained growth, it may help spare these countries some of the political turmoil that industrialization so often involves. (Olson 1971:227)

Although the Olson argument uses class terminology, the fundamental concern is with social mobility and with individuals. A Marxist class orientation to the question would more heavily emphasize class conflict. For Marxists, the transition from fundamentally feudal societies, which exist or have recently existed in many less developed countries, to capitalist societies will necessarily involve class conflict. Without such conflict (or perhaps external force), the transition cannot be made. So, too, will the longer-term transitions from capitalist to socialist societies involve conflict between capitalist and worker classes. Any process that accelerates economic development (in the absence of countervailing repression) is potentially going to accelerate the pace of overt class conflict.

> Even where imperialism is successful in advancing the forces of production in the periphery, it generates certain contradictions which threaten the stability of the process and offer opportunities for revolutionary change. . . . First, the unequal character of capitalist growth in the periphery is likely to give rise to serious tensions. . . . Rising aspirations conflict with a largely unchanging reality for the masses of the people who benefit little from economic growth. (Weisskopf 1978:511)

EMPIRICAL ANALYSES

Case studies   Many of the classic studies of revolution, particularly those that place revolutionary episodes in the context of longer-term socioeconomic development, are in essence case studies of the relationship between economic advance and political stability. Among the most important generalizations that have come from those studies is that revolutions seldom occur in stable or even stagnant societies but, rather, appear in those undergoing significant economic change. A second generalization is that revolutions often appear when change has engendered expectations of continuing change that are then, for any number of reasons, frustrated by failures in the economic growth process. These two generalizations have been captured by Davies (1969) in his theory of the "J-curve" (the economic growth pattern that gives rise to and then dashes growing expectations looks something like an upside-down and leaning "J"). He explored the French Revolution, the American Civil War, the Nazi takeover in Germany, and black and student rebellions in the United States during the 1950s and 1960s using this theory and found considerable support for it.[12]

---

[12] The argument of Gurr (1970) on "relative deprivation" has much in common with J-curve theory but is more general—it would also incorporate the status discrepancy arguments of Olson. Gurr argues that the important gap is between the conditions one faces and the conditions to which one feels rightfully entitled. An objective outside observer may not judge some to be in want who feel deprived, or may perceive some to be in abject poverty who accept it without question.

Comparative case study analyses also suggest hypotheses relating the speed of change and the violence associated with the process. Huntington (1985:266–267), in a comparative review of democratization, characterized that process in Britain as a "stately progression from civic rights to political rights to social rights, gradual development of parliamentary supremacy and cabinet government, and incremental expansion of the suffrage over the course of a century." That linear and steady description also fits Sweden relatively well, according to work he cited.

In contrast, Huntington argued, two nonlinear and arguably more violent models have characterized much of the Third World. One of the two models is alternating despotism and democracy. The other Huntington called dialectical, a process involving the emergence of a middle class and installation of a democratic government, followed by a normally right-wing reaction against and overthrow of that government. In time, this collapses and is replaced by a more stable democracy. Huntington did not, but could have, interpreted the difference in First and Third World models as a function in part of the slower pace of economic change in Britain and Sweden compared with that of later arrivals on the industrial scene. Instead, he points (1985:269) to the "major increases in social mobilization (such as urbanization, literacy, and media consumption)" that encourage mass participation early in the developing world and before a democracy-building process historically pursued in the First World primarily by elites.

Statistical analyses A substantial number of statistical studies on the relationship between growth and stability exist. An extensive review of the literature can be found in Zimmerman (1983:94–102). There are two separate questions investigated by this literature, corresponding to the political-theoretical arguments sketched earlier. The first is whether higher economic growth rates are generally associated with greater political stability or greater instability. The second concerns the impact on political stability of downturns in growth. The first question is easily investigated with cross-sectional analysis, whereas the second lends itself more readily to longitudinal analysis.

The evidence concerning the impact of higher growth on stability is mixed but most often supports the contention that higher growth is stabilizing. In a factor analysis of 33 countries, Alker and Russett (1964) found a quite strong negative relationship between rate of GNP growth (1950–1962) and deaths from domestic group violence. Flanigan and Fogelman (1970) also supported this majority finding. In a cross-sectional analysis of 26 countries, Parvin (1973) reported the rate of economic growth to be inversely related to political unrest (deaths from violence). In a 108-nation study, Hibbs (1973) again found a weak negative relationship between higher economic growth rate and violence levels. On the other hand, the Feierabends and Nesvold (1969) documented a high association between modernization rate and instability. And in a study of 14 states between 1955 and 1960, Tanter and Midlarsky (1967) uncovered a moderate positive correlation between economic growth rate and deaths from political violence.

Turning to the impact of slowing growth within a country, as opposed to higher or lower growth across countries, Gupta and Venieris (1981) undertook a longitudinal analysis of Britain in the period 1948–1967. They identified a positive correlation between slower economic growth or increased unemployment and social violence, especially industrial disputes. Hughes (1985b) focused on the impact of the oil-shock-related economic downturn of the mid-1970s and found that in industrial countries, the downturn was associated with greater domestic conflict (although in LDCs, where the downturn was much less pronounced, the result was contradicted).

Ironically, these studies do not directly tackle the question of whether significantly accelerated economic growth within a given country (as opposed to continuous high growth rates) will be stabilizing or destabilizing. Although the cross-sectional evidence linking higher growth to greater political stability may suggest that accelerated growth is stabilizing, and longitudinal analyses that link slowing growth to instability carry the same implication, longitudinal studies linking accelerating growth rate to stability or instability appear to be missing. There is no reason to believe that the relationship would be symmetrical—that is, that because slowing growth rates appear to be associated with instability, accelerating growth rates would lead to stability. It is quite possible that both would be socially disruptive and therefore destabilizing.

To this point, we have focused on the relationship between the *rate* of growth and stability (and on acceleration or slowing in the rate). But in the long run, the relationship between the *level* of development and stability is also important to the Idealist/Internationalist argument. Most studies support the Idealist/Internationalist view—namely, that more-developed countries experience less domestic violence. An extensive and systemic investigation of the linkage between economic level and political stability was undertaken by Hibbs (1973). He reviewed earlier theoretical and empirical work and found that a curvilinear relationship is identified in much of that work. Specifically, the argument is that the early stages of industrialization encourage a great deal of violence relative to preindustrial society but that in advanced industrial states, the working class "is now at peace with the industrial system, and ideology has lost its former relevance as the absence of a suppressed class leaves little hope for radicalism" (Hibbs 1973:22).

Some earlier cross-sectional statistical analysis lent support to this curvilinear thesis. For instance, Feierabend et al. (1969) found a moderate curvilinear relationship between level of economic development and political instability across 84 countries. In contrast, Flanigan and Fogelman (1970) used longitudinal analysis between 1800 and 1960 on a variety of countries and found a linear and negative relationship. Hibbs simultaneously tested both linear and curvilinear models (as well as the hypothesis that there is no relationship) in a cross-sectional analysis of 108 countries. In general, the curvilinear model performed better, although the percentage of variation explained (24–26 percent) was not high.

Model-based analyses   The work of Hibbs resulted in a quite complex multiequation model of the relationship between many measures of development (both rate and level) and many of domestic political violence. He did not, however, attempt to apply the finished product to individual countries or to undertake dynamic analysis with it (and, hence, we discussed it with statistical analyses).

Richardson (1987) created a dynamic computer model of domestic violence in Argentina and further tested that model by extension to Mexico. He adopted the relative deprivation theory of Gurr as a basis and anticipated increased violence when economic performance falls below expectations (based on past performance). The model also incorporates government repression and a "contagion" or self-reinforcing representation of violence. In a test of model-generated results against Argentine data from 1900 to 1980, the correlation of model and observed values was 0.66 (1987:18). The model also performed well for Mexico. The implications of a model of this structure is that accelerated economic growth rates would be stabilizing in the short run but over a longer period would be built into expectations. At that point, a reversion to earlier rates would be destabilizing.

To summarize the evidence on this linkage of the Idealist-Internationalist theory, the majority of the research studies suggest that more rapid economic growth in the South will be stabilizing so long as the higher growth, once it has come to be anticipated, is maintained. Moreover, should Southern countries achieve levels of economic performance in the long run comparable to those in the North, the research suggests that it would further contribute to domestic political stability in those countries.

Southern Economic Performance and North-South Relations

POLITICAL-IDEOLOGICAL LITERATURE

This aspect of the Idealist/Internationalist argument builds on a perception of mutual interests between the North and the South. The Brandt Commission stated it in this way:

> There is ample historical evidence that expansion of trade is and has always been one of the mainsprings of the world economy. For most countries balanced trade expansion is a less inflationary form of raising the level of economic activity than stimulation through increases in domestic public expenditure. The large-scale transfers we will propose are seen therefore as measures both to support growth in developing countries directly, and to permit a significant expansion of world trade. It is in this sense that we view them as contributing to growth and employment creation in the North as well as in the South. (1980:68)

In other words, the South can be an "engine" of global economic growth. The Brandt Commission authors feel such mutual economic benefit will underwrite improved political relationships as well.

> . . . there is no doubt that many people view with considerable unease (for security reasons, not to speak of others) the continuance of existing inequalities and inequities in the world economy. . . . Failures of development can certainly give rise to instability *within* countries, in ways which generate additional conflict internationally. (1981:397)

The argument linking lagging Southern economic performance to political instability in the South and deteriorating North-South relations has deep roots. Among others, the Pearson Commission report popularized it (Pearson 1969). Others have spelled out specifically the linkage between economic performance in the South and North-South relations.

> By 1974 there was a great deal of pent-up frustration in the developing countries over the slowness with which international economic inequities were being reduced. This potential bargaining energy was rendered kinetic when a few countries in the group acquired "oil power" and were inclined, politically, to deploy it on behalf of the Third World generally. (Lewis 1983:15)

In reviewing the evolution of North-South relations, Moon (1987) recognized the widespread appeal of this mutual-interest perspective:

> The venerable argument of internationalists that Southern demand for Northern products sustains growth for developed nations . . . culminated

in the so-called "global Keynesianism" of the first Brandt Commission report. (1987:228–229)

But Moon saw less "win-win" and more "win-lose" (zero-sum character) in the North-South relationship. He pointed out that the growth in Northern protectionist sentiment and action has followed in part from the successful penetration of sensitive Northern markets by NICs, and he argued that by the end of the 1970s, a "political backlash" had appeared in developed countries. That backlash may grow further in intensity.

> Moreover, the major readjustment in the North lies ahead. As the global division of labor increasingly turns away from Northern specialization in manufactured goods (except those in high technology), employment effects must persist and expand. (Moon 1987:243)

Tied to the general North-South problem is the more specific decline in America's global role. Many have pointed out the difficulty of sustaining free trade as an international economic leader or hegemon declines (Kindleberger, 1973, was perhaps the first). Further growth in the South, especially at rates more rapid than those in the United States, accelerates the relative decline of the United States and may undercut its willingness and ability to carry the burden of support for free trade.

Somewhat surprisingly, Moon optimistically concluded that North-South relations will "slowly grow into the interdependence mode which has long marked West-West interactions" (1987:245). He could as easily have dwelled on his point that the backlash would intensify as Southern growth proceeds. It is not clear whether the mutual benefit (win-win) or basically neomercantilist (win-lose) understanding of North-South relations will prove more accurate in describing the linkage between improved Southern economic performance and North-South relationships. The nature of the impact of faster Southern growth on North-South politics may actually depend more on whether the *perceptions* of the key economic actors are win-win or win-lose than on the reality of economic impact.

EMPIRICAL ANALYSES

There is in reality very little systematic analysis of the relationship between Southern economic performance and North-South relations. Most previous linkages in the Idealist/Internationalist theory that we have discussed are ones that can be investigated at the country level. This issue obviously focuses our attention on the international system as a whole, as did our discussion of East-West relations. Thus, the kind of cross-sectional or (state-level) longitudinal statistical analysis reviewed as evidence in support of or contradicting earlier linkages becomes at best difficult, and perhaps even inappropriate. We report none here.

Case studies   Some appropriate analysis comes from historical study of international trade regimes, especially the free or liberal trading orders of the nineteenth century and of the post–World War II period.[13] For instance, studies by Krasner (1976) and Lake (1983) emphasize the relationship between the breakdown of liberal trading orders and decline in the strength of dominant economic actors (like the United Kingdom or the United States). Both note the tendency of smaller and less economically developed countries to take advantage of open markets created by the dominant actors and to contribute little to creating open markets themselves. Economic development of the smaller countries (and trade expansion) can make such opportunistic behavior more important and potentially more disruptive in the international environment. These studies are generally pessimistic that economic development could in the foreseeable future make many Southern countries into what Lake calls "supporters" of the free-trade order. Thus, to the extent that Southern growth is faster than Northern growth and makes Northern states, including the United States, less relatively able to dominate the trading system, such growth would seem, in historical context, to be disruptive.

This question would perhaps best be investigated by studying the export-promoting newly industrialized countries. Those countries have had the greatest impact on the international economic system of all LDCs. Have they evolved toward supporters of free trade and global economic cooperation?

Disruption of a liberal trading order is not, of course, the same as disruption of North-South political relations; yet, the citations from the Brandt Commission at the beginning of this section did make that same connection. And the North-South struggle over the proposals of the New International Economic Order suggests that they are closely related. The North has proven reluctant, in the face of an increasingly forceful South, to make such exceptions to the liberal system as tariff preferences or commodity price stabilization schemes.

Another literature of relevance to the relationship between Southern economic performance and North-South relations is that which focuses on the relationship between systemic distribution of military capabilities and propensity for conflict in that system. Southern gains

[13] Unfortunately, liberal in the context of this argument refers to the "classical liberal" and free-trade perspective, while liberal up to this point has been used in the context of modern political terminology in the United States. The confusion is inherent in the juxtaposition of popular writing (which uses liberal as we have to this point) and the more scholarly literature on political economy (which retains the classical terminology and has no widely accepted term for the "modern liberal").

economically can be translated into military strength. In fact, that has happened in the last two decades as growth of military expenditure in the South has outstripped that in the North (see the data in Sivard 1986:32). Evidence on this issue was summarized earlier in connection with consideration of the implications of arms control for East-West relations. Beer has carefully evaluated the arguments and empirical evidence (1981:171–172):

> We might expect international inequality to help make wars both more frequent and more serious. The more unequal any international environment is, the more violence we might expect. This would be particularly true from the perspective of Marxist theory. Marxism—in both traditional and contemporary forms—highlights the inclination of monopoly capitalism to export the class struggle, exploitation, and revolution on a global scale through imperialism. Marxism predicts that the expansion of monopolistic cartels will eventually produce the violent total breakdown of the international system.
>
> Alternatively, however, inequality might work to produce fewer wars since inferiors should be cautious about fighting superiors and equals afraid of losing their rank.
>
> Empirical research does not confirm either relationship. . . . Some suggest that war is more likely between groups of equal size and resources. . . . Some find that countries that are unequal are more likely to go to war. . . . Others find that foreign conflict, including both war incidence and casualties, are unrelated to differences in size and economic development. . . .

Model-based analysis We know of no computer simulations that have addressed this linkage of the Idealist/Internationalist theory. Because of that and because the issue must be addressed globally and not at the level of an individual state, the multicountry GLOBUS model may itself be uniquely situated to shed some light on the issue.

Overall, the evidence on the relationship between improved Southern economic performance and North-South relations is so partial and peripherally related to the central question that it can scarcely be used as a guide to expectations of model behavior.

ON METHOD AND THE CURRENT STUDY

The foregoing brief literature review suggests the difficulty of reaching firm conclusions about any of the relationships addressed in this study. The implications of reductions in arms spending for international political behavior are uncertain. It appears that such reductions should benefit the economies of states undertaking them. But, again, it is not clear that increased foreign assistance (whether made available as a result of reductions in defense spending or by some other means) will benefit the economies of recipients. More rapid economic growth in the South is nearly as likely to be destabilizing as stabilizing, according to the research on that linkage. And a narrowing of the North-South gap might as easily lead the South to forcefully advance its grievances with the North as to improved North-South relationships.

From the review of the literature, we learn something of the weaknesses (as well as the strengths) in each of the methodologies as applied to the questions under consideration in this volume. For example:

> Case studies have some contributions to make, notably that concentration on a single country can allow examination of a larger number of variables and possible causal connections than is possible in the typical statistical analysis. A weakness is the inability to systematically control for the effects of confounding variables.
>
> Both cross-sectional and longitudinal studies help formalize the analysis. They can allow a researcher to control for the effect of selected additional variables on the relationship of interest to him. But in both statistical procedures, it is difficult to infer causality.
>
> Models can help a researcher directly contrast the presence and the absence of policies such as reductions in military spending or increases in aid, since they allow "what-if" analyses in which only a single external change is introduced into the system represented. This can help clarify patterns of causality. Moreover, models can assist the researcher in considering explicitly the interaction of two or more policies such as reductions in military spending and increases in aid, and there is reason to believe that there are important effects from that interaction. But a model's results may be critically flawed if an important real-world linkage is not included or is represented incorrectly.

The analysis we undertake in the following chapters is based on a large-scale global computer model called GLOBUS. It has some features of several of the methodologies considered earlier and thus can build on some of their collective strengths. For instance, because of its forty-year time horizon, it allows what are in essence long-term longitudinal analyses of individual countries as well as cross-sectional analysis of the twenty-five nations it contains. In addition, an individual country can be selected for much more intensive analysis in a case-study fashion. It allows us to experiment with alternative policies—for example, increased aid versus no aid increase—and observe how the results differ as a consequence. Such experiments are directly relevant to the causality question because they permit us to see the impact of a specific alteration while controlling for the effects of all other factors. Moreover, secondary policy changes can be simulated in combination with changes in military spending or foreign aid receipts. Although the use of a GLOBUS cannot solve all difficulties associated with the complex analysis of these questions (and limitations will be noted), it can extend our ability to understand the issues.

In the chapters that follow, we will explore each of the linkages in Figure 2-1 with a parallel strategy of inquiry. After modifying the GLOBUS model to introduce the appropriate policy interventions, we examine the behavior of the model to determine whether the predicted changes in behavior occur. For example, in Chapter 3, we will introduce significant arms reductions in the simulated West and East nations beginning in 1990 to determine what impact that may have on their domestic economies and diplomatic relations with one another. Chapter 4 discusses the introduction of a marked increase in foreign aid given by the West and seeks to determine whether such a policy is advantageous to the South. The question of the degree to which internal reforms in the less developed nations can bring about more growth with or without additional aid is the focus of Chapter 5. Chapter 6 looks at the supposition that more growth in the South should promote domestic political stability there, while Chapter 7 considers the impact of increased growth in the South on North-South diplomatic relations. Chapter 8 brings together our overall findings and relates them to the broader question of how the world might change in the next two decades, with or without policy changes of the kind proposed by the Idealist/Internationalist theory.

APPENDIX: AN OVERVIEW
OF METHODOLOGICAL TERMINOLOGY

This appendix defines and places in a general context the methodological terms used in the chapter. Science begins with **concepts,** which are names or labels given to a generalized set of objects or ideas. *Chair* is a fairly concrete concept; although individual chairs vary greatly, we recognize the term as referring to a set of objects having much in common. *Wealth* and *military capability* are somewhat more abstract concepts; yet, although somewhat less easily defined than is chair, they also have a generalizable character. The United States clearly has wealth and military capability, as does Japan.

Many concepts describe phenomena that vary in degree or in quantity. Although it makes little sense to speak of more or less chair, it is sensible to refer to more or less wealth. Such concepts become *variables* when they are operationalized—that is, when rules for measuring variations in degree or quantity are set. Wealth of countries might well be measured by their Gross National Products (GNP), a variable measure of wealth. The military capability of countries might be measured by looking at their levels of military spending. That might not be a totally satisfactory measure of such capability for several reasons; for instance, the same spending by different countries might buy very different amounts of military manpower or equipment. Nonetheless, the measure would allow us to look in rough terms at the variation of military capability across countries.

We relate concepts to each other in **propositions.** Propositions suggest **covariation** in the measurement of two concepts. For example, we would generally expect that wealth and military capability of countries would be related. Moreover, we would expect the relationship to be **direct** or **positive.** That is, as the wealth of a country increases, we expect military capability to increase. When upward variation in one variable is associated with downward movement in a second, the relationship between them is considered **inverse** or **negative.**

A **theory** is a set of interrelated propositions that we use for explaining and predicting. (Appendix A, at the end of this volume, defines theory more fully and identifies different definitions.) The six propositions of Figure 2–1 constitute a theory of the global implications of disarmament and development. The propositions in that theory are not sufficiently well supported to constitute **laws,** and instead they are **hypotheses** concerning the relationships. When we wish to test hypotheses and examine individual propositions, we rely heavily on three methodologies: case studies, statistical analyses, and formal models.

A **case study** is an analysis based on one episode or case. For instance, we might wish to test the proposition that overly large military expenditures by countries seeking expanded military capability will damage the countries' economies and lead to an erosion or a collapse of wealth. We could test this proposition through a detailed examination of the collapse of the Roman Empire, and we would look carefully at the intermediate linkages between Roman military spending and the strength of its economy (for instance, how spending affected maintenance of a transportation network and availability of food).

One difficulty with this analytical approach (and the others as well) is that it is very hard to know whether other variables (concepts) are confusing the relationship between those in our proposition. For instance, climatic changes preceding the Roman Empire's collapse could have both weakened the agricultural potential of the empire and encouraged exterior populations (barbarians) to intensify their intrusions into it, thus necessitating higher military spending. That is, a third variable might be leading to both high military spending and economic collapse, so that our proposition about causality appears on the surface to be correct but is in reality wrong. It is very difficult in a case study to make the assumption of **ceteris paribus** (that is, all else remaining equal or unchanged) as we look at the relationship between change in our two concepts.

A second approach to the analysis of a proposition is statistical and involves more than one observation or case. Statistical analysis can be either **cross-sectional** or **longitudinal.** In cross-sectional analysis, two variables are compared at a single point in time across many cases. For instance, Figure 2-2 shows the relationship between GNP and military spending for the East and the West European countries represented in the GLOBUS model. It is fairly obvious from that figure that there is a direct relationship between the two across countries; that is, the two variables rise and fall together.

A line has been drawn on that figure to indicate the way in which military spending appears to increase with economic size. When the points on such a figure fall generally along a straight line, we say that the relationship is **linear.** Should the points fall along a curved line, the relationship would be **curvilinear.** The statistical procedure that is most often used to determine the nature of that line or relationship is called **regression analysis.** A **correlation** is a statistical measure of how

FIGURE 2–2   European Defense Expenditure and Gross National Product in 1985. *Source:* ACDA 1988.

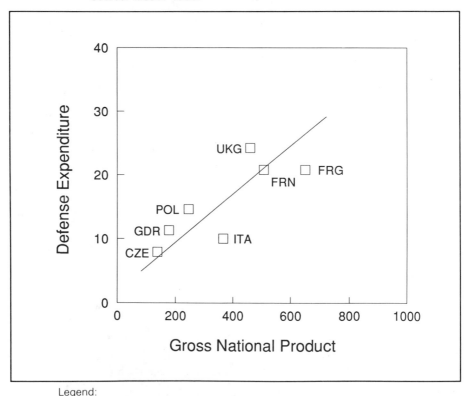

Legend:
CZE   Czechoslovakia   ITA   Italy
FRG   West Germany   POL   Poland
FRN   France   UKG   England
GDR   East Germany

close the points are to the line. Normally, a correlation value of 0 indicates that no line appears to trace the relationship between the variables. A value of 1 indicates that all the points fall on an upward sloping line (on the line of a direct or positive relationship), whereas a value of −1 indicates that all the points fall on a downward sloping line (on the line of an inverse or negative relationship).

Longitudinal analysis looks at the relationship of two variables over time for the same case. Figure 2-3 traces GNP and defense spending from 1975 through 1985 for West Germany. In this figure, each point represents a year rather than a country as in Figure 2-2. It indicates the same positive or direct relationship between the two variables as did the cross-sectional analysis. The two types of analysis often, but by no means always, support each other with respect to a given relationship.

To the degree that the two variables shown in these figures appropriately measure or **operationalize** the concepts of wealth and military capability, the figures provide support for a proposition that the two concepts are highly related. Our propositions generally suggest not simply

FIGURE 2–3   West German Defense Expenditure and Gross National Product, 1975–1985. *Source:* ACDA 1988.

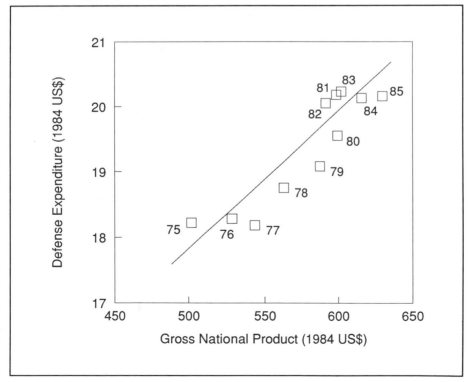

that there is covariation but also that there is causality. For instance, we might believe that an increase in wealth will lead to an increase in military capability.

As suggestive as our figures are, we can never prove such **causality.** As in our case study analysis, there is always the possibility that there is another variable that is accounting for the relationship between the two we examine. The ceteris paribus assumption may be violated. When we are conscious of another variable that might influence the relationship specified in the proposition, procedures exist to bring that variable into the statistical analysis. But because we can never possibly consider all external variables that could lead to the appearance of a causal relationship when none is present in reality, it is in fact impossible to verify causality. Although we might strongly doubt it, the positions of the stars, the occurrence of sunspots, or the machinations of the mafia might influence both our economies and our decision making about defense spending.

Another problem with respect to causality is the difficulty in determining the probable direction of it. For instance, it may be plausible to argue that military capability leads to wealth, rather than the reverse. Longitudinal analysis does offer us some assistance here. If we focus on **change** in GNP and **change** in military spending (rather than the **levels** of the two variables), we can ask whether changes in one tend to precede or follow the changes in the other). Precedence does support (again it does not prove) causality. This is a focus on **lagged effects.**

The third analytical approach is **formal modeling,** an abstract mathematical representation of the relationship among several variables. Appendix A describes **simulation,** a computerized approach built upon formal modeling. Often, the relationships among variables in a formal model are based on cross-sectional or longitudinal analyses.

Very often, propositions like those in Figure 2-1, especially in the policy arena, concern the relationship between two variables that are linked in the real world by very complex mechanisms. If these mechanisms are represented in the model, it may be no more obvious in advance how one variable in the model will respond to changes in another than it is in the real world. But we can use the model to investigate the relationship by experimenting with changes in the first variable. An important advantage of the model over case study or statistical analyses is that we can control it so that only one change is introduced externally. That is, we can impose the ceteris paribus assumption on the model. A serious problem with a model is that we cannot be sure that the intermediate linkages between the variable we change and the one linked to it in the proposition are correctly specified in the model.

Swords into Plowshares?

CHAPTER 3

The first element in the Idealist/Internationalist design for a better future under investigation here is arms reduction among the nations of both the East and the West, and in this chapter we will explore what the long-term implications of that might be. We begin by discussing some principal alternative ways in which arms reduction might be brought about and then describe the implementation of the particular arms reduction scenario we will use. Following that, we examine the direct and the indirect effects of arms reduction upon domestic and international political and economic conditions to see if the predictions of the I/I theory are borne out.

IMPLEMENTING ARMS REDUCTION

Alternative Paths to Arms Reduction

It is generally assumed that any significant arms reduction by East and West would have to come about as a consequence of extended negotiations among those nations. Up to this time, such negotiations, and the treaties that they have sometimes produced (for example, the antiballistic missile [ABM] and intermediate nuclear forces [INF] agreements), have focused on limiting particular classes of weapons. As valuable as those agreements have been, they have not brought about any significant reduction in the burden of armaments as called for in the

I/I proposals. Nevertheless, it is conceivable that a successful contin-uation of such negotiations (particularly the mutual and balanced force reduction, or MBFR, talks) might lead to significant defense savings. If the United States and the Soviet Union were to drastically cut (and demobilize) their conventional forces in Western and in Eastern Europe, for example, substantial defense reductions in all nations in the West and the East blocs might follow.

A less realistic alternative (but one generally favored by the United Nations) would be for West and East nations to agree upon limits to defense spending. Under such an agreement, the parties to it would be allowed to create and deploy whatever force structures they chose as long as the total resources allocated to this did not exceed some specific budgetary threshold. Discussions of general arms reduction usually focus on this type of agreement.

There is, of course, the possibility that a significant reduction in East and West armaments could emerge not from direct negotiations but from "tacit bargaining." If some "security dilemmas"[1] in Central Europe could be resolved by a slow but steady reduction in tension in that area, then East and West nations might cautiously but meaningfully reduce their arms.

Since the design for the future under investigation here *assumes* that significant arms reduction is accomplished, the specific way in which that comes about is not of central concern to us. That is not to say that the question is unimportant but only to assert that it is outside the scope of our analysis, since our focus is on the possible *effects* of arms reduction rather than on its *genesis*. Nevertheless, we must specify our arms reduction scenario in precise terms in order to be able to introduce it operationally into the simulation model.

We considered several different arms reduction scenarios and ex-perimented extensively with one that assumed a significant shift in the relative power of the government bureaucracies vying for resources within the *East*[2] and the *West* nations (Bremer and Hughes 1987). In the end, we opted for a simple scenario in which we assume that, beginning in 1990, the nations of the *West* and the *East* reduce their defense burdens (that is, defense expenditures in relation to GDP) by

---

[1] When one state increases its military strength to protect itself, it simultaneously increases the threat it potentially poses to other states (the distinction between defensive and offensive weapons is seldom great). Other states respond by increasing their own strength. The ironic consequence of an attempt to increase security can be either no change (after costly expenditures) or even lessened security. This pattern of interaction frames a security dilemma. More generally, the term refers to the inability of individual states to provide their own security in a world without central authority.

[2] In this and the remaining chapters, italics are used to denote the GLOBUS regions. That is, *West, East, South,* and *Opec* designate the specific sets of nations listed in Chapter 1, whereas West, East, South, and OPEC refer to the more general groups.

about one-third over the following five years. The specific target defense burdens for the eleven nations are given in Table 3-1. Such reductions are feasible, for as we saw in Chapter 1, the United States by itself implemented roughly that reduction between 1958 and 1965 and accomplished a nearly 50 percent reduction between 1968 and 1979.

Three considerations figured in the selection of these target values. First, the target defense burdens should not lead to a fundamental shift in the *East-West* balance of power, which meant that, given the smaller size of their economies, the nations of the *East* should have generally higher defense burdens than the nations of the *West.* Second, the resulting cuts in defense spending had to be significant rather than trivial for a meaningful test of the I/I theory to be carried out. To us, that meant reducing total expenditures by at least one-third over the long term, and we used one-third reductions of the simulated 1990 values as our beginning point for the derivation of these values. Japan was an exception to the one-third reduction rule, since their defense burden is already quite low. Third, for the sake of exposition, the set of values should be easy to understand and remember. That led us to select the round percentages shown in Table 3-1.

To explain further how we experimentally introduced this type of arms reduction, it is necessary for us to discuss how decisions concerning the allocation of resources to defense are normally made in GLOBUS. Once that is accomplished, we can turn to the specific changes that were made to these altered defense burden targets.

National Security Decision Making in GLOBUS

The process by which simulated GLOBUS nations decide how much to spend on defense is relatively complicated but fully described in Cusack (1987). Thus, we only need sketch out some of the more im-

TABLE 3–1 Target Defense Burdens of *West* and *East* Nations with Arms Reduction

WEST NATIONS	DEFENSE AS A % OF GDP IN 1995	EAST NATIONS	DEFENSE AS A % OF GDP IN 1995
United States	5.0	Soviet Union	8.0
Canada	2.0	East Germany	5.0
United Kingdom	2.0	Poland	2.0
France	2.0	Czechoslovakia	3.0
West Germany	2.0		
Italy	2.0		
Japan	1.0		

portant aspects of that process here, and we refer the reader seeking more detail to the aforementioned source. The national security decision-making process is composed of three principal steps: (1) the setting of a desired level of defense spending, (2) the reconciliation of that desired level with other desired levels of expenditure to produce a final defense expenditure value, and (3) the transformation of that expenditure into actual military capability. We will discuss each of these steps briefly.

A simulated nation's desired defense spending is set in accordance with the results of assessments of the external security situation of the nation and the internal bureaucratic needs of the military. The first assessment involves surveying the diplomatic flows received from and the military capabilities of all other nations in order to identify probable future friends and foes. This yields measures of expected threat and support, and the difference between the two is compared with the nation's existing capability in order to determine if and by how much the nation needs to add military capability to counter future threat. The outcome of the second assessment depends upon the military bureaucracy's determination of the minimum expenditure required to sustain itself. These two assessments are combined to produce a desired defense expenditure figure.

In addition to desired defense expenditures, the simulated budgetary process also generates desired civilian expenditures, desired government investment, desired total expenditures, and expected debt management payments. The last of these are considered obligatory; hence, the reconciliation process involves matching the sum of desired defense, civilian, and investment expenditures with the difference between desired total expenditures and expected debt management payments. The process by which the final defense, civilian, and investment expenditures are derived is complex, but three important parameters that reflect the budget bargaining power of the relevant bureaucracies play a significant role, for they determine the distribution of budget cuts and increases across the three main categories.[3]

In GLOBUS, two types of military capability are distinguished: conventional and strategic-nuclear. Both are measured in terms of indices that reflect stocks of military equipment, and, for conventional capability, military manpower also contributes to the index.[4] All twenty-five GLOBUS nations possess conventional military capability, and five of them

---

[3] Parameters are normally unchanging numerical coefficients in the mathematical formulas describing the relationships among variables. Within the model, these particular parameters are called *top2, top3,* and *top4,* and correspond to the budget bargaining power of defense, civilian, and investment bureaucracies, respectively.

[4] For more information on the derivation of these indices, see Cusack (1982).

have strategic-nuclear capability as well. On the conventional side, separate expenditures are made for defense labor and defense capital based on nation-specific ratios, while on the strategic-nuclear side, all expenditure is assumed to be for capital items. The actual amounts of capability added to a nation's arsenal depend upon the expenditure level in each category and the changing cost structure of each type of capability.

Experimental Introduction of Arms Reduction

The first step in introducing arms reductions of the sort described earlier was to alter the process by which desired defense spending is determined. Rather than being a function of external threat and internal bureaucratic needs, beginning in 1990 desired defense in the *West* and the *East* nations is set equal to a nation-specific share of GDP. Between 1990 and 1995, these shares decline linearly toward the target defense burdens shown in Table 3-1 and remain at those levels thereafter.

Lowering the desired defense spending is not sufficient to guarantee reduced spending levels, however, because of the way in which the budget reconciliation process functions. Any sudden reduction in desired defense spending will release resources for reallocation, and a large share of those resources would be allocated back into defense, given its relatively large budget bargaining power. To prevent that, we reduced the budget bargaining power of defense[5] to 0 and increased the budget bargaining power of the civilian and capital bureaucracies proportionately.

DIRECT EFFECTS
OF REDUCED DEFENSE SPENDING

Defense Expenditure

Figure 3-1 shows the level of real defense expenditure by the *West* and the *East* blocs at five-year intervals over the period 1985–2010 in two runs of the simulation. In the reference run, no interventions or changes of any kind are made, whereas in the arms reduction run, we introduce, beginning in 1990, the changes described previously.

It is readily apparent that a substantial reduction in arms spending has been brought about by the changes. In the reference run, arms spending in the *West* and the *East* grows by about 3.2 percent and 3.7

---

[5] Within the model, this is known as the *top2* parameter.

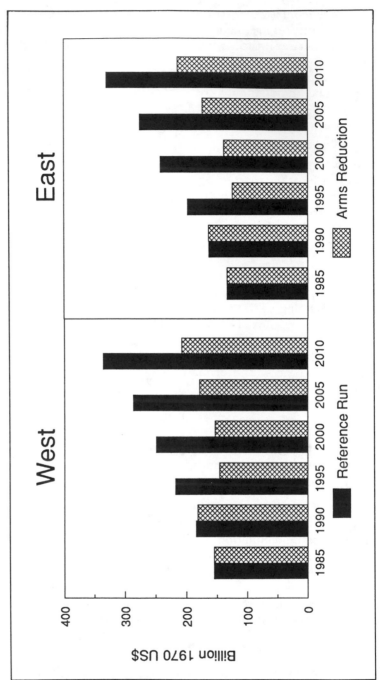

FIGURE 3–1 *East* and *West* Defense Expenditure with and without Arms Reduction

percent per year, respectively, whereas in the arms reduction run, these rates of growth are about two percentage points lower—that is, 1.2 percent and 1.9 percent for the *West* and the *East*, respectively. By the year 2010, the *West* is spending about 40 percent less on arms with arms reduction, and the *East* is spending about 35 percent less.[6] We see that in the two runs, the *West* and the *East* are spending about the same; hence, we have been successful in realizing our aim of maintaining a balance between the *East* and the *West* while reducing arms.

Defense Savings

Since defense spending is a flow, it can be argued that a better measure of the impact of any arms reduction plan is the sum of the total reductions realized by the plan over a span of time. We can derive such a measure by integrating defense expenditures over time and examining the differences between the integrated series to obtain cumulative savings. Figure 3-2 shows the cumulative real defense savings that the arms reduction plan under consideration produces, and they are quite large. By the year 2000, ten years after the introduction of arms reduction, both the *East* and the *West* blocs have realized a cumulative defense savings of about 600 billion 1970 U.S. dollars, and ten years later, these savings have grown to approximately 1.7 trillion 1970 U.S. dollars. In current dollars, the combined *East* and *West* savings would be something like $4 trillion in 2000 and $11 trillion in 2010.

We have reason to believe that not all nations will save equally on defense under this arms reduction plan, and Table 3-2 shows the defense spending of *West* and *East* nations in the years 2000 and 2010 with and without arms reduction. The values shown in this table are defense expenditures in 1970 dollars, and we can see that for all *West* nations except Japan, defense spending is significantly lower with arms reduction; Japan's defense spending is about 50 percent higher, because in the reference run, Japan's defense burden drops below the 1 percent level we are imposing in the arms reduction run. In the *East*, all four nations have lower defense outlays with arms reduction.

Comparatively speaking, by the year 2010 defense spending by the United States and the Soviet Union is reduced by about one-third by the arms reduction plan, while the reductions for their allies are proportionately larger. For these nations, the average reduction in defense expenditure is about 50 percent (with the already-noted exception of Japan).

---

[6] This amount of reduction is roughly comparable to that introduced by Leontief and Duchin in their 1983 study.

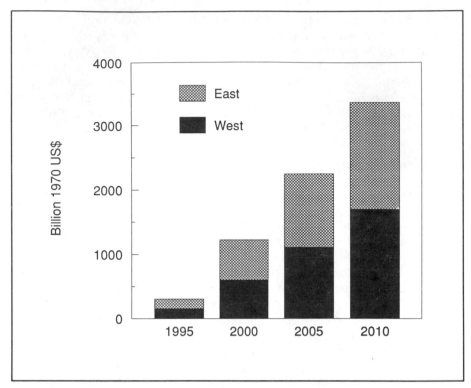

FIGURE 3–2   *East* and *West* Cumulative Defense Savings with Arms Reduction

TABLE 3–2   Defense Spending of *East* and *West* Nations with and without Arms Reduction (Billion 1970 U.S.$)

NATION	2000		2010	
	REFERENCE RUN	ARMS REDUCTION	REFERENCE RUN	ARMS REDUCTION
Canada	7.2	4.8	11.0	6.2
France	13.5	7.6	21.3	9.7
Italy	12.4	5.1	19.7	7.1
Japan	5.1	7.4	7.7	10.1
United Kingdom	10.2	10.1	25.8	7.2
Unites States	178.1	114.9	229.2	157.6
West Germany	16.8	8.0	21.2	9.3
Czechoslovakia	4.3	4.3	9.5	4.6
East Germany	7.2	4.4	8.6	5.3
Poland	2.8	2.7	5.8	4.0
Soviet Union	225.8	127.9	305.9	199.9

The East-West Military Balance

Before we consider what happens to the resources released by these arms reductions, we will briefly examine the balance of conventional military power that they produce.[7] Conventional military forces are expensive,[8] and the defense cuts brought about by our arms reduction plan should produce substantial reductions in conventional capabilities. Since something on the order of 50 percent of any defense budget is devoted to personnel costs, which must be paid each year, of course, and since the depreciation rate of conventional weapons systems is relatively high, reduced military budgets should translate into reductions in large conventional forces. Table 3-3 shows the index values of conventional military power in 2010 with and without arms reduction.

As expected, the reductions in conventional capability are substantial, and their distribution suggests that an extensive demilitarization of Europe is entailed. The rough parity between *East* and *West* is maintained through arms reduction, as we desired, and one can imagine the reduced levels as corresponding to what might be obtained if the United States and the Soviet Union were to withdraw and demobilize their conventional forces in Central Europe, coupled with a general reduction in forces among European nations. The most significant reduction to be found

TABLE 3–3 Conventional Capability of *East* and *West* Nations with and without Arms Reduction in 2010

WEST NATIONS	REFERENCE RUN	ARMS REDUCTION	EAST NATIONS	REFERENCE RUN	ARMS REDUCTION
United States	393	265	Soviet Union	602	372
Canada	18	11	East Germany	16	10
United Kingdom	54	15	Poland	20	16
France	57	27	Czechoslovakia	29	14
West Germany	55	25			
Italy	85	32			
Japan	52	70			
Total	714	445	Total	667	412

[7] As explained earlier, the model also generates levels of strategic-nuclear capability for five nations. We will not examine those here because (1) they relate to only four of the eleven nations under consideration; (2) the resource demands of such weapons are relatively small and, therefore, they are not as sensitive to budgetary reductions as conventional forces; and (3) we do not have as much confidence in the validity of the strategic-nuclear index as we do in the conventional military index.

[8] It has been estimated that, for example, not more than 10 percent of American military expenditure is devoted to strategic-nuclear capability (Collins 1985:295). Hence, any significant cuts in defense expenditure would have to substantially reduce conventional military power.

in this table is in the United Kingdom, and this reflects the fact that this nation has historically devoted a greater proportion of its GDP to defense than have other European nations. Under our arms reduction plan, that is no longer true; therefore, what we see here is a conventional military capability that is much more commensurate with its economic size.

Disposition of Savings

In a previous section, we saw that our arms reduction plan has produced considerable savings on defense. GLOBUS governments allocate resources among eight categories of expenditure: defense, education, health, welfare, administration, foreign aid, investment, and interest payments. We have already seen that defense expenditures are down by almost 250 billion real dollars by 2010 under the assumptions of our arms reduction scenario. Hence, the question arises, Which of these categories of expenditure have increased? Tables 3-4 and 3-5 provide the answers to this question for the *West* and the *East* nations, respectively.

Adding together health, education, and welfare outlays yields what we will refer to as social expenditures, and Tables 3-4 and 3-5 show how these increase in both the *West* and the *East* as a consequence of arms reduction. It is apparent that a large share of the released resources is channeled in this direction in both groups of nations, and although the absolute increases in the *East* are somewhat lower than in the *West,* the proportionate (or per capita) increase is much greater in the *East.* Hence, our first conclusion is that sizable portions of the savings from arms reduction are spent on health, education, and welfare programs in both regions under the assumptions of this arms reduction scenario.

Another principal category in which substantial increases might be seen under arms reduction is government investment. Tables 3-4 and

TABLE 3–4   Disposition of *West* Defense Savings (Billion 1970 U.S.$)

YEAR	CHANGE IN DEFENSE EXPENDITURE	CHANGE IN SOCIAL EXPENDITURE	CHANGE IN GOVERNMENT INVESTMENT	CHANGE IN ADMINISTRATIVE EXPENDITURE
1995	− 72.0	+ 42.9	+2.2	+16.1
2000	− 95.8	+ 60.2	+1.5	+22.3
2005	−107.7	+ 85.9	+2.0	+31.3
2010	−128.6	+122.3	+2.9	+44.4

The positive changes do not exactly equal the negative change in defense because a few categories of expenditure, such as foreign aid, are excluded. In general, the expenditure increases in the categories shown here *exceed* defense reductions because of increased economic growth and greater government revenues.

TABLE 3–5 Disposition of *East* Defense Savings (Billion 1970 U.S.$)

YEAR	CHANGE IN DEFENSE EXPENDITURE	CHANGE IN SOCIAL EXPENDITURE	CHANGE IN GOVERNMENT INVESTMENT	CHANGE IN ADMINISTRATIVE EXPENDITURE
1995	− 73.8	+17.2	+57.0	+ 2.9
2000	−103.5	+45.0	+82.6	+ 7.7
2005	−101.4	+70.1	+68.1	+12.3
2010	−116.0	+97.1	+73.1	+17.5

The sum of the changes in social outlays, government investment, and administrative expenditure *exceeds* the change in defense expenditure because of increased total expenditures. This is primarily due to an increase in government revenues brought about by economic growth.

3-5 show that significant additional outlays in this area are forthcoming only in the *East*. That is not altogether surprising because of the large size of government investment in these nations and the relatively high priority that it has been historically assigned in government decisions about resource allocation. *West* nations have traditionally given this a relatively low priority and have focused on creating the economic conditions that would foster increases in private investment.

The third category shown in these tables is administrative expenditures. This category includes a wide variety of items, ranging from communications to tax collection to law enforcement. These are closely tied to the size of government civilian programs in both the *West* and the *East*, and, consequently, increases in this category are to be expected in response to increases elsewhere.

Clearly, with the great increases in social and administrative expenditures in the *West*, not much remains for increases in foreign aid. The amount of aid given by the *West* does increase somewhat with arms reduction.[9] The foreign aid total in the reference run increases from about 6 billion in 1970 to about 23 billion by 2010, and the introduction of arms reduction increases the latter figure to about 27 billion, which is an 18 percent increase. Between 1990 and 2010, total *West* foreign aid grows by about 3.3 percent per year without arms reduction and by about 4.1 percent with arms reduction. Since, as we shall see, *West* real GDP is only slightly higher with arms reduction, the proportion of *West* GDP devoted to foreign aid does rise as predicted by the I/I theory—from 0.37 percent to 0.41 percent of GDP in 2010. The question of whether this has the predicted beneficial impact upon the economies of the nations of the South will be dealt with later in this chapter.

[9] Currently, only *West* nations are assumed to give foreign aid in GLOBUS. This restriction is discussed further in the next chapter.

DOMESTIC CONSEQUENCES IN THE NORTH

The potential benefit of arms spending reduction most often cited is an increase in economic growth. Thus, we want to examine the impact of the cuts on the Gross Domestic Products (GDP) of the North economies. Even in the absence of change in GDP, however, the cuts could affect standards of living in the North—for instance, through increases in personal consumption. And it is virtually certain that significant reductions in arms spending would alter the size of the armaments sector within the overall economy and have secondary impacts on other sectors. Thus, in this section we look in turn at the differences between the reference run and the arms reduction scenario in aggregate economic growth, standards of living, and sectoral structure of the economies.

Economic Growth

Figure 3-3 displays percent change in GDP brought about by the arms reduction scenario for both *East* and *West* GLOBUS countries. By the year 2010, both groupings exhibit improved economic performance relative to the reference run. But there are important differences in the timing and the extent of the improvement. Whereas the *East* improves its collective GDP by 7.7 percent, the gain in the *West* is only 0.6 percent. Moreover, the *East* gains come quickly—the rise over the reference run in 1995 is 0.8 percent. In contrast to that, the *West*'s performance is better in the reference run until 2005, a decade after the completion of the reductions.

There are three components to the explanation for these quite dramatic regional differences in economic reaction to the reductions in arms spending. First, the magnitude of resources freed by the reductions is very different. Military spending as a percentage of GDP in the *East* is more than twice as high as it is in the *West*. In the reference run, for the year 1990, the figures are 13.2 percent and 5.3 percent respectively. The essentially symmetrical cuts analyzed here reduce the percentage of GDP allocated by 2010 to defense in the *East* by 4.6 percent, compared with a reduction in the *West* of 2.1 percent.

A second portion of the explanation lies in the disposition of the savings. In *East* nations, the budget bargaining power of the civilian bureaucracy has been estimated to be only one-third of that of the capital bureaucracy, whereas in *West* nations, the relevant ratio is, on the average, 10 to 1 in the opposite direction.[10] Hence, we expect at the outset that, ceteris paribus, in *West* nations, defense savings will tend

[10] A description of the methods used to derive these values is to be found in Cusack (1987:411–415).

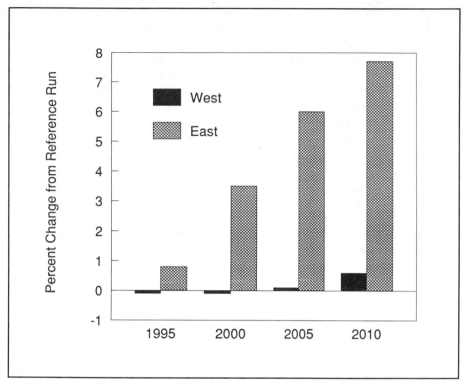

FIGURE 3–3 GDP Increases in the *West* and *East* with Arms Reduction

to be channeled more into the civilian sector, whereas in *East* nations, defense savings will tend to be directed into the capital sector. Although current reforms in the U.S.S.R. and elsewhere in Eastern Europe are directed at reducing government subsidies for underperforming industries and at decentralizing important investment decisions, none of the reforms seriously threatens to challenge the principle of public ownership of capital or the practice of state direction of investment. In contrast, *West* governments increase spending in a variety of categories, including investment, but the bulk of the funds freed moves toward consumption categories or is provided through transfer payments and tax reductions to households and then largely used to supplement private consumption.

    This pattern in the *West* leads us to the third part of the explanation for differential economic impact of spending reductions. Although the increases in governmental and private consumption do create demand that can stoke the market-oriented economies of the *West*, that demand appears in sectors other than armaments, where, as we will see, significant surplus capacity quickly develops. The *West* economies immediately face a structural imbalance between production and demand, which results in interim underutilization of capital and labor. The flip side of the fiscal stimulus provided by increased defense spending (as in the Reagan years) is both negative fiscal stimulus and structural adjustment problems.

We must caution against accepting the full magnitude of the difference shown here in *East-West* economic impact. That difference could be overestimated because the ease of transition between defense and nondefense spending in the *East* may be too great in GLOBUS. Although there is apparently the desire and even some planning for such a transition in the U.S.S.R., a shift of more than 4 percent of GDP among end uses within an economy is likely to be constrained by bottlenecks that cannot be specifically anticipated.

In addition, GLOBUS may underestimate some benefits, in both the *East* and the *West*, of the reductions in arms spending. For instance, in the *West*, the reduction in defense spending leads to increases of 2.0 percent in government spending for education by 2010. That would have an impact on labor quality and productivity that is not calculated within GLOBUS; however, the omission does not significantly affect the results reported here.[11]

Standard of Living

Standards of living can vary quite substantially within the same total figure for GDP, simply because very different proportions of GDP can accrue to consumers. Thus, we want to move from the highly aggregate consideration of the impact of arms reduction conveyed by changes in GDP to a closer examination of what the reduction might mean for households. A full picture of household well-being requires an examination of more than simply income levels. To obtain a reasonably full picture, we will consider three measures of the standard of living. These are social expenditures (as defined earlier) per capita, disposable income per capita, and personal consumption per capita.

Figure 3-4 shows the increases in these indicators at several time points in the *West* as a result of arms reduction. The figure indicates on a per capita basis the increases in social expenditures, disposable

---

[11] According to cross-sectional and longitudinal studies by Nadiri (1972) and Maddison (1987), the contribution of education to the economic growth of industrialized countries appears to average around 0.3 percent annually. Over the twenty-year period between 1990 and 2010, the average increase in *West* educational spending brought about by reductions in arms spending is no more than 1 percent. A 1 percent average increase in spending, should it raise the growth contribution of education by 1 percent of its average 0.3 percent, would make an annual contribution of 0.003 percent to GDP growth. Compounded over twenty years, the missing positive impact on growth should not much exceed 0.06 percent. Since the *East* raises educational spending by 23 percent, the potential productivity gains there are larger (adding perhaps 0.6 percent to growth over twenty years) and could further widen the differential impact on East and West of reductions in arms spending.

income, and personal consumption brought about by arms reduction. These gains exceed those in *West* GDP. Both disposable income and personal consumption surpass the reference run by about 2.5 percent as a result of tax reductions. Social expenditures rise by 7.7 percent because of the shift from military spending. The relatively large gain in social expenditures also suggests some probable improvement in income distribution. Thus, standard of living benefits considerably more in the *West* from arms reduction than does GDP.

Figure 3-5 shows the comparable increases in the standard of living indicators for the *East* region. Here the benefits are again larger than in the *West* and larger than for *East* GDP. *East* disposable income rises 11 percent and consumption gains 14 percent. Social expenditures climb a full 25 percent. All these gains exceed the already substantial GDP increase of 7.7 percent.

Thus, when we move beyond GDP, both *East* and *West* gain substantially from arms reduction. Although the benefits are asymmetrical, with income increases in the *East* nearly three times those in the *West*, all parties to arms reduction benefit economically.

FIGURE 3—4 Standard of Living in the *West* with Arms Reduction

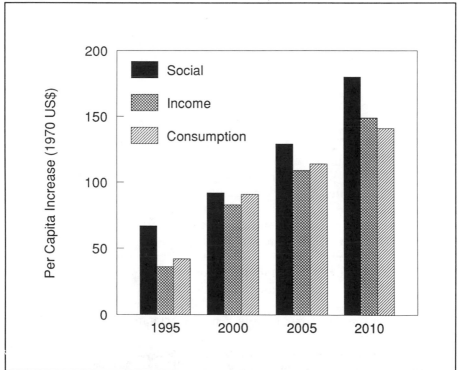

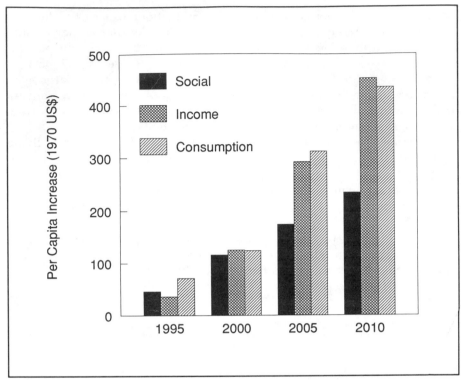

FIGURE 3–5 Standard of Living in the *East* with Arms Reduction

Sectoral Implications

The armaments sector of the economies, both *East* and *West*, bear the brunt of the adjustments required by the reductions in defense spending. The value added in that sector in the year 1995 is 23 percent lower in the *West* with spending reductions and 18 percent smaller in the *East*. Profit rates in the armaments sector drop dramatically in the *West* and never recover to reference run rates.[12] Capacity utilization falls 10–25 percent by 1995, depending on the country. Employment in the United States armaments industry steadily erodes after 1995 with arms reductions and is 22 percent below the reference run by 2010.

○ The agricultural, manufacturing, and service sectors gain shares in the total economy as the armaments sector loses. In the *West*, the primary energy and raw materials sectors also decline relatively, because the personal consumption that largely replaces armaments is not as energy

[12] A 1986 GAO study showed defense contracting to have been 120 percent more profitable than commercial manufacturing between 1980 and 1983 (Sivard 1987:38).

or materials intensive as armaments. In the *East*, the much greater relative emphasis on increased investment leads to the maintenance of the sectoral shares of energy and raw materials.

The significant sectoral decline of armaments is of considerable importance because it has been argued that the military-industrial complex of the *West* and the "metal-eater" alliance of heavy industry and the military in the *East* hold disproportionate political power in both societies. If that is true, it might well indicate substantial social obstacles to the arms reductions.

The disruption to the armaments sector, although great, is ameliorated in part through arms trade. Arms exports of the *West* drop with spending reductions relative to the reference run (because *West* states export many arms to each other), but the declines are not as great as the declines in imports, causing a net increase in the export of armaments. As we shall see, this gain is made in the markets of the GLOBUS *South*. In the *East*, arms exports increase absolutely over the reference run, again a result of capturing market share in the *South*.

It is important to realize how small the armaments sector actually is within the Northern economies. Table 3-6 shows the value added in that share as a portion of total GDP for both *East* and *West*, with and without the reductions in arms spending. In the *West*, the sector is never more than 2 percent of the total economy, and in the *East*, it only slightly exceeds 3 percent. The sector sizes are smaller than the GDP share of military spending because so much of that spending is for military personnel. Given these small sector sizes and the finding that the aggregate economies improve with reductions in arms spending, the military-industrial complex in the United States and the Soviet equivalent, the "metal-eater" alliance, should logically not be able to prevent significant arms reductions. Whether they in fact could is beyond the scope of this investigation.

TABLE 3–6 **Armaments Sector Shares in *West* and *East* with and without Arms Reduction (Percent of GDP)**

| | West | | East | |
PERIOD	REFERENCE RUN	ARMS REDUCTION	REFERENCE RUN	ARMS REDUCTION
1990	1.58	1.58	3.39	3.39
1995	1.58	1.28	3.23	2.48
2000	1.57	1.26	3.24	2.33
2005	1.58	1.34	3.15	2.74
2010	1.64	1.32	3.14	2.78

In conclusion, the aggregate economic impact of the arms reduction is quite asymmetrical. Although both *East* and *West* benefit from the reduction, and although standards of living in both regions improve as a result, the impact of the cuts in arms spending is substantially greater in the *East.* Structural adjustment of the economies would, of course, be necessary in both groupings of countries.

ARMS REDUCTION AND EAST-WEST RELATIONS

Having seen what the impact of arms reduction is on the economic performance of the North, we can now turn to the second postulate of the I/I theory—that is, that arms reduction should lead to better East-West relations.

East-West Climate

In the GLOBUS model, flows of hostility and cooperation are generated at the bilateral level, and the index that has been developed to measure the overall state of affairs between the *West* and the *East* is based on the ratio of hostility to cooperation exchanged between members of the two regions (Smith 1987a:620–621). The *East-West* climate index is, therefore, the ratio of the sum of the 28 (7 *West* nations × 4 *East* nations) hostile flows to the sum of the 28 cooperative flows. This indicator tells us in an aggregate sense whether *East-West* relations become relatively more or relatively less hostile over the course of a simulation run.

The value of the *East-West* climate indicator is shown at five-year intervals over the period 1990–2010 in Figure 3-6 for the reference and arms reduction simulation runs. Contrary to I/I expectations, the introduction of arms reduction makes the *East-West* climate relatively more hostile. That is, at the aggregate level, relations between the two blocs are slightly but noticeably worse after arms reduction.

Decomposing the *East-West* climate indicator into its parts reveals that hostile flows from *West* to *East* and from *East* to *West* are uniformly higher with arms reduction. The flow of cooperation from *East* to *West* is also higher across the period with arms reduction, while the reverse flow is lower at first but ultimately rises relative to the reference run. By the year 2010, levels of both hostility and cooperation are up, indicating increased *East-West* diplomatic activity, but hostility has increased by about 15 percent while cooperation has increased by about 10 percent. Hence, relatively speaking, *East-West* relations have been made worse and not better, as postulated by the I/I theory. Given that we are dealing with fifty-six quasi-independent flows, untangling the

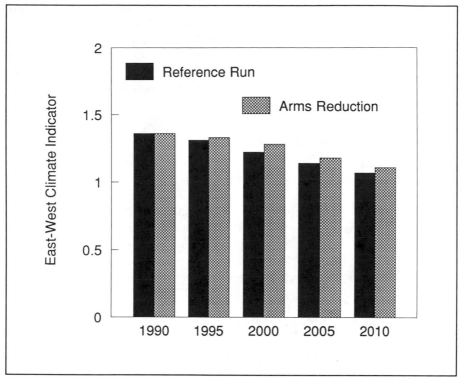

FIGURE 3–6 *East-West* Climate with and without Arms Reduction

changes in *East-West* relations brought about by arms reduction is no simple matter. Let us begin with how relations between the bloc leaders, the United States and the Soviet Union, change as a result of arms reduction.

Superpower Relations

Although overall *East-West* relations are slightly more conflictual with arms reduction, this need not be true of the critically important Soviet-American dyad. Figure 3-7 shows the ratio of hostility exchanged between the United States and the Soviet Union to cooperation exchanged between the two nations. What we see there is that overall Soviet-American relations improve, relatively speaking, in the long term with the introduction of arms reduction. That is, without arms reduction, the diplomatic climate of these two nations becomes slowly but steadily more negative in the twenty years following 1990, whereas arms reduction halts this trend. A deeper examination reveals that the flow of hostility in both directions between the two nations is virtually unchanged by arms reduction while the flow of cooperation in both directions is significantly increased. By 2010, for example, the United States is sending33 percent more cooperation toward the Soviet Union and the Soviet Union 13 percent more toward the United States. Thus, relatively speaking, arms reduction does improve American-Soviet relations. This leads us to conclude that whatever is causing *East-West* relations to deteriorate slightly under arms reduction it is not to be found in the relationship between the superpowers.

European Relations

If we shift our attention to Europe, we begin to see where the problem lies. Figure 3-8 shows the European diplomatic climate (that is, the ratio of hostility to cooperation exchanged between the *East-West* European dyads[13]) over the period 1990–2010 with and without arms reduction, and it is apparent that relations between these states are more conflictual throughout the period with arms reduction.

FIGURE 3–7 Soviet-American Relations with and without Arms Reduction

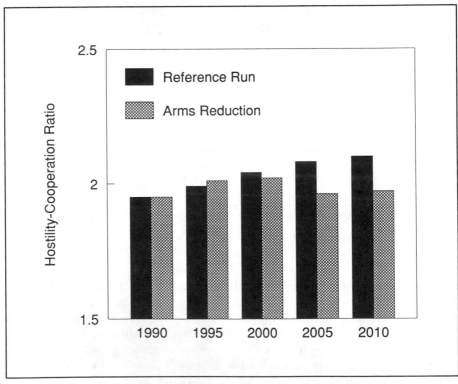

---

[13] The European *East-West* dyads are those that involve the United Kingdom, France, West Germany, or Italy on the one side and the Soviet Union, East Germany, Poland, or Czechoslovakia on the other.

An examination of the component flows of this indicator shows that by 2010, *West* to *East* hostility is up by about 22 percent while *East* to *West* hostility increases by about 32 percent with arms reduction. In contrast, cooperative behavior in both directions is only slightly (about 3 percent) lower. These results clearly point to a marked increase in the exchange of hostility between at least some European members of NATO and the Warsaw Pact as a primary cause of more hostile overall *East-West* relations with arms reduction.

A detailed examination of the sixteen dyads included in the European *East-West* grouping is clearly out of the question here. What we propose to do instead is to focus on the West German–East German dyad in search of an explanation of how decreased arms can lead to increased hostility.

The Two Germanys

Changes in hostility and cooperation induced by arms reduction are clearly evident in this dyad. By 2010 West German to East German hostility is up by 50 percent and the hostile flow in the opposite direction is 35 percent higher with the introduction of arms reductions. Coop-

FIGURE 3–8 European Diplomatic Climate with and without Arms Reduction

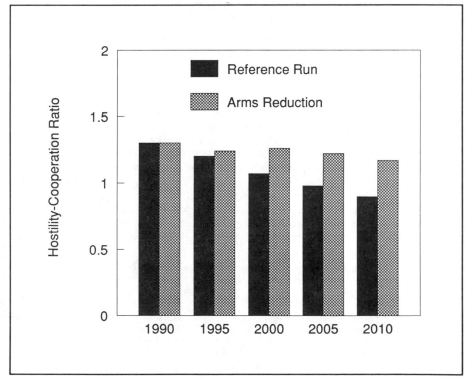

eration is lower by 2010 with arms reduction; the flow of cooperative behavior from West Germany to East Germany is down by 50 percent while the comparable reduction in the East German to West German flow is only 2 percent. Why do we observe these unexpected changes in behavior?

To answer that question, we must delve into the structure and the parameters of the international political submodel contained in GLO-BUS.[14] How one nation reacts to hostility it receives from another depends additively upon four factors:

The relative conventional capability of the two nations
The degree of imbalance in bilateral trade relations
The balance of hostility to cooperation in bilateral relations
The balance of hostility to cooperation in *East-West* relations

Because convincing theoretical arguments can be made that these factors should both increase and decrease hostile reactivity, in his estimations of dyad-specific parameters Smith (1987a) placed no restrictions on the direction of these effects. Given the heterogeneity present in the modern world, it is not altogether surprising that his estimations revealed that different nations responded differently with respect to the aforementioned factors in how their reactivity changed toward hostility received from specific other nations.[15]

What that means is that a general explanation of how nations will react to other nations is difficult to frame. To help the reader understand how this process works, we lay out the following rules.

Relative Power Rule. Ceteris paribus, the greater a nation's superiority in military power relative to another nation, the less it will react to hostility received from that nation. Conversely, the more inferior a nation is in relation to another, the more sensitive and reactive it will be toward hostility from that state. This is sometimes referred to as the "compensatory dynamic," since it implies that weakness is compensated for by bellicosity.

Trade Imbalance Rule. Ceteris paribus, the less favorable a nation's bilateral trade balance is with another nation (and the less favorable the nation's overall trade balance), the more it will react to hostility received from that nation. Conversely, the more favorable the bilateral and overall trade balances are, the less reactive a nation is likely to be to hostility received

---

[14] The process by which nations determine how they will respond to hostility and cooperation received from other nations is fully described in Smith (1987a). It is too complex to be explained here in any detail, and the reader not satisfied with this abridged discussion should consult this source.

[15] The estimated relative importance of these four factors is reflected in the values of four GLOBUS parameters. These are *hbeta1*, *hbeta2*, *hbeta3*, and *hbeta4*, and their values are to be found in Smith (1987a:697–721). A very small number of the values given in these tables have been revised; see Smith (1987b).

from the other nation. The logic of this rule is most clearly evident in current relations between Japan and the United States.

Dyadic Climate Rule. Ceteris paribus, the higher the ratio of hostility to cooperation received from another nation, the more the receiving nation is likely to respond in kind to hostility from that other nation. Conversely, the more cooperative, relatively speaking, another nation is, the less reactive a nation will be to hostility from that nation. In other words, nations will tend to ignore hostility they receive from nations with which their relationship is fundamentally cooperative.

East-West Climate Rule. Ceteris paribus, the more hostile *East-West* relations are in a relative sense, the more a nation will respond to hostility received from another nation with hostility. Conversely, the better overall *East-West* relations are, the more tolerant a nation is likely to be toward hostility received from another nation. This rule assumes that the overall state of *East-West* relations contaminates bilateral relations.

Having laid out these general rules, we must immediately note that exceptions to them abound among the hundreds of GLOBUS dyads. That is to say, it is not difficult to find dyads in which the directionality stated in the foregoing rules is reversed. For example, the Relative Power Rule for some nations in some dyads is that the more superior they are in relation to another nation, the more hostile they are in response to conflict received from that other nation. This is equivalent to "bullying" behavior. Exceptions to the Dyadic Climate and *East-West* climate rules are particularly plentiful. In spite of the exceptions, however, it will be useful to bear these rules in mind as we turn to the analysis of relations between the two Germanys under arms reduction.

We should note at the outset of this analysis that there is a fundamental asymmetry in relations between the two Germanys that reflects their long-term policies. Beginning in 1970, East Germany sends about three times as much hostility toward West Germany as West Germany does toward East Germany, while their cooperative flows are approximately equal. That is in part due to the fact that West Germany tends to view the Soviet Union and not East Germany as its principal adversary, while East Germany sees West Germany as its principal adversary. Thus, traditionally West Germany has tended to ignore a great deal of hostility emanating from East Germany.

With arms reduction, the military balance between West Germany and East Germany changes in such a way that West German superiority drops from 3.2:1 in 1990 to about 2.5:1 in 2010, while this ratio increases slightly in the reference run to about 3.4:1. This loss of relative superiority leads West Germany to be less restrained in its response to hostility received from East Germany and, therefore, relatively more hostile in its relations with that nation. A similar but reverse effect is to be seen with respect to West German responses to cooperation from the East Germans with arms reduction. That is, the West Germans send relatively less cooperation toward the East Germans as the military balance becomes less favorable. The East Germans, on the other hand, see this development as favorable and lower their hostile reactivity toward West Germany. If this were the only significant factor affecting their relations, then we might see a shift in the fundamental asymmetry discussed in the preceding paragraph but little overall increase in their exchange of hostility. However, the lessening of West German tolerance for East German hostility is accompanied by a reduction in West German imports from East Germany. This reduction in trade causes resentment among the East Germans and leads to a significantly more hostile policy toward West Germany by the year 2000. The net result of all this is that relations between the two Germanys become relatively more hostile as a result of arms reduction.

Returning to the general question of whether arms reduction would improve East-West relations, our answer would have to be yes and no. Relations improve between many *East-West* dyads as a consequence of arms reduction, but relations within a few become significantly worse. What is clear to us from this analysis is that arms reduction per se will not lead necessarily to an improvement in East-West relations, since it may upset relatively delicately balanced power relations and thereby exacerbate tensions rather than diminishing them. The degree to which that happens will depend, of course, on the particular arms reduction plan adopted. Focusing as we have on only one of many possible arms reduction plans, we are unable to assert that all such plans are unlikely to significantly improve East-West relations. On the other hand, our analysis has persuaded us that, given the diverse propensities of the states involved, developing a plan that did result in clearly improved relations would not be a trivial exercise.

ARMS REDUCTION AND THE SOUTH

Let us recapitulate our results with respect to the I/I theory up to this point. As predicted, we did find economic gains in the North as a consequence of reduced defense expenditures, and these were especially pronounced in the *East.* We did not find, however, that arms reduction led to better overall East-West relations, although some important bilateral relationships were slightly improved by it. The third arrow in Figure 2-1 postulated that some of the resources released by arms reductions would lead to an increase in foreign aid, which, in turn, would produce better economic performance in the South. In spite of the fact that most of the realized defense savings were used for domestic purposes, we did find that arms reductions led to slight increase in foreign aid. In addition to that, we found that some restructuring of the global armaments market had occurred, a development that might have some impact on the developing nations. In this part of the chapter, we will consider how arms reduction in the North affects the South.

Economic Conditions in the South

Regardless of which indicator we examine—GDP, disposable income, personal consumption, or social expenditures—almost no change is present in the South as a whole. The absolute increase in foreign aid that accompanies arms reduction is too small to have any impact. Whatever positive impact such increased aid might have is probably negated by developments in the armaments sector. It will be recalled that one of the consequences of arms reduction in the North was a depressed arms sector there. Other things being equal, that will lead to relatively lower North arms prices, which, in turn, should lead to South nations importing more arms and relying less on domestic production. Hence, we should find that arms reduction in the North tends to depress the armaments sector in the South.

When we compare *South* imports and exports of armaments across the two runs, we find that arms reduction in the North causes *South* imports of arms to increase by a third (roughly 9–12 billion real U.S. dollars) and exports to decrease by about the same proportion (1.7–1.2 billion). As a consequence, arms production in the *South* is down and some dislocations occur as production shifts to other sectors; the small size of this sector greatly limits the impact of this development on the economy as a whole. Thus, arms reduction in the North does not, by itself, seem to have much of an effect on economic conditions in the South. It may, nevertheless, have an impact on the *relative* economic positions of the North and the South, and it is to this question that we turn next.

North-South Gap

As we pointed out in Chapter 1, the economic disparity between the more and the less developed nations may be measured in a variety of ways. Our principal measure will be the ratio of the GDP per capita in the North to that in the South.[16] Figure 3-9 shows how this ratio develops over time in the reference and arms reduction runs. As we can see, arms reduction in the North leads to an *increase* in the economic disparity between North and South. The reason for this is not that the South has become significantly poorer but, rather, that the North has

---

[16] More specifically, it is the total GDP of the eleven *East* and *West* nations divided by their total population over the total GDP of the fourteen *South* and *Opec* nations divided by the total population of the *South* and *Opec*.

become significantly richer. In the year 2010, GDP per capita in the North rises from about $8,350 to almost $8,600 with the introduction of arms reduction while the GDP per capita in the South remains essentially unchanged at about $750.

North-South Relations

The arms reduction plan explored in this chapter called for no such reductions in the South. Moreover, the economic implications for the South of arms reduction in the North have been found to be small. Hence, we might be tempted to conclude that the impact of arms reduction, as specified here, on North-South relations is likely to be small.

That conclusion is borne out when we compare the flows of hostility and cooperation between the North and the South in the reference and arms reduction runs. Computing a North-South climate indicator, which is comparable to the *East-West* climate indicator discussed earlier (that is, the ratio of hostility exchanged between all North-South dyads to

FIGURE 3–9 North-South Gap with and without Arms Reduction

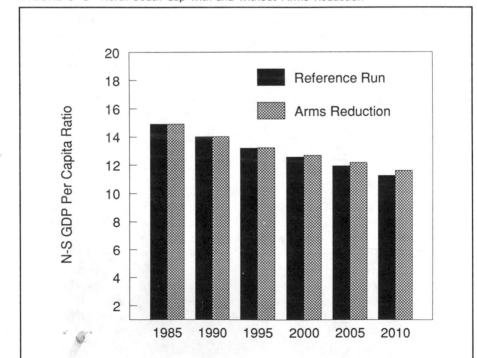

that of cooperation), for the two simulation runs reveals that it is virtually unchanged by the introduction of arms reductions. Decomposing these indices into their parts reveals some slight patterns. As a group, the *West* sends somewhat more hostility and somewhat less cooperation to the South with arms reduction, while exactly the opposite is true with respect to the *East*. The South, in turn, responds as expected; that is, it sends slightly more hostility and slightly less cooperation to the *West* but does the opposite with respect to the *East*. Hence, we might conclude that West-South relations would deteriorate to a small degree with arms reduction while East-South relations could improve slightly under this condition. Chapter 7 will explore North-South relations in much more detail.

In one sense, however, our arms reduction scenario is producing a rather fundamental restructuring of the international system, and that is in the distribution of global conventional military capability. Figure 3-10 shows the shares of this capability that each of the four regions holds in 2010 with and without arms reduction, and the relative growth of the South is readily apparent under arms reduction. Without arms reduction, the *West* and the *East* each have about one-third of this capability and the *South* and *Opec* combined have the remaining third. With arms reduction, the shares of the *West* and the *East* each decline to about one-fourth of the world total and the less developed nations have the remainder. Thus, relatively speaking, we see a rather dramatic shift in the global military balance emerging from arms reduction in the North.

Two factors should be mentioned in conjunction with this, however. First, the shift evident here is a relative one; that is, the South is not spending more on defense and amassing larger capabilities under arms reduction, the North is simply spending less on defense and as a consequence reducing their conventional capabilities. Second, this diagram ignores the distribution of strategic-nuclear capability, and in this area, with or without arms reduction, the dominant position of the North is unchanged. Hence, we must avoid concluding that this shift means a radical reduction in the global influence of the West and the East generally and the United States and the Soviet Union in particular.

Given the wide disparities in conventional capability between most North nations and most South nations, even after arms reduction, this shift in power should not lead to dramatic changes in relations between members of these two groups. The notable exception to this is China, of course, since its conventional capability is generally larger than all other nations' save the United States and the Soviet Union. Thus, we will conclude this discussion of North-South relations by briefly examining the impact arms reduction has on relations between these three "top dogs."

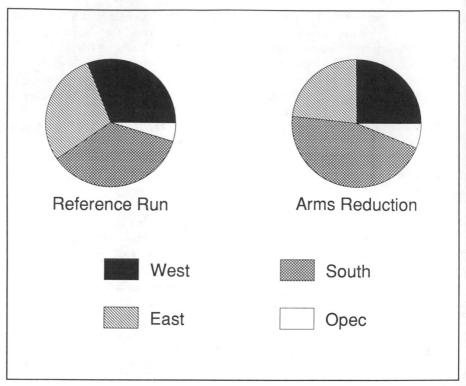

FIGURE 3–10   Distribution of Conventional Capability with and without Arms Reduction—2010

We have already seen that overall Soviet-American relations are slightly improved as a consequence of arms reduction. The same is true of Sino-American relations, although the change is not symmetrical, because most of the overall change comes about as a consequence of a reduction in Chinese hostility toward the United States and not the opposite. The Sino-Soviet relationship is much more strongly affected by arms reduction than the other two relationships, and its net result is to significantly improve those relations. What appears to be happening is that Soviet arms reductions lead to a decreased perception of threat on the part of the Chinese and much lower levels of hostility in relation to the Soviets. This, in turn, leads the Soviets to be less hostile, and their relationship improves over time. Thus, one of the unexpected consequences of arms reduction in the North might be a lessening of Sino-Soviet tensions. Again, we will examine this in more detail in Chapter 7.

CONCLUSION

In this section, we have investigated three important linkages shown in Figure 2-1. The results are mixed with respect to the validity of the Idealist/Internationalist view of the world. We found that arms reduction did improve economic conditions in the North, albeit somewhat marginally, in both the short and the long terms. However, we did not find a consistent positive effect with respect to the state of East-West relations. In the first decade after arms reduction, these relations improve slightly, and although relations between the Soviet Union and the United States remain less hostile with less arms spending, those between some of their key allies do not. Hence, by 2010 the *East-West* climate as a whole is slightly more hostile with arms reduction than without. With respect to foreign aid, we found that arms reduction per se does not bring about much change in its level. That is, there is very little "trickle down" effect that would translate defense savings into increased aid. This suggests that a commitment by the North to reduce arms is not, by itself, sufficient to promote development in the South, but rather an additional commitment to divert defense savings to this goal is required. In the next chapter, we will investigate the impact of such a policy change.

A Helping Hand?

CHAPTER 4

In the spring of 1974, the United Nations adopted the Declaration and Action Program on a New International Economic Order (NIEO) sponsored by the less developed countries.[1] Among the calls for action within the Declaration was the repetition of an earlier UNCTAD target—namely, that donor countries should provide 0.7 percent of their GNPs as foreign aid. As unlikely a prospect as it appears politically that this or many other targets of the NIEO should be accomplished (in spite of general Northern agreement in the 1960s to so increase aid),[2] proposals for increased foreign assistance, and this 0.7 percent target in particular, have been advanced so frequently and fervently that an evaluation of the potential impact on recipient countries of such increased assistance has merit.

Chapter 3 showed that reductions in arms spending would not automatically lead economically developed countries to increase foreign aid by anywhere near enough to reach the NIEO target. Instead, we must assume an act of political will by the North. Although we have no way to assess the likelihood of such a manifestation of international political will, with or without reductions in arms spending, we must add it to the Idealist/Internationalist (I/I) theory to be able to proceed

[1] For brief introductions and background, see Blake and Walters (1987) and Spero (1985, chapter 6).

[2] In 1964 UNCTAD had proposed 1 percent of GDPs, and in the mid-1960s the Development Assistance Committee had agreed to work toward that target (Mikesell 1983:6).

88

further with our testing of that theory. In particular, this chapter examines the degree to which an increase in aid to the NIEO target level might improve economic conditions in the South.

Before doing that, however, we must first discuss how foreign aid processes are represented in GLOBUS and how they are changed to incorporate the 0.7 percent aid target. Following that, we turn to an assessment of the impact of this increased foreign aid on both the donors and the recipients.

FOREIGN AID DECISION MAKING IN GLOBUS

The representation of foreign aid in GLOBUS differs in several ways from what we find in the "real" world. First, only the nations of the *West* are assumed to give aid and only the nations of the *South* and *Opec* (minus South Africa and China) and a Rest-of-World entity receive aid. Second, all aid is considered to be in the form of grants; that is, no repayment is expected. Third, all aid is assumed to be in the form of money rather than goods. These simplifications do not, in our judgment, constitute a serious misrepresentation of aid flows in the contemporary world.[3]

Amount and Distribution of Aid

The processes by which *West* nations decide how much and to whom aid will be given are described in Cusack (1987:371–374). As in the defense sector, a desired foreign aid total is first formulated and then reconciled with the other desired expenditures at a later stage in the budget process. The desired foreign aid total varies in accordance with increases or decreases in the political and economic alignments of recipient nations with donor nations. The distribution of the aid is also dependent upon political and economic alignment as well as the relative need of potential recipients. At the end of the foreign aid decision-making process, each aid donor has set a desired aid total and a dis-

---

[3] The first of these restrictions stems from the lack of adequate data concerning East-bloc aid deliveries. Almost all available data report the aid *commitments* of East-bloc members, which may or may not correspond to actual aid given. The total amount of East aid is certainly small in comparison with that of the West—for instance, Soviet foreign aid is about 10 percent of American aid; consequently, omitting these flows does not substantially change our results. A fuller treatment of this question would require us to include them, however, and we are considering how that might be done in our future work on this topic. With respect to the second restriction, it should be noted that the official OECD definition of aid is only that it must contain at least a 25 percent concessionary component. It is almost impossible to determine in general how much aid is truly of a grant nature at the time it is given and equally impossible to determine how much of the nongrant aid is or will be repaid.

tribution pattern across the potential recipients. After the final aid figure emerges from the budget reconciliation process, the distribution pattern is applied to divide up the aid, and transfers of aid are made to the recipient governments. That income is then available to the recipient governments in the next decision cycle.

Implementation of Aid Increase

Increasing foreign aid requires deciding where and when to intervene in the process just described. Two intervention points are feasible: the setting of the *desired* foreign aid total or the setting of the *final* foreign aid total. We chose the former because it seems more realistic to assume that aid givers would be willing to try harder to increase aid than that they would guarantee a specific amount of aid under all circumstances. Thus, in the increased aid scenario, we intervene and set desired foreign aid as a fixed proportion of GDP.

Movement toward the 0.7 percent target could be done gradually or quickly, and we chose to introduce the full change in 1990. That is, at the beginning of 1990, the desired foreign aid total is set to 0.7 percent of GDP for all seven *West* nations. Since some nations are further from the target than others at the time of intervention, the shift will be more significant for some than for others. Moreover, since it is the *desired* and not the *final* foreign aid figures that we are altering, some time is likely to elapse after the intervention before the target is reached. We should add that there is no guarantee that the exact aid target will be achieved, however. If demands from other areas, such as education or welfare, increase (or decrease), then the final foreign aid figure may be slightly lower (or higher) than the desired value.

COSTS AND BENEFITS OF INCREASED AID

Introducing the policy shift in 1990 during a run of the simulation allows us to assess some of the direct and indirect effects of a serious commitment of resources by the West to development in the South. In this section, we will compare the reference run with one that incorporates increases in aid to determine the probable costs and benefits of such a policy.

Level of Foreign Aid

Figure 4-1 shows the total amount of foreign aid given by the seven *West* nations in the reference and aid increase runs at five-year intervals. As we hoped, the amount of foreign aid flowing from the

West to the South increases substantially, and the level reached is roughly 0.7 percent of the *West*'s GDP. The amount of aid is somewhat more than twice as high within the first decade following the policy shift, and in absolute terms the increase in aid amounts to about 30 billion (real) dollars by 2010. To place this number in perspective, it should be noted that it represents a little more than 1 percent of the total GDP of *South* and *Opec* nations in 2010 in the reference run.

Table 4-1 shows the amount of foreign aid given by the seven *West* nations with and without the 0.7 percent aid target in the years 2000 and 2010. The degree of change is, of course, related to how close the nations are to the 0.7 percent target in 1990 in the reference run. France is slightly above the target in 1990, and as a consequence, its aid level is basically unchanged. Canada is also relatively close to the target value; hence, its modest 25 percent increase in aid. The total amount of aid given by the United Kingdom, the United States, and

FIGURE 4–1 *West* Aid with and without Aid Increase

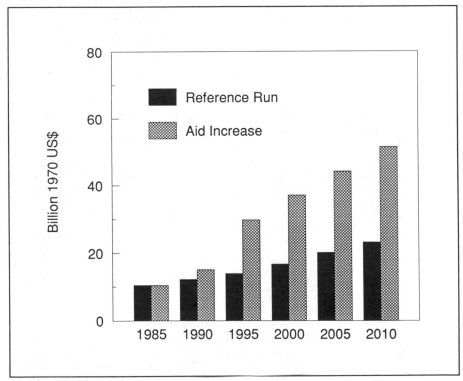

West Germany is more than doubled, while the amounts given by Italy and Japan are more than quadrupled by the aid increase policy.

Some changes in the aid-donor hierarchy in 2010 are worthy of note. Under this aid plan, the United States retains the position of number one donor, and its share of all aid given increases from 46 percent to 50 percent. In the reference run, France is the second-largest aid donor with 21 percent of total aid but falls to third in the aid increase run with 10 percent of total *West* aid. Japan rises from third position (9 percent of total aid) to second (15 percent of total aid) with the aid increase policy in force. Canada moves from being the fourth-largest donor to being the smallest donor, West Germany rises from fifth position to fourth, Italy rises from seventh to fifth, and the United Kingdom remains in sixth position.

Table 4-2 shows the increases in aid that the seven oil-importing aid recipients experience as a consequence of the adoption of the 0.7 percent target.[4] For most, this results in more than a doubling of their aid, which suggests that the distribution patterns of the aid donors are not changing dramatically over time. At the bottom of Table 4-2 is shown the amount of aid flowing to the rest of the developing world, and it is evident that this is not an inconsequential sum.

These results reveal that we have been successful in increasing the flow of aid funds from North to South with this policy change. Before we turn to the question of how much impact such an increase has on economic conditions in the South, we will first look at some of the costs of this policy for the *West.*

TABLE 4–1   Foreign Aid Given by *West* Nations with and without Aid Policy
Change (Million 1970 U.S.$)

DONOR NATION	2000		2010	
	REFERENCE RUN	AID INCREASE	REFERENCE RUN	AID INCREASE
Canada	1,378	1,906	1,968	2,500
France	3,061	2,876	4,938	4,908
Italy	406	1,983	772	3,006
Japan	1,616	6,105	2,117	8,376
United Kingdom	914	2,041	1,251	2,756
United States	8,192	19,199	10,598	26,185
West Germany	1,169	2,977	1,551	3,800

[4] Although some oil-exporting nations do receive foreign aid, they are excluded from most of the analyses that follow. We do this because these are not the developing nations that are the intended beneficiaries of an expanded aid program. Results reported for the LDC group thus pertain to the seven nations listed in Table 4-2.

TABLE 4–2   Foreign Aid Received by Selected LDC Nations with and without Aid
Policy Change (Million 1970 U.S.$)

RECIPIENT NATION	2000		2010	
	REFERENCE RUN	AID INCREASE	REFERENCE RUN	AID INCREASE
Argentina	53	120	72	160
Brazil	483	1,070	623	1,451
Egypt	142	497	239	731
India	2,205	5,161	2,863	6,734
Mexico	154	301	224	462
Pakistan	1,152	2,775	1,567	3,853
Turkey	471	1,092	670	1,538
Rest-of-World	12,076	26,071	16,937	36,602

Costs of Increased Aid to the West

STANDARD OF LIVING

Figure 4-2 shows at five-year intervals the change in the *West*'s standard of living resulting from increased aid. These are the same three indicators (social expenditures per capita, disposable income per capita, and personal consumption per capita) that were shown in Figure 3-4, and the results shown here are dramatically different from those produced by the scenario for arms spending limitation.

In the decade following the implementation of the aid increase policy, all three indicators are lower as a consequence. In 1995, for example, the decrease is approximately $20 per capita for all indicators. After the year 2000, slight real income gains begin to be seen, but the reduction in social expenditures per capita remains and the drop in real consumption per capita is growing. In percent terms, all these losses are small, since none represents much more than a 1 percent reduction. Nevertheless, these declines in the standard of living constitute part of the costs of the aid program, and to see how these costs arise, we will focus on how the aid increase policy affects the United States.

The first question we need to consider is how the government finances the increase in foreign aid expenditure brought about by the policy change. In the reference run, in 1995 the United States spends 7.2 billion (real) dollars on foreign aid, while the comparable figure in the aid increase run is $15.6 billion. This increase in foreign aid in that year is almost totally offset by a reduction in social expenditures (welfare, health, and education outlays) of about 2 percent, with a slight increase in revenue accounting for the rest. In the longer term, tax rates rise

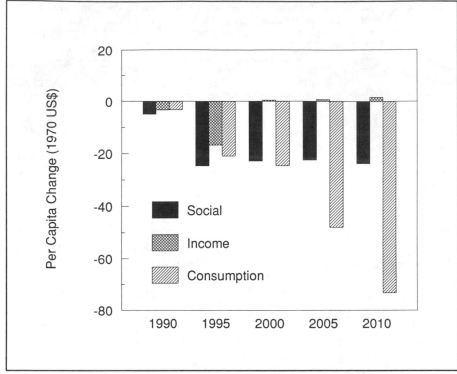

FIGURE 4–2   Standard of Living in the *West* with Aid Increase

more significantly, and the net result is that foreign aid increases are covered by decreased social outlays and increased tax revenues in roughly equal measure. Thus, the first impact of increased foreign aid is a slight "crowding-out" of social programs and a modest increase in taxes. This explains to a greater extent the reduction in social expenditures per capita shown in Figure 4-2 and to a lesser extent the reductions in disposable income and personal consumption per capita.

The increases in foreign aid do not, however, represent an automatic economic loss for the United States, for these grants of aid constitute infusions of purchasing power into the global economy. As a matter of fact, American exports grow significantly as a consequence of increased aid. By 1995 they are already 1 percent higher, by 2000 they climb 3 percent above the reference case, and by the end of the period, 2010, they rise nearly 6 percent with the aid increase policy in force. Indeed, by 2010 the annual increase in exports ($17 billion) exceeds the annual increase in foreign aid ($15 billion). An analysis of where this increased demand for American goods originates reveals that about three-fourths of the increase is due to higher imports by the developing nations, while the remaining one-fourth is attributable to increased imports by other *West* nations. Hence, a significant increase in exports is a second effect of increased aid on the American economy.

The increase in exports has its own effects on the economy of the United States. The increased export demand calls forth an increase in investment and in the real interest rate, as well as a rise in the inflation rate. These lead, in turn, to relatively lower consumption and higher savings on the part of households, which is the explanation for the reduction in real personal consumption per capita shown in Figure 4-2.

In short, increased aid does impose immediate and midrange standard of living costs on the *West*, but that is only part of the story. There are indications that the *West* may in the longer term derive growth benefits from increased aid, and it is to this topic that we now turn.

ECONOMIC GROWTH

A comparison of the total real Gross Domestic Product of the *West* nations with and without the aid increase reveals that increased aid does promote growth in the *West*. Already in 1995 their collective GDP is 0.2 percent higher with increased aid, and that percentage grows slowly but steadily to nearly 1 percent by the year 2010. To see more clearly how this growth is being generated, we will again focus on the United States.

As we indicated in the preceding section, United States exports climb 1 percent above the reference run in 1995 with increased aid, and by 2010 the comparable figure is 6 percent. Two-thirds of the 17-billion (real 1970)-dollar increase in American exports in 2010 is in the manufactures and services sectors, which is not surprising given their sizes; yet, all sectors experience increased demand. Agricultural exports are approximately 7 percent higher by 2010, primary energy and raw materials exports are up 6 percent, and arms exports are 9 percent greater in the same year, while manufactures and services prove to be 5 percent and 6 percent larger, respectively, with increased aid. These increased exports lead to higher production in all sectors by 2010. The value-added increases in 2010 in the six sectors are as follows: manufactures, armaments, and primary energy are 1.5 percent higher; services and raw materials are on the order of 1 percent greater; and agriculture proves to be 0.5 percent higher. Altogether, these increases mean that the American GDP is about 1.1 percent greater in 2010 with the aid increase than without.

These increases in export demand call forth not only more production but also more investment, for as prices and profits increase in the various sectors, incentives for investment grow as well. In the

American case, the increased investment produces an additional 50 billion (real) dollars in capital stock by 2010, which represents an increase of about 0.6 percent over the reference run. By the year 2005, this increased productive capacity is just beginning to have a significant impact on disposable personal income, and we conclude that a general improvement in the American standard of living after 2010 is quite certain as a delayed consequence of increased aid. Seen in that light, foreign aid is not only a charitable act but also a profitable investment, and in some important ways the American economy is stronger as a consequence of increased aid.

Having seen the short-term standard-of-living costs that the *West* bears and the long-term growth benefits it reaps as a result of increased aid, we now turn to the questions of whether and in what ways the South is helped by this increased aid.

Economic Conditions in the South

STANDARD OF LIVING

When we compare the standard-of-living indicators of the increased aid scenario with those from the reference run, we do see some improvements in the South as a consequence of additional aid. Table 4-3 shows the increases that are produced by more aid. It describes the three standard-of-living indicators at several time points. Several conclusions seem evident. First, increased aid produces small but not insignificant improvements in the South's standard of living. Second, these benefits increase in size as time passes. Third, the largest gains appear to be on the private side (disposable income and personal consumption) rather than the public side (social expenditures).

We are disappointed with the overall size of these gains, the largest of which (personal consumption) is about 2.5 percent larger in 2010 than in the reference case. When one notes that the degree of inequality in most of these nations is relatively high, it becomes clear that if the

TABLE 4–3   Increases in LDC Standard of Living Resulting from Aid Increase (Real 1970 U.S.$)

YEAR	SOCIAL EXPENDITURES PER CAPITA	DISPOSABLE INCOME PER CAPITA	PERSONAL CONSUMPTION PER CAPITA
1995	0.50	4.31	3.73
2000	0.76	6.42	6.41
2005	1.48	8.61	9.14
2010	2.26	10.37	11.82

gains were distributed in accordance with the prevailing pattern of income distribution, most citizens of these nations would see minimal improvement in their standard of living as a result of this doubling of aid.

ECONOMIC GROWTH

Some would assert that the primary criterion for evaluating aid is not whether it improves the standard of living in developing nations in the near term but whether it leads to economic growth that will ultimately free the developing world from its dependence upon the North for assistance. Table 4-4 shows the percent change in real Gross Domestic Product resulting from increased aid for the seven less developed aid recipients.

As a whole, the results shown in this table are disappointing, for it is clear that for most aid recipients, the increase in GDP amounts to less than 1 percent. Egypt and India are notable exceptions, and it is clear that not all nations are benefiting equally from the increased aid. Since they do not receive equal amounts of aid, we should not expect that to be so, but it should be noted that the nation with the lowest growth gains, Turkey, is the third-largest aid recipient in this set of nations. In any event, we need a better measure of the effectiveness of aid, and in the next section we will consider such a measure.

RETURNS FROM AID

To derive a measure of the GDP and income returns from increased aid, the following procedures were followed. GDP and income are both flows (goods and services in the first case and money in the second), and to gauge their overall development over a period of time, it is appropriate to integrate (sum) them over that time period. The same is true with respect to foreign aid. If we compare these integrated flows across two simulation runs, the difference between them shows us the

TABLE 4–4 Change in GDP of LDC Aid Recipients with Aid Increase (%)

RECIPIENT	1995	2000	2005	2010
Argentina	0.1	0.2	0.4	0.4
Brazil	0.1	0.4	0.7	0.9
Egypt	0.5	1.0	1.6	2.5
India	0.5	0.8	1.4	2.3
Mexico	0.1	0.2	0.2	0.3
Pakistan	0.6	0.8	0.7	1.0
Turkey	0.3	0.3	0.2	0.1

aggregate change in economic activity in the case of GDP and income and the additional total resources transferred in the case of foreign aid. To measure the economic return of an additional dollar in foreign aid at a particular time point, we divide the aggregate change (or cumulative change) in economic activity up to that point by the total additions (or accumulated increases) of foreign aid up to that point. Performing this operation separately for GDP and disposable income gives us two measures of the returns from aid that control for differences in the amount of aid nations receive.[5] Moreover, they take into account the fact that aid given in one time period is likely to have a continuing impact on the economy thereafter rather than simply a sudden and short-lived impulse.

Figure 4-3 shows the values of these two indices in the years 2000 and 2010 for the seven less developed aid recipients. Three conclusions are supported by this figure. First, in all cases except Brazil, income gains are greater than GDP gains. Second, in all cases except Pakistan and Turkey, both GDP and income gains grow through time. Third, the break-even point, defined as when an additional dollar in aid generates more than an additional dollar in GDP or income, is reached considerably sooner and by more nations with respect to income than with respect to GDP. Pakistan and Turkey, for example, are realizing only about eighteen cents of increased GDP from each additional dollar of aid received in the year 2000, and this rate of return is virtually unchanged ten years later. In terms of income (and standard of living), all seven nations are showing a low but acceptable return from aid by 2010, but with respect to economic growth, this can be said only for Argentina, Brazil, and India.

When we stand back and assess all of this evidence regarding changes in economic conditions in the South arising from increased aid, it becomes clear that aid tends to be used to generate a higher standard of living rather than a higher rate of economic growth. Since such a use of aid runs the danger of *increasing* the dependence of the South upon the North to maintain this higher standard of living, it behooves us to better understand what the impact of foreign aid is on the developing economy. To do that, we will focus on Pakistan in the next

[5] Another way to view such an index is to imagine a time-plot containing two GDP series drawn from different runs of the model. The total change in GDP would be represented by the difference between the areas under the two lines. If the two series are the same, then this difference would be 0, of course, but if the GDP associated with aid increase is systematically higher than the reference run, then the difference in area would be positive. Plotting the levels of foreign aid received in the two runs and again taking the difference in areas under the two lines would give us an overall measure of the difference in aid received. The GDP return index is the ratio of the GDP (area) difference to the foreign aid (area) difference, and the income return index is of the same nature.

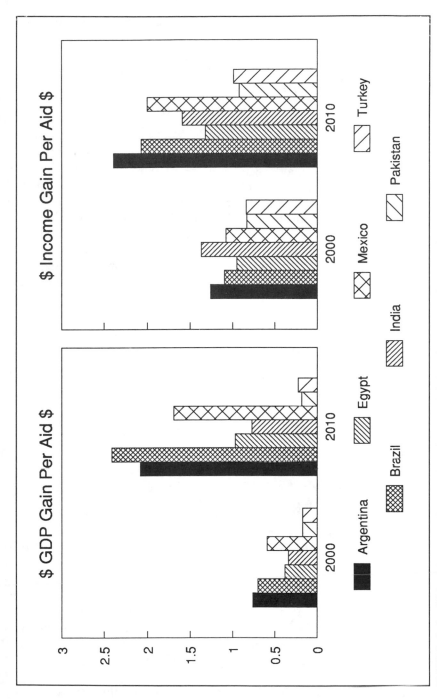

FIGURE 4-3 GDP and Income Returns from Increased Aid to Seven Less Developed Nations

section and try to determine if more-effective strategies of aid utilization are possible.

A CASE STUDY OF PAKISTAN

To see more clearly the impact of additional foreign aid on the less developed nations, we will here look more deeply into the case of Pakistan. Since it is one of the poorest nations to be found in GLOBUS and one of the largest aid recipients (relative to GDP), it is a good example of a nation that should benefit significantly from a program of increased aid. As shown in the previous section, however, the amount of additional GDP per additional aid dollar after two decades of increased aid is about eighteen cents for this nation. Income gains are about five times higher than that, but an essential part of the rationale for giving foreign aid is to enable less developed nations to accelerate their growth and become more self-reliant. Why don't we observe this in Pakistan?

As might be expected, the full answer to this question is rather complex, and we offer Figure 4-4 to enable the reader to better understand the explanation that follows. In this diagram, wide arrows designate the primary impact of aid on the Pakistani economy, and narrow arrows denote secondary effects. None of the primary paths connects increased aid to higher economic growth. This discussion will explain why that is so.

The Primary Effects of Increased Aid

As Figure 4-4 shows, one of the two immediate effects of aid is to increase government revenues, and the government must "decide" to what degree it will increase spending or reduce taxes, or do both. Aid is treated no differently from other government revenues, and the response made by the Pakistani government to the increased revenue favors lowering taxes rather than raising expenditures, an action that is quite reasonable if the government is seeking to maximize short-term political gains. Figure 4-5 demonstrates that although government spending in Pakistan initially does increase, it gradually returns to that of the reference run, while tax rates continue to fall until almost the entire aid increase is reflected in lower taxes. By 2010 approximately three-fourths of the aid increase has effectively been allocated to tax reductions. The other one-fourth moves almost entirely into a variety of government consumption categories, and very little finds its way to increased investment.

This assumption of nearly complete substitutability, or fungibility, of aid and other government revenues contradicts the intent of aid

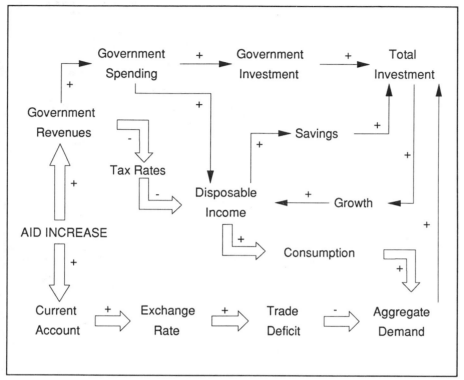

FIGURE 4–4 The Impact of Aid on Growth and Welfare

donors, but the response reflected in the estimated parameters leads Pakistan to reduce other tax revenues by nearly the full amount of the aid over a five- to ten-year period. This outcome is supported by the statistical analyses in the literature that were reported in Chapter 2. This government behavior suggests a policy scenario that we want to subsequently examine; namely, what would be the consequences were Pakistan (and other aid recipients) to use the aid to bolster government spending and, in particular, to increase government investment (as donors hope and expect)? In sum, most of the additional aid flows, through tax rate reductions, into the disposable income of Pakistani households (see again Figure 4-4), while another portion of the aid increases household income through slightly higher transfer payments from the government.

Depending in part on which households benefit from this increased income, there can be little doubt that the overall welfare of the inhabitants of the recipient country is enhanced. This model does not differentiate households by socioeconomic category; therefore, we cannot pursue welfare analysis further. Obviously, however, tax reductions

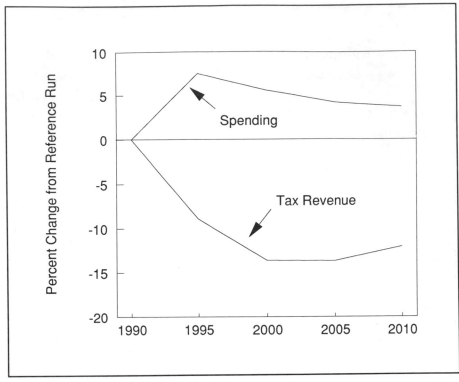

FIGURE 4–5   Change in Pakistani Taxation and Spending

throughout the world tend to benefit primarily the higher-income house-holds most subject to taxation.

Returning to the analysis of the possible linkages between aid and growth, the household disposition of income becomes critical. It would still be possible for savings and investment in Pakistan to increase in response to the aid, were households to devote much of their increased income to savings. That would, in turn, lead to higher growth. In fact, household savings rates are very low, lower than government savings rates. Thus, the increase in household savings in response to higher income is negligible. In fact, increases in the money supply resulting from the aid depress interest rates and further erode household incentives to save (see Taylor 1979 on the close connection of LDC monetary growth rates to foreign exchange earnings). Overall, domestic savings are thus reduced, while consumption based on the increased income rises. Figure 4-6 traces this phenomenon over time for Pakistan, comparing domestic savings and personal consumption in the increased aid case with the values in the reference case.

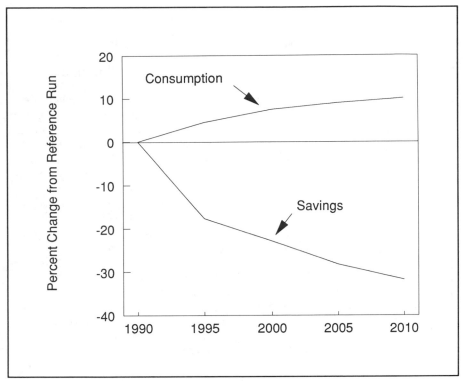

FIGURE 4–6 Change in Pakistani Savings and Consumption

Returning to Figure 4-4, investment and therefore GDP growth in an aid-recipient country could be increased by higher savings (which facilitate investment through lower interest rates) or by increases in direct government investment, but those two paths do not seem to be very effective in the Pakistani case. A third potential route to higher investment and growth lies in increased aggregate demand. Increased demand (and therefore capacity utilization and prices) creates incentives for producers to invest. As opposed to the supply-side generation of savings and investment as a route to growth, increase in aggregate demand could pull growth forward. Because we have already seen that private consumption in Pakistan has increased, such increase in aggregate demand appears to be a serious possibility.

It is at this point that we must turn to the impact of aid on the current account (see Figure 4-4 again) and that an important argument contained in the literature reviewed earlier becomes relevant. Through improvements in the current account and settlements balance, aid can lead to relative increases in the real exchange rate. (See the box for a definition of terminology used here.) In LDCs this can be almost un-

BOX 4-1 *International Economic Concepts*

This and subsequent chapters assume knowledge of some of the terminology used in international trade and finance. Many of the terms center on the exchange rate of currencies and we therefore begin by defining it.

Exchange rate   The **nominal exchange rate** (often simply called the exchange rate) between two currencies is the number of units of one currency (for example, Japanese yen) that it takes to buy a single unit of another (for example, the U.S. dollar) in the global marketplace. Based on the nominal rate and the difference in inflation rates among countries, we can calculate a **real exchange rate.** As a crude example of a real exchange rate, consider the Big Mac Index, the real cost to Americans of Big Macs purchased around the world. If the prices of Big Macs (and other goods) in Brazil are going up faster than those in the United States but nominal exchange rates between the two countries remain unchanged, Americans will find it more and more expensive in dollars to buy enough Brazilian currency to buy a Brazilian Big Mac. The Brazilian Big Mac Index, like the real exchange rate of Brazilian currency, will be **overvalued.** That will discourage Americans from buying Brazilian Big Macs and other goods. At the same time, Brazilians will find United States Big Macs inexpensive and will increase their purchases. The result will be an imbalance in trade, and one solution would be for the Brazilians to **devalue** their nominal exchange rate to offset the more rapid rise in their prices.

Devaluation   Downward change in the nominal value of the currency of one country relative to the value of the currencies of its trading partners.

Revaluation   Upward change in the nominal value of the currency of one country relative to the value of the currencies of its trading partners.

In a floating exchange rate system, such as that which now prevails in much of the world, nominal exchange rates respond to the balance of financial flows among countries. (That balance determines the supply and demand for currencies internationally.) Some additional terminology assists in understanding the mechanism of exchange rate change in this supply-and-demand system.

Settlements balance   Also known as the overall balance or the official settlements balance, it is the balance in international accounts after all trade, aid, long-term lending, and private short-term flows are reconciled. It must be settled by short-term transactions between governments and, if the imbalance is substantial, can indicate urgent needs for changes in trade policy or exchange rates. In a floating exchange rate system, the need for governments to send their currency abroad to cover a settlements imbalance increases the international supply of that currency and automatically puts downward pressure on its price.

> **Current account** A component of the international balance of payments accounting scheme that ultimately produces the settlements balance. Trade, aid, and property income are part of the current account.
>
> **Property income** Payments crossing international borders for capital use abroad. For instance, investors who repatriate profits, dividends, or interest on assets abroad are obtaining property income. This is part of the current account and settlements balance. It therefore affects exchange rates.

noticeable to policymakers because high inflation rates normally are offset by regular devaluations of the nominal exchange rate so as to keep the real exchange rate stable; should the devaluations be less than normal, or the inflation rate higher, the real exchange rate will rise. In the increased aid scenario here, that is exactly what happens. Although the nominal exchange rate of Pakistan falls, it falls less rapidly than in the reference run because the current account and settlements balance picture is less threatening. Moreover, the inflation rate with aid is higher; thus, the real exchange rate rises. In many policy environments, the tendency to overvalue a currency is further reinforced by explicit decisions (rather than a failure to adapt to the changed situation) to use an overvalued rate to dampen demand (exports), increase imports, and slow inflation.

In the increased aid scenario, these joint influences result in a real exchange rate that is higher than the reference case, which encourages imports, discourages exports, and leads to increased trade deficits. In essence, the result is a use of aid to finance increased imports (and to offset falling export revenues). Potential increases in aggregate demand resulting from higher personal consumption are largely cancelled by decreases in demand on the trade side. Figure 4-7 shows this pattern for Pakistan, utilizing the higher real exchange rate and the lower exports to illustrate it.

The reader should turn again to Figure 4-4 to review the entire argument concerning the impact of aid on Pakistan, and by implication on the other aid recipients. The increase in government revenues led to lower taxes, higher household income, more consumption, and greater aggregate demand. The improvement in current account (and settlements balance) brought about simultaneously by the aid led to a higher real exchange rate, a deterioration in trade (more imports and fewer exports), and lower aggregate demand. The net impact of the two paths on aggregate demand is positive, but it is insufficient to stimulate much increase in investment and therefore does not substantially encourage GDP growth. Figure 4-4 essentially represents a model of a model (a

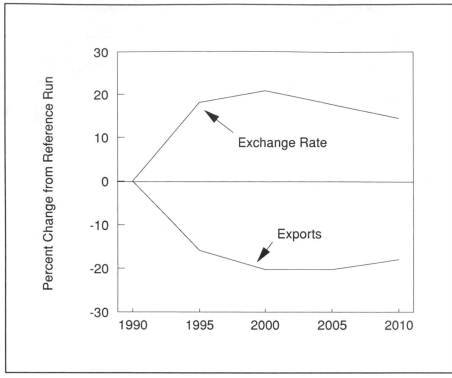

FIGURE 4–7 Change in Pakistani Trade Deficit and Aggregate Demand

simplification of the GLOBUS system) and has helped us clarify the relationship between increased foreign aid and GDP growth.

Some Secondary Issues

The overall result for Pakistan and generally for the other aid-recipient countries in GLOBUS is increased consumption and greater trade deficit (offset by the aid) but little increase in aggregate demand, investment, and growth. There are, however, some interesting changes that occur within the economies and that are not visible in such aggregate indicators.

Specifically, aid causes some restructuring of the economies. Two of the six economic sectors grow in response to the aid. The first is agriculture, which responds to the higher level of private consumption and the high proportion of that consumption spending directed toward food. The second is services, which respond to private and government consumption. Services, although traded in GLOBUS, are primarily domestically produced, as is food. The additional demand upon those sectors requires expansion of domestic production,[6] and this restructuring has a secondary impact on aggregate economic growth. Although the nature of the impact is too complex to describe in any detail here, this structural change in production results in a slight downward pressure on GDP (relative to the reference run).[7]

One reason behind the assumption in two-gap models that imports may raise growth is that imports carry imbedded technology. The GLOBUS model recognizes that by tying technological advance in production to the availability of imported manufactured goods.[8] Thus, the increase in manufactured imports does provide an upward impetus to GDP relative to the reference run. Much of the import surge is in consumer goods, however, and many two-gap models may be overly optimistic in the degree to which they posit that imports relieve growth bottlenecks.

There are two possible interactions of aid and growth that are not captured in the GLOBUS domestic economic model. First, private investment and governmental investment may not make equal contributions to economic growth, and aid might lead to an increase in investment by government at the expense of private investment. In fact, such a substitution of governmental investment for private investment is exactly what happens in the GLOBUS increased aid scenario, even if the shift is small. Although this change in the nature of investment could change growth rates in the real world, government and private investment are not distinguished by destination within GLOBUS. There is no public or infrastructure capital stock variable, and government investment flows with private investment to the six economic sectors. Thus, in this model, the slight shift of investment from private to governmental has no impact on growth, a possible structural weakness of the model.[9]

Second, at the microlevel, the absorption potential of the aid recipient is an important issue. That is, does it have the managerial skills, resources, access to markets, and so on, to make additional aid profitable? Aid can also, of course, assist in identifying new high-return projects and in creating absorption potential, and aid can contribute to

[6] This phenomenon has been noted in descriptions of the impact of the oil shocks on OPEC economies. Inflation was particularly rapid in nontraded services.

[7] Although GLOBUS does treat the issue of sectoral restructuring, it does so somewhat incompletely. Specifically, increases in disposable income will alter consumption and savings patterns in ways that depend in reality on the distribution of that income across socioeconomic classes. GLOBUS contains no such classes at this time.

[8] This linkage has been added to the model since the publication of the documentation volume (Bremer 1987), and it is the only significant structural difference between the model described there and the one used in these analyses.

[9] It may also *not* be a weakness, because it is unclear whether government investment is marginally more or less effective than private investment in contributing to GDP growth. In the absence of such knowledge, placing government investment into a pool with private investment may be reasonable.

increased government spending on health and education, which might improve labor productivity.[10] But a model at GLOBUS's level of aggregation cannot treat fundamental microquestions directly.

THE NORTH-SOUTH GAP

One of our primary concerns in this book is the degree to which the policies implicit in the I/I theory of Figure 2-1 could bring about a significant reduction in the economic disparity between the North and the South. As indicated earlier, the measure that we employ in assessing this disparity is the ratio of the North GDP per capita to the South GDP per capita.

Figure 4-8 shows this ratio over time for the reference run and increased aid scenario. Given what we found concerning the impact of aid, it is not surprising that the North-South GDP per capita ratio is only slightly lower by the year 2010 with increased aid than without. Although the South (including *Opec* for this figure) benefited marginally from increased aid, the North gained as much.

Rather than narrowing the North-South gap, by increasing aid we have generally raised GDPs around the world. In fact, the global GDP is nearly 1 percent higher as a result of the aid, and most countries benefit, whether they give aid, receive aid, or export to the aid recipients. As we have seen, however, the aggregate picture presented by GDP conceals considerable differentiation in the impact of aid. Income levels rise significantly in the aid recipients and fall slightly in the donors. Aid recipients develop larger agricultural and service sectors to meet the demand of consumers but import more of other goods, including energy. Manufacturing sectors grow and exports increase in the North.

Overall, the implications of the aid are substantially different from those posited in the I/I theory of Figure 2-1, primarily because the aid does not facilitate as much growth in the South as that theory anticipates. We turn next to an investigation of how aid might in fact encourage more Southern growth.

CONCLUSION

Let us recapitulate what we have found in this part of our analysis. We have found that if the *West* adopted the 0.7 percent aid target, a doubling of aid would result. Giving this amount of aid does entail short-term standard-of-living costs for the *West* but brings substantial long-term

---

[10] Krueger (1979) emphasized this value of aid in her study of Korea.

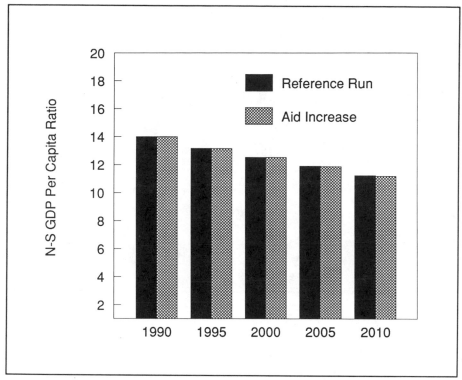

FIGURE 4–8   North-South Gap with and without Aid Increase

economic gains as well. However, this increased aid does not bring about greatly accelerated economic growth in the South. It does produce a slight improvement in the standard of living in the South but makes the South more dependent upon the North for the maintenance of that standard of living.[11]

Our detailed analysis of the impact of foreign aid on Pakistan suggests, however, that developing nations may be able to make better use of the aid they receive, and in the next chapter we will focus on the utilization of aid in the South to determine whether the adoption of particular policies in that portion of the globe could significantly enhance the effectiveness of aid.

---

[11] This is precisely the effect that conservative critics of domestic welfare programs claim is the result of "government give-away programs." And some radical critics on the opposite end of the political spectrum concur that welfare creates dependence that perpetuates an inferior social and political position.

Self-Help?

CHAPTER 5

The previous chapter showed that, were international assistance flows increased to meet the NIEO target levels, welfare in less developed nations would increase, but domestic production would be largely unaffected. Overall, the effectiveness of aid proved fairly low. Figure 5-1 provides a measure of the "return" to the additional aid given to the LDCs, an indicator that we introduced in the previous chapter and will continue to use. It shows the cumulative gains in income and GDP relative to the cumulative increment of aid received in the seven principal aid-recipient countries (see also Figure 4-3). Although in 2010 income increases by $1.50 for every aid dollar received, GDP is only $0.50 greater. As we saw in Figure 4-8, these increases are far too small to have any significant impact on the North-South gap.

That result demanded both explanation and elaboration, and to investigate the reasons for it, we initially narrowed our focus to the economic behavior of a single recipient country. Pakistan receives more aid relative to its GDP than any other country in the GLOBUS *South* (4–5 percent in the reference case and 7–9 percent in the high aid case). Pakistan thus served well for a deeper examination of the result. It appears that two factors explain much of the general failure of increased aid to promote rapid and sustained economic growth. The first is the failure of governments to direct the aid to productive investments; instead, they use it to relieve spending pressures in other categories and to reduce taxes. The second is the overvaluation of exchange rates that results from aid and leads to deterioration in trade balances.

110

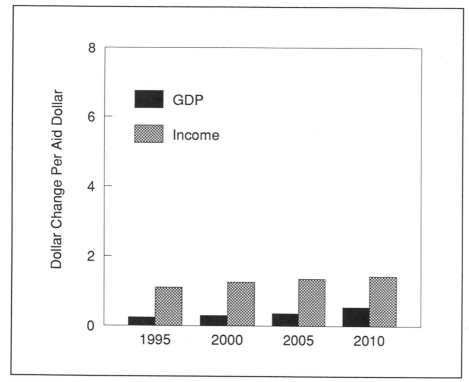

FIGURE 5–1   GDP and Income Returns to Increased Aid

The importance of placing aid receipts into a specific policy context was emphasized by Papanek (1983), an active earlier participant (1972 and 1973) in the debate over whether aid has net positive or negative consequences for economic growth. In looking in detail at five South Asian countries, he found that

> For instance, in Pakistan in the 1960s, increasing aid was accompanied by declining defence expenditures and rising development expenditures. However, in the 1970s increasing aid was, conversely, accompanied by rising defence and declining development expenditures. . . . The consequences of aid seem to depend less on the quantity of aid provided or on the projects financed by the aid donors, than on how the government receiving aid wanted to use it. (Papanek 1983:176–177)

DOMESTIC POLICY REFORMS IN THE SOUTH

The case study of Pakistan in the last chapter suggested two areas of governmental policy that merit further attention: fiscal policy (both revenues and expenditures) and currency valuation. This chapter undertakes an analysis of the interaction of both with increased foreign aid. We return our attention to LDC aid recipients as a whole.[1] Specifically, this section presents results from three further model runs. Fiscal policy is the focus of one, which directs foreign aid into government investment and also maintains government revenues in the face of higher foreign aid. The second model run explores the interaction of aid with exchange rates. The final analysis considers the three-way interaction of increased aid, fiscal reforms, and exchange rate interventions.[2]

Fiscal Policy

If foreign aid is not treated differently from any other national revenue stream, it is hardly surprising that most is consumed, both by households and by government. The parameters of the GLOBUS model (as reflected in the results of the last chapter) suggest that most governments will, in the long run, treat aid very much like other revenue streams.

Although a considerable amount of aid is, in fact, intended for consumption (especially food aid), donors certainly want much aid to be budget enhancing rather than budget relieving, and often aid is intended specifically to supplement capital formation. As a result of donor pressure and the desires of the recipients themselves to maximize the impact of aid receipts upon long-term growth prospects, many recipient states might be moved to attempt to channel supplemental aid directly into governmental investment activities.[3]

To implement a scenario that assumed governmental success in that attempt, we directed 50 percent of all foreign aid in the increased aid case (beginning in 1990 and continuing thereafter) into incremental desired total governmental expenditures and specifically into additional desired governmental investment.[4] Fifty percent of foreign aid is ap-

---

[1] We focus on the principal aid recipients of the GLOBUS South: Argentina, Brazil, Egypt, India, Mexico, Pakistan, and Turkey.

[2] We also analyzed but are not reporting a third policy cluster—namely, monetary policy. The increased aid scenario results in high monetary growth that leads to higher inflation. Constrained monetary growth, like that which would be obtained by sterilizing foreign exchange increases, did constrain inflation but had no significant affect on growth. This result possibly says as much about the GLOBUS model as about the reality of monetary restraint implications. The GLOBUS model incorporates no money illusion— no agents react significantly to higher or lower nominal money levels—and price levels adjust quite rapidly. Dervis et al. (1982:152) and many others argue that money is relatively neutral in the longer term and, hence, is less important to long-run models or analyses than to those of the short run. That is the case in GLOBUS.

[3] We are aware that this policy of expanding government's role as an investor is contrary to the policy advice put forth by increasing numbers of development experts who favor private initiatives instead. Nonetheless, it remains the preference of those taking the Idealist/Internationalist position.

[4] This was done in the subroutines of the governmental budgeting model (BNODEF and BEXPEC). The variables to which the aid was added were DGINV and DTOTEX.

proximately all of the increase relative to the reference run (the higher aid scenario effectively doubled the aid of the reference run). Because the government budgeting model must reconcile all demands for expenditure, it cannot be guaranteed that final changes in investment will be precisely those desired. In fact, the result of this change was that government investment in Pakistan increased in 1995 by 44 percent of the aid increment.

It is theoretically possible (although very unlikely) that recipient governments would direct all additional foreign aid to government investment. Certainly, donors would be pleased to see that. The slightly more limited success in using aid for investment that we examine here is a much more reasonable upper limit. In combination with the scenario of the last chapter, in which all aid was in essence treated as general revenue, these two analyses should represent the outer limits of the impact of aid on savings and investment.

The impact of the aid is quite dramatically different when the desires of donors that aid supplement investment are translated into model behavior. Figure 5-2 shows the returns to increased aid when it is combined with the fiscal "reforms" noted previously. It should be compared with Figure 5-1, which indicated the effects of increased aid without reform. Clearly, aid directed into investment has quite dramatic potential for improving both growth (GDP) and welfare (income). With fiscal reforms, every dollar of additional aid provides a GDP return of $4.90 and an income return of $5.30.

The more rapid growth in this scenario, relative to the former one, can be attributed almost entirely to higher rates of investment for the economy as a whole. The increases relative to reference run investment levels are perhaps not as great as might be expected, however. For the seven aid recipients, the initial investment increment is approximately 3 percent and thereafter total investment levels remain 3–4 percent above the reference.

Again it should be emphasized that Figures 5-1 and 5-2 portray extreme, and perhaps equally unlikely, uses of foreign aid. In the first instance, the aid is essentially all consumer or welfare aid. Although it improves consumption levels, it creates little growth and largely finances imports. In the second case, the aid is heavily investment-directed. It creates rapid growth and actually contributes more to income and consumption growth than when the aid is treated like any other income flow.

There are, of course, problems with the high investment scenario. Most fundamental is the political difficulty of maintaining the discipline necessary to avoid the diversion of aid to other short-term purposes—especially by restructuring the "nonaid" budget. Such diversion can be accomplished gradually and almost unnoticeably to donors or recipients. In fact, the diversion of domestic funds from investment can make the

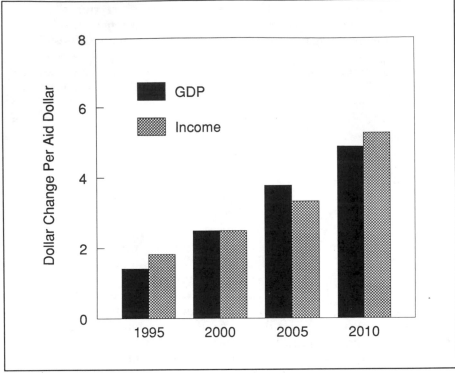

FIGURE 5–2 GDP and Income Returns to Increased Aid and Fiscal Reforms

case for continued or increased aid even stronger, because over time, aid may come to constitute a critical portion of investment. In addition, inflation remains a problem, although the use of aid funds for investment gives rise to less additional inflation than when aid supplements consumption. Finally, and perhaps most important, the real exchange rate appreciation and considerable transformation of trade patterns (no matter how the aid is used internally) leaves the recipient country very vulnerable to a reduction or elimination of the aid.

Exchange Rate Policy

In the increased aid model run, the real exchange rate[5] of the recipient countries reacts rapidly to the additional inflow of funds from abroad. In the case of Pakistan, for example, the additional aid amounts to about 3 percent of GDP and 19 percent of exports; the real exchange

[5] The "real" rate here is the nominal exchange rate adjusted by the ratio of local to United States price indices (which is equivalent to annual adjustment by the inflation differential).

rate is 18 percent higher than the reference run by 1995. Because trade patterns then shift and begin to offset the aid inflow, the real exchange rate of the high aid case gradually drifts back toward that of the reference run after 2000.

The tendency for aid recipients to have overvalued currencies is a common one. Krueger (1979) suggests that aid promotes overvalued currencies, because a considerable surplus of imports over exports supports a developing nation's plea for aid to fill the gap. In the case of Korea, she notes that only as aid began to decline in the early 1960s were devaluation and export promotion undertaken.

Within GLOBUS, the pattern of overevaluation is not so much political as economic. The model posits market-responsive exchange rates as reacting to the settlements balance, which aid improves. Even though most LDCs set or strongly influence exchange rates rather than letting them float freely, they generally look to the settlements balance for information in so doing, thereby making the GLOBUS structure a reasonable one.

Thus, it may be useful to examine a scenario in which the real exchange rate is largely unaffected by the additional foreign aid. Some countries introduce substantial periodic devaluations to remedy overvaluations; many others rely upon repeated "minidevaluations" to maintain a reasonably valued currency. We rely upon the second strategy in implementing the scenario.[6] Specifically, we devalue the currencies of recipient countries by 3 percent each year after the beginning of the aid increase. In addition, we "hide" the increment of aid (50 percent of the total) from the settlements balance, which would otherwise become more favorable and exert downward pressure on the currency.[7] As in the preceding fiscal scenario, this should be considered a maximum effort to protect the exchange rate.

The results for all GLOBUS aid recipients of this variation on the increased aid scenario are quite interesting. The minidevaluation strategy accomplishes the objective of largely maintaining reference run trade patterns. In combination with the higher domestic demand levels that result from increased government and household revenues, the continued export strength results initially in pressure upon production capacity, which, in turn, leads to increased investment and GDP growth, relative to the reference run. Because aggregate demand is considerably higher, the devaluations also contribute to more rapid inflation.

[6] A useful and readable discussion of the benefits of devaluation, especially repeated small ones, can be found in Bird (1984).

[7] The scenario was introduced through changes in the economic subroutine EFINAN. For years beginning in 1988, the variable SETBAL is reduced by 50 percent of foreign aid and DOLRXZ is decreased by 3 percent of DOLRX.

In this scenario, investment is increased because of higher aggregate demand and capacity utilization, not because of direct governmental action; the increase to investment is for the most part private rather than governmental. Interestingly, total investment increases almost as much as in the previous scenario, which supplemented it directly. Specifically, investment is 3 percent higher than the reference case by 2000; thereafter, it moves closer to that of the reference run because the exchange rate, in spite of the interventions just described, begins to climb relative to the reference run.

Figure 5-3 translates these intermediate effects into the relationship between aid and real aggregate economic performance. The GDP and disposable income returns to aid exceed $1.00 before 2000 and continue to grow for some time. The acceleration in economic performance does not, however, endure beyond fifteen years. Unlike the fiscal policy scenario, in which the growth contribution of the policy change not only endures but compounds, the contribution of the exchange rate policy is substantial initially, but erodes.

FIGURE 5–3 GDP and Income Returns to Increased Aid and Exchange Reform

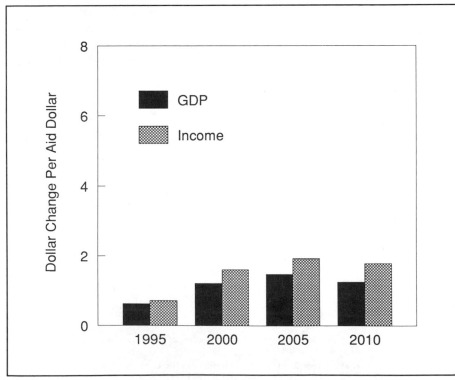

There are two reasons for this. First, the increased domestic demand does raise interest rates and the cost of investment, which, in turn, dampens investment. Here, perhaps, a more expansive monetary policy could be helpful (although in the face of high inflation it hardly seems prudent). Second, and more important, the near-reference-run levels in exports and imports, coupled with the continued inflow of substantial foreign aid, allow some aid recipients to move from debtor to creditor nation status. Foreign assets have returns (interest, dividends, profits) that themselves further improve the settlements balance. Although this scenario made the additional foreign aid largely "invisible" to the settlements balance and the currency valuation process, it did not hide net property income payments from it. Thus, more slowly than before, but steadily, the real exchange rate of aid recipients rises relative to the reference run and begins to again shift trade patterns and weaken growth.

This situation could be seen as analogous to that of Japan, which has invested much of its trade surplus abroad and in so doing has helped avoid appreciation in the value of its currency and thereby facilitated continued trade surpluses (investment of trade earnings abroad strengthens demand for foreign currencies like the dollar while failing to increase demand for the yen). But as the assets purchased increasingly return interest, dividends, and profits to Japan (assuming that such property income is not constantly reinvested abroad), those financial flows themselves increase demand for the yen and result in revaluation. The resulting increase in price of Japanese exports is among factors now forcing Japan to raise domestic demand to replace the role of exports. Similarly, the upward pressure in the late 1980s on Taiwanese exchange rates was a result of the success of earlier efforts in that country to maintain low real rates and the financial resources accumulated by Taiwan as a result. Figure 5-3 suggests that the erosion of export-promoting low exchange rates may have economic growth costs for such countries.

There are several potential policy responses to this situation. First, it could be recognized that the only way to maintain a particular exchange rate in the long run is to accommodate the inflow of aid with a parallel inflow of goods. Thus, demand for imports must be created and our attention returns to fiscal policy instruments, such as increased governmental spending. The central policy question simplifies to whether the imported goods should support consumption or investment. It is easy to say that they should be investment goods and thereby increase productivity. It is much harder, as many countries know from experience, to assure that imports add to investment. Second, if other states do not threaten to retaliate or actually do so, a government could postpone this seemingly inevitable choice by forcing further devaluations.

Combined Policy Change

It cannot be simply assumed that combining the changes in the fiscal and exchange rate policies results in greater contributions of aid to economic growth than either policy does individually. It is possible that the two policies could be activating the same potential contribution of aid to growth—it is even possible (if improbable) that, when combined, each policy would negate the effects of the other. Therefore, another scenario was examined that combines the previous two. The implementation is simply the combination of the increment to governmental investment and the protection of the exchange rate already described.

Figure 5-4 presents the aid returns in the combined policy case and shows that the policy efforts are essentially additive. Clearly, the GDP return of $5.50 per $1.00 of aid argues that the economic growth return to aid *can* be very high. This type of return is important to donors, but to recipients the more important indicator may be the extent of absolute improvements in welfare. Figure 5-4 shows an income return of $6.00 in 2010. Not only can the growth return to aid be high; the human impact of aid *can also* be very high.

Substantial increases in North-South aid would require international cooperation on a fairly extensive scale. Many in the North question the desirability of such aid, and many others question its feasibility. Thus, we should also consider the possibility that the South can accomplish a meaningful increase in growth through a reliance on the reforms without aid.

REFORMS WITHOUT AID

Aid without reforms provides limited benefit, primarily to consumption; aid with reforms yields considerable growth and welfare benefits to recipient countries. Could it be that the reforms are responsible for these benefits and not the aid? The reforms introduced earlier in association with aid are in fact quite similar to those that have often been proposed by the International Monetary Fund and other development agencies as important measures in generating growth.

To investigate that possibility, we will here compare the impact of reforms alone with that of aid plus reforms. Again we restrict our analysis to the seven principal aid-recipient states of GLOBUS and consider that group as a whole.

Reforms alone do not result in as great an improvement in economic performance as aid with reforms. GDP growth with reforms but without aid is less than half that with both aid and reforms. Perhaps even more important, the reforms by themselves require the sacrifice of current

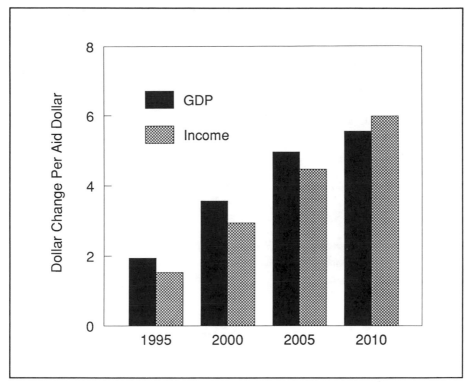

FIGURE 5—4 GDP and Income Returns to Increased Aid and Combined Reforms

consumption for future consumption. Figure 5-5 traces the development of consumption in the two instances. Aid and reforms significantly raise the levels of income and allow rises in consumption. In fact, by 2010 the seven aid recipients are able to boost private consumption expenditures by 4 percent, relative to the reference case, when they receive NIEO aid levels and institute fiscal and exchange rate reforms. But should they attempt to introduce the reforms without additional aid, losses occur in consumption (relative to the reference run) until 2010. That is, it requires nearly twenty years of relative sacrifice before consumers begin to reap the benefits of reforms. The political difficulty of such policies should be obvious.

Aid thus can serve important purposes in raising the level of economic achievement above that which could be attained with reforms alone and in allowing consumption to grow during the period of disruption that accompanies more rapid growth. There are other *economic* reasons to believe that the reforms would be difficult to accomplish without the additional aid. (In the next chapter, we will address the *political* side.)

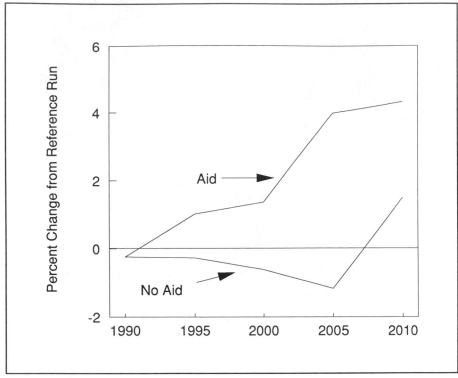

FIGURE 5–5 Consumption after Reforms in Seven Aid Recipients

Inflation is a cost of the reforms. The maintenance of lower real exchange rates encourages exports and puts pressure upon the domestic capacity of exporting sectors. That, in turn, draws forth investment funds that facilitate higher production. In this way, lower exchange rates lead to the higher growth that we have seen. In the process, however, the pressure upon production capacity contributes to inflation. In addition, lower real exchange rates raise the price of imports. Higher-priced imports directly contribute to inflation also, as well as allowing domestic producers some freedom to raise their own prices. Although monetary or fiscal restraint could compensate for these inflationary pressures by dampening domestic demand, the political will seldom exists to so obviously discourage consumption. Fiscal reform, involving the use of existing aid funds for investment, can in the longer run actually reduce inflation by raising production capacity. But in the shorter run it, too, is inflationary because of the demands it places upon the economy to purchase the tools of production. Thus, inflationary consequences constitute a second strike against developing countries that seek to implement the reforms without aid.

We must point out, however, that the reforms with aid are even more inflationary, because the increases in aid stoke government and private demand while reform in the exchange rate seeks to choke off the transmission of that additional demand abroad. Figure 5-6 indicates the annual increases in price levels brought about by the two reform scenarios. There is still reason to believe, however, that aid with reform would be more palatable than the reforms alone. Namely, the aid and reform combination has nearly immediate benefits for consumers and the overall GDP that can compensate for the higher inflation, whereas the reforms alone do not.

An additional problem associated with reforms alone is external rather than domestic. Maintaining lower real exchange rates to encourage exports is a fundamental part of most export promotion strategies and does increase the exports of those countries implementing it (while constraining imports). Exports from the seven aid-receiving countries of GLOBUS rise more than 4 percent with reforms (no aid) relative to the reference run by 2010.

FIGURE 5–6 Inflation Rates after Reforms in Seven Aid Recipients

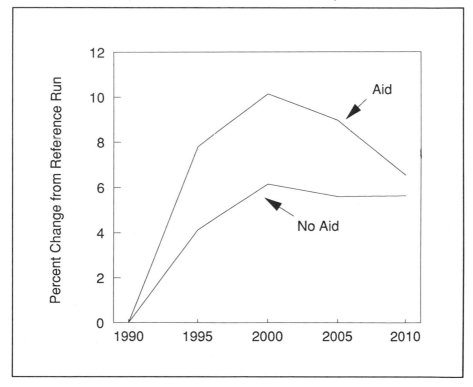

As many observers have noted, export promotion as a development strategy depends on willing importers. When only a small number of exporters pursue such a strategy, shifts in global and national market shares are scarcely perceptible. But the pressure that the United States has at times exerted on Japan, South Korea, Taiwan, and other export-promoting countries to raise their real exchange rates indicates that even a limited number of such countries can be perceived as an important threat to the markets of importers. Should larger numbers of aid recipients similarly strive to grow by means of increased exports, the systemic strain could become very substantial. Although exporters also import, they seek to do so only after some time lag, a fact that we earlier saw causes the early growth benefits of export promotion to erode. The issue can be expected to cause leading industrial countries to resist the widespread introduction of the exchange rate reform.

An indication of how large that resistance might be can be gained from Figure 5-7. This figure shows that the cost to the *West* of the Southern export promotion strategies is relatively low, about 0.6 percent of GDP. Nonetheless, the growth of the *West* is somewhat reduced by the reforms alone, whereas it is slightly increased by the reforms with aid (because of the long-term economic benefits of aid to the donors that we saw earlier). Because the sensitivity of the West to these trade issues is very high, not only might the aid and reform combination be superior for the South, it may also be more acceptable to the West.

In short, reforms without aid are at best difficult and in many cases would be politically impossible to undertake. Increases in aid to the levels of the NIEO targets not only hold out the promise of economic benefits (at least when combined with reforms) but appear nearly essential if the political costs of the needed reforms are to be made tolerable.

THE TOTAL POLICY PACKAGE

The I/I theory of Chapter 2 called for less arms spending and more international aid. We have seen here that increased aid alone, even a doubling of global transfer levels, does not accomplish what the proponents of that theory desire. Thus, for the purposes of continuing evaluation of that theory, we will add a third element to the overall I/I policy package—namely, the combined fiscal and exchange rate reforms by aid recipients that have been elaborated in this chapter.

The next two chapters will return to the political consequences, both domestic and international, of this extended I/I package. Before that, however, we need to consider the combined impact of the package on the global economic system. Two primary conclusions emerge from this section. First, the package is in fact of global economic benefit,

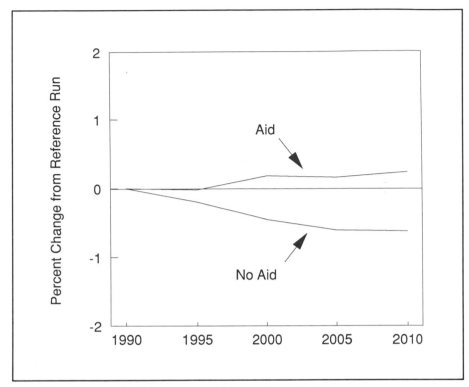

FIGURE 5–7 *West* GDP Gains from Reforms with and without Aid

although the magnitude of benefits may be considerably less than those expected by the advocates of the policy measures. Second, the distribution of those benefits across regions is somewhat surprising.

Both of these conclusions can be drawn from Figure 5-8, which indicates the percent change in GDP, income, and social expenditures for the four world regions between the reference run and the policy package scenario. All four groups of nations benefit from the package on all measures, although the benefit to the *West* is not large. We saw in Chapter 3 that the GDP gain to the *East* from the arms reduction was 7.7 percent, and that is preserved in the total package. The *West* gained 0.6 percent in GDP by 2010 from arms reduction, but that already-small gain is mostly lost in the extended I/I scenario, largely because of the increased trade competition from the *South*. The *South* itself adds nearly 4 percent to its combined reference run GDP figure, and, somewhat surprisingly, the *Opec* states, which for the most part receive very little aid, actually increase their collective GDP by more than 13 percent. Some do benefit from aid (for instance, Nigeria and Indonesia) and from the reforms (which were introduced there as well as in the *South*). But most important, they benefit from the increased energy exports elicited by greater global demand.

Income gains from the policy package are, on the whole, larger than GDP gains. *West* income is up more than 2 percent and *East* income rises a bit more than 11 percent, in comparison with the reference run. The exception to the rule is *Opec*, where income gains are roughly identical to those of GDP.

The gains in overall social benefits, including welfare, health, and education, differ once again across regions. Figure 5-8 makes clear that in this instance, the Northern regions (*East* and *West*) gain more than the combined South (*Opec* and *South*). Arms reduction frees governmental resources for other spending. In contrast, the fiscal reforms of aid recipients starve other categories of government expenditure to increase investment.

Arms reduction is not a panacea for growth in the North, nor will aid, even with reforms, overcome all the economic problems of the South. We saw earlier that these policies in combination add no more than 13 percent to the GDP of any region; they collectively raise the

FIGURE 5–8 Regional Economic Gains from the Policy Package in 2010

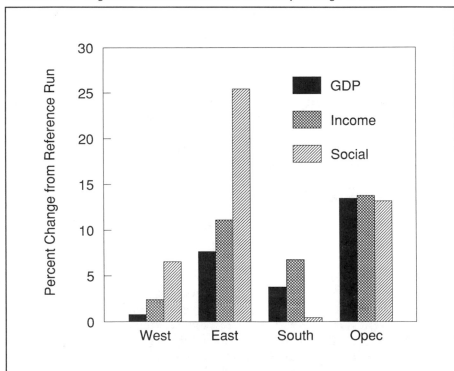

global GDP by only 3.6 percent. To put such numbers into proper context, the GDP of the *South* grows by 185 percent between 1990 and 2010, even without aid. And the global economy grows 110 percent over the same twenty years. It is not possible for the I/I policy proposals to resolve completely the growth problems of the South, much less of the larger world economic system.

Will the combined I/I package substantially close the North-South gap? Not with such a relatively small impact on GDP. Figure 5-9 shows the gap in 2010 in each of our scenarios. Arms reduction actually causes the gap to become slightly wider than it is in the reference run, whereas the aid and reform scenarios produce slight narrowings of the gap. Yet what this figure makes clearest is that increase or reduction in the North-South gap as a result of the adoption of any or all these policies would be minor.

Does the relatively small contribution of the combined package to GDP growth or to closing the North-South gap mean that the policies are unimportant? No, for two reasons. First, the impact on standards of living in the South could (with policy changes by recipient countries)

FIGURE 5–9 North-South Gap in 2010 for All Scenarios

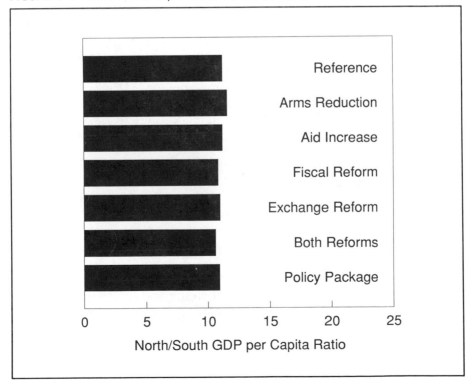

be very substantial. In just twenty years after the increases in aid, average disposable incomes in the *South* could be $45 per capita higher than in the reference run. Although only $20 of this would appear in private and social consumption, that $20 would be available to each of several billion people. Moreover, the remaining $25 would constitute long-term growth-enhancing savings and investment.

Second, for heavily targeted countries like Pakistan, the impact could be far greater. Figure 5-10 makes that clear. There the income gains by 2010 are $92 per capita, or 32 percent more than the $292 income expected in the reference run. Private and social consumption gains are nearly $67 per capita. Were aid targeted at the neediest, this increased income and consumption potential could mean the difference between life and death for many and between health and disability for a great many more. We might well feel that such a gain would be worthwhile even in the absence of improved production performance, but overall GDP rises 30 percent relative to the reference case.

Although the economic benefits of arms reduction in the North are considerably less important in relative terms for those already-prosperous countries, they should also not be underestimated. While the percent income gains in the *West* are very small (only 2.4 percent), the combined package of policy changes raises average disposable income in the United States by $222 in 2010—more than twice the absolute gain of Pakistan (see Figure 5-10 again). In addition, we saw previously that in both *East* and *West*, social expenditures would rise proportionately more than GDP or income because of the natural redirection of governmental military spending to other governmental purposes. Since social expenditures are of great importance to the neediest, such gains are especially desirable. In the United States, those gains would be $206 per capita and could potentially be concentrated on a small segment of the population.

In conclusion, East, West, South, and OPEC can benefit economically through adoption of I/I policies, but the impacts are limited and unevenly distributed. And self-help, especially in the South, works best in combination with outside help. That is, reforms are greatly facilitated and made more palatable by additional aid.

Economic consequences are only part of our concern here. We saw in Chapter 3 that the reductions in arms spending also have significant, albeit complex, international political consequences. We return our attention in the next two chapters to domestic and international political consequences for the South of the total package of proposed policies.

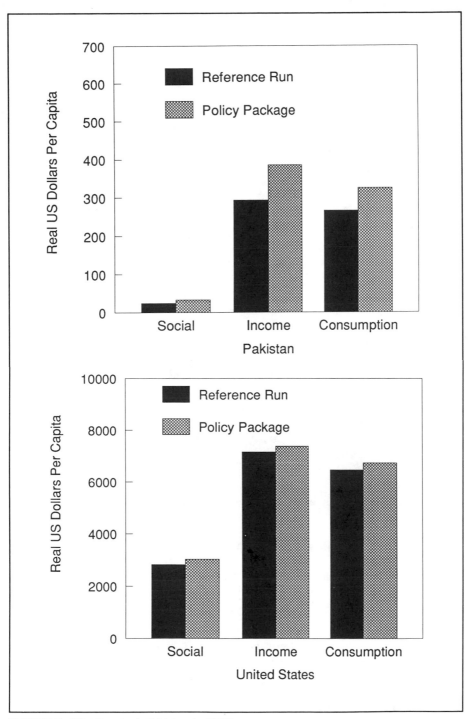

FIGURE 5–10 Standard of Living in 2010

Domestic Tranquility?

CHAPTER 6

Chapter 5 showed that foreign aid can, in combination with fiscal policy and exchange rate reforms, facilitate economic growth. Does the total package of Idealist/Internationalist policy changes and the resultant economic growth contribute, in turn, to political stability? This chapter seeks to answer that question, thereby focusing on the fifth of the relationships originally outlined in the theory of Figure 2-1. In addressing the issue, we look here primarily at the seven primary aid recipients of the GLOBUS *South.* The potential impact on the nonaid-receiving South is, however, also of interest. China constitutes an especially interesting case because it contains a full 20 percent of the world's population; we thus turn briefly to it after considering the aid-receiving South.

THE PROBLEMS OF MEASUREMENT AND ANALYSIS

Analyses of economic growth almost invariably rely on Gross Domestic Product or Gross National Product as their principal measure. That simplified our earlier task of assessing growth, but even economic growth is a far more complex phenomenon than can be captured by a single measure. Therefore, we also considered the implications of foreign aid for citizen welfare and found that disposable income, personal consumption, and social expenditures of government often react to policy changes quite differently from GDP.

As we move to a consideration of domestic political stability, the issue becomes much more complicated. There exists no really standard measure of political stability. One root of the confusion about measures, and a reason for their proliferation, lies in the fact that the consideration of domestic stability forces us to change our focus from society as a whole to interactions of groups within it. Societies, whether they formally recognize it in their political structures or not, are pluralistic.

Seldom, if ever, does any development uniformly favor all elements in society. Even when economic growth occurs, it is highly probable that some groups will be adversely affected. And even if all within a country actually benefit from growth, it would be impossible for them to benefit equally. Since satisfaction with the political and social order derives in large part from one's relative place within it, not merely from objective conditions, even a relative decline will elicit dissatisfaction.[1] Relative deterioration in position will have uncertain implications for political stability, depending on whether the disadvantaged groups have or can obtain power.

The literature review of Chapter 2 surveyed some theoretical arguments and studies that contradict the Idealist/Internationalist theory and that argue that economic growth tends to destabilize societies. Many of the reasons for such arguments lie in this inevitable inequity in the impact of growth. It is possible that in the longer run the absolute condition of nearly everyone will improve with continued growth and that the improvements will increase the stake each has in maintaining the social and political system. Moreover, wealthier societies should be more capable of addressing residual distributional problems. Thus, long-term growth may on the average be stabilizing. Nonetheless, the creation of losers, both absolute and relative, as well as winners, often cannot help but be destabilizing in the short run. In addition, growth has a large number of noneconomic implications, many of which are destabilizing. These include the challenges to traditional religious and social value systems inherent in the changed life-styles of people with higher incomes.[2]

There is still another issue in our discussion of stability measures and theory. Not only does growth differentially benefit or harm societal subgroups or classes, it also has complicated impacts even upon individuals. Increases in income almost universally please those who receive them, but rigorous work schedules, more intense supervisory control,

[1] Hirsch (1977) emphasized the distinction between absolute and relative position in his analysis of the social limits to growth.

[2] Although we have consistently referred here to growth, and have restricted our attention to economic issues, the real issue at the root of political stability is development, which involves broad economic, political, and social transformations of society. See K. J. Holsti (1975), especially pages 833–834.

and the necessity of moving from one's place of birth may accompany the higher income. Whether the net result for the individual is one of satisfaction or dissatisfaction may not be predictable.

THE MIXED BLESSINGS OF GROWTH
FOR AID RECIPIENTS

Two important implications flow from the foregoing discussion of the difficulties of political stability measurement and analysis. First, in this area, relative to the others covered by the analysis here, it will be more difficult to reach conclusions with confidence. Second, we would be wise to consider a plurality of indicators and measures rather than rely solely on one or two. In the subsequent discussion, we consider in turn four categories of indicators that should help us understand the implications of policies for political stability: aggregate economic conditions, relative economic changes, shorter-term political summary measures, and longer-term political trends.

Some Aggregate Economic Costs

Figure 5-8 summarized the aggregate economic benefits that can accrue to the South through the combination of approximately doubled foreign aid and domestic reforms. GDP, disposable income, and personal consumption all gained nearly 5 percent over the reference case.

There are costs associated with those gains, however, that were not given much attention at that time. At least three are of importance: higher inflation, higher interest rates, and the short-term sacrifice of current consumption for the promise, inherent in growth, of greater future consumption. We discussed earlier how the influx of foreign aid in most countries would be inflationary (with or without reforms). Although theoretically action could be taken to prevent the aid from increasing the money supply (it could be "sterilized"), that outcome is in practice difficult to realize and monetary growth is near certain. This accelerated monetary growth would also stoke inflation. So, too, would the exchange rate reform of our package, which consciously seeks to dampen imports and maintain exports. Rather than allowing the additional private and governmental demand created by the aid to move abroad, the exchange reforms channel it into the domestic economy.

The response of the monetary authority to the inflation itself, as well as to the increased demand for investment capital, is very likely under these circumstances to cause a rise in interest rates. Monetary authorities would feel compelled to react as inflation began to build. Higher interest rates, while helping create longer-term wealth, can have two destabilizing consequences: greater concentration of that wealth and the reduction of consumption. Although we cannot with this model measure the concentration of wealth, Figure 6-1 does trace how the policy package gives rise to the three other generally destabilizing aggregate economic developments: increased annual inflation, higher interest rates, and an interim reduction in personal consumption as a share of GDP.

These negative implications of growth and the policy package that underlies it must be set against the positive contributions to GDP, income, and absolute consumption levels. There is no easy way to weight their combined impact on political and social stability.

The decline in consumption as a portion of GDP compared with the reference run does not contradict the finding of Chapter 5 that absolute levels of consumption would rise above those of the reference run. Although the consumption slice is smaller relative to the total, the GDP pie is larger. Again we must stress that political and social reactions are often keyed to relative, not absolute, position. Consumers are as likely to note that they are getting a smaller share of the pie as to see

FIGURE 6–1   Aggregate Economic Costs for Aid Recipients

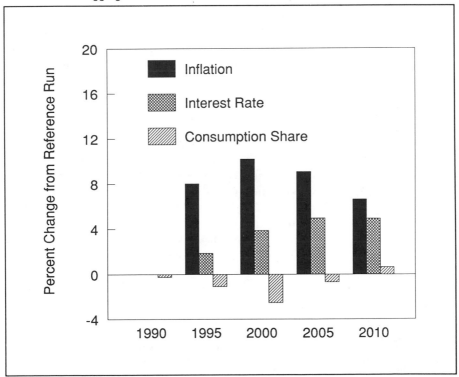

that the pie has grown and made their piece bigger. We need to turn more directly to relative performance.

Relative Economic Performance

With economic growth, the structure of an economy changes. Specifically, a country in the early stages of economic growth normally experiences a significant increase in the size of manufacturing, a relative (if not absolute) decline in agriculture, and a slight increase in the size of the already-large service sector, as well as a change in its composition. Subsequently, as in the currently more developed countries of the West, a relative decline in manufacturing accompanies the absolute growth in and further transformation of services.

In the West, the relative decline of agriculture has been a more or less gradual process over the last two centuries, although the decline accelerated in the post–World War II era. It has posed significant social problems as the income of farmers has fallen behind that of urban workers and as many farmers have been forced to leave the land and seek other employment. Subsidies to agriculture, which have exceeded $30 billion annually in both the United States and the European Community, testify to the difficulty of the adjustment.

Because nutrition remains a serious problem in much of the Third World, it may surprise some that a similar relative decline in agriculture is occurring there. Economic growth brings improvement in average nutrition by providing the necessary increases in disposable income. At the same time that large portions of additional income are spent on food and thereby help Third World farmers, the share of additional income spent on food declines.[3] Growth thus brings relative, not absolute, decline in agriculture. Accelerated economic growth would therefore, on the whole, also accelerate the relative decline in the agricultural sector. Figure 6-2 indicates the rapidity of the decline that seems likely in any case and how increased aid could marginally accelerate it. Because the continuing relative decline of the agricultural sector is so much greater than the change brought about by the policy package, we should not make too much of this issue. In fact, by 2010 the agricultural share returns to that of the reference case because of the increase in personal consumption within GDP (after the relative sacrifice of consumption during the early years of the reforms). Nonetheless, any acceleration of decline in a weakening sector could promote additional discontent in what will be an already-dissatisfied social group.

[3] Consumption at the margin is quite different from average consumption. For example, Third World consumers devote a substantial proportion of their incomes to the purchase of food, but a considerably smaller fraction of additional income they receive is spent in that way.

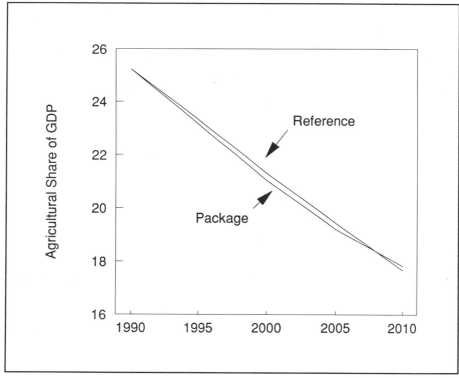

FIGURE 6–2   The Agricultural Sector as a Share of GDP in Aid Recipients

The Idealist/Internationalist package of changes would, all else being equal, thus favor cities and urban dwellers working in manufacturing and services, relative to rural residents and the agricultural sector. Naturally, government policy could compensate for this. For instance, social expenditures could help ease the transition. Yet government budgets are limited, and in the addition of fiscal reform to the package introduced here, we have earmarked as much of the aid itself as possible to investment, not to social programs.

In fact, the emphasis on investment and growth is difficult to obtain without some relative sacrifice of other governmental expenditures. Figure 6-3 shows the percent change from the reference case of the military, health, and education GDP shares in the instance of the complete policy package. Although initially all hold up well or even gain compared with the reference case (the aid is, of course, channeled through the government), over time the portion of the total GDP directed into each governmental spending category declines relative to the reference run. Again we must emphasize that the declines are relative—in absolute terms, educational and health expenditures exceed those of the reference run.

The largest relative expenditure share decline in Figure 6-3 occurs in military spending. Civilian governments in many less developed countries have purchased uneasy coexistence with military establishments in part through high levels of military spending. Obviously, this attempt to placate military establishments has not always worked; high spending also gives the military the wherewithal to challenge civil authority. But, according to conventional wisdom, reducing the military's share of societal resources in developing nations entails fairly substantial risks for civilian authorities. Hence, reduced relative spending on the military is probably destabilizing.

Short-Term Political Considerations

In the 1980 United States presidential election campaign, candidate Ronald Reagan popularized a measure of aggregate economic performance called the misery index. He suggested that voters sum the rates

FIGURE 6–3 Government Expenditure Shares of GDP in Aid Recipients

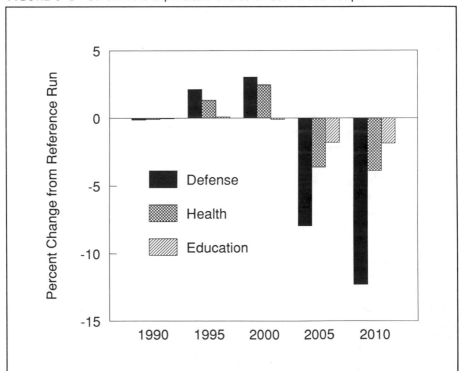

of inflation and unemployment to obtain a total measure of their pain. He went on, of course, to point out how they should translate their dissatisfaction into votes against the incumbent President Carter. Social scientists may cringe at the failure to differentially weight inflation and unemployment, since most United States citizens would almost certainly accept a 1 percent increase in inflation if it brought about a percentage-point reduction in unemployment. Yet individuals and countries differ in their feelings toward this trade-off. For example, Germans in the 1980s still recall the hyperinflation of the 1920s and continue, therefore, to view inflation as the greater of the two evils.

We will nevertheless employ the Reagan misery index as a useful indicator of immediate satisfaction with the government. As a challenger, Reagan did not argue that economic growth could in any way offset the misery. Yet governments around the world are obviously convinced that their citizens will accept some pain if it facilitates economic growth. Many Latin American populations tolerate incredible inflation rates in an effort to improve marginally the pace of economic growth. Thus, we here introduce a second measure of short-term satisfaction, which adds the economic growth rate to the inflation and unemployment rates. This "approval index" almost certainly underrepresents the importance of economic growth, but again we have no rigorous basis for selecting other than equal weightings. The fact that we will focus on changes in the values of the two indices, and on relative levels across runs of the model, rather than considering absolute levels, compensates somewhat for the failure to weight the components of the indices.

Figure 6-4 compares the misery and approval levels in the seven aid-recipient countries of GLOBUS across the reference and policy package runs. Specifically, the figure indicates the difference between the index levels in the two runs (unlike the ratios or percent changes shown in earlier figures).[4] Misery is up and approval down when the package is introduced. The pattern holds no great surprises. The misery increase can be traced to inflation increases and not to rises in unemployment, which with a heated economy actually declines marginally. Approval initially falls less than misery rises because higher economic growth partially offsets the rise in inflation. There is the real possibility that with a higher weighting of economic growth, the approval index could turn positive. Yet the overall conclusion of this analysis must be that the I/I package could be politically destabilizing in the short run.

---

[4] Generally, we have shown variations from the reference run in terms of percent changes from it. Because the misery and satisfaction indices can take on negative signs and can change signs over time, percent changes from the reference run are not meaningful. Thus, we fall back on differences. Differences are much more difficult to interpret (they lack a clear base), and we should look primarily at signs and changes in magnitudes over time.

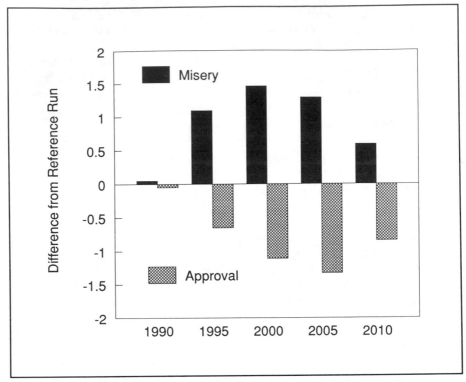

FIGURE 6–4 Short-term Satisfaction in Aid Recipients with Policy Package

Longer-Term Political Considerations

Theories of political and social change and stability often emphasize the interaction between two phenomena.[5] One is the degree to which the basic needs of citizens are satisfied, since whether or not government is capable of meeting those needs, it will be held responsible for them. A second is the level of social mobilization within a population. Social mobilization involves the spread of participatory attitudes and behavior. Support for (or opposition to) the specific authorities in power, for the broader nature of the political regime (the structures and processes of politics), or even for the character and integrity of the polity (the nation-state itself) depends on the level of need satisfaction and the level of social mobilization. The GLOBUS domestic politics submodel calculates these two fundamental indicators based on an estimation of their relationships with assorted economic variables in the model.

[5] This linkage and the relationship between it and the domestic political model of GLOBUS are described in Eberwein (1987). His discussion defines and explains the various political stability indicators presented in this section.

Figure 6-5 traces the development of basic needs satisfaction and social mobilization in the seven aid recipients when we apply the entire package of changes, in comparison with the reference run. After some immediate disruption when the elements of the policy package are introduced in 1990, both indicators increase substantially above the reference run levels and stay there. (In this difference comparison of indices, units are not meaningful.) The impact of the I/I package on both of these indicators is positive for the society.

Satisfaction with the provision of basic needs and the level of social mobilization interact to determine the nature and the extent of disruption to the political system. We want to distinguish between violence and protest as manifestations of longer-term dissatisfaction. Violence is a concept frequently used in studies of stability and is measured often by the incidence of assassinations, armed attacks, and the like. Protest behavior, such as antigovernment demonstrations and political strikes, can occur in a political system relatively free of violence. For that reason, we treat these as separate indicators of political instability. As we did with international hostility and cooperation in Chapter 3, we can state some general rules (with many exceptions) concerning the occurrence of protest and violence in GLOBUS:[6]

With increases in social mobilization, both protest and violence *increase*.

With increases in the satisfaction of basic needs, both protest and violence *decrease*.

Given equal increases in social mobilization and basic needs fulfillment, violence will *decrease* and protest will *increase*.

The last rule stems from the fact that the empirically estimated parameters specify that basic needs fulfillment (or lack thereof) has a stronger influence upon violence than does social mobilization and that social mobilization has a stronger impact upon protest behavior than does basic needs fulfillment (see Eberwein 1987).

One common pattern in development is thus the following: Both basic needs provision and social mobilization increase, roughly in proportion to each other, causing violence to decline and protest to rise. This is essentially the pattern suggested by Figure 6-5 in conjunction with Figure 6-6. For the seven aid recipients, the total package of policies facilitates development over the long term that reduces violence but increases protest.[7]

---

[6] These "general rules" are based on the parameters estimated for the GLOBUS domestic political model.

[7] For this figure, we have reverted to the normal pattern of presenting percent differences from the reference run.

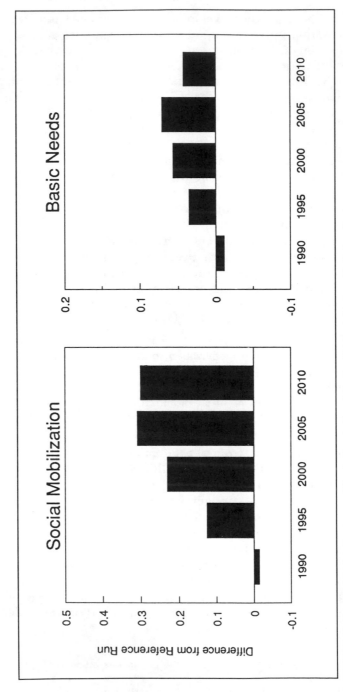

FIGURE 6–5 Social Mobilization and Basic Needs Provision in Aid Recipients with Policy Package

Figure 6-6 indicates, too, the additional sanctions that the government of aid-recipient countries impose on their populations because of the policy package. Normally, the ability of government to utilize sanctions and its willingness to do so increase with both basic needs provision and social mobilization. Sanctions generally increase also with both violence and protest. Thus, it is not surprising that the acceleration of development accomplished with the package of policy measures results in a higher level of sanctions than does the reference case.

One hopeful aspect of Figure 6-6 is the greater proportional decline of violence, relative to the rises of protest and sanctions. No society is ever free of instability, but some manifestations of dissatisfaction are much more desirable than others.

A GLANCE AT CHINA

The Chinese population slightly exceeds one billion in a total world population of just over five billion. Thus, although China is not an aid recipient, it contains a very substantial portion of the world's people

FIGURE 6–6 Protest, Violence, and Sanctions in Aid Recipients with Policy Package

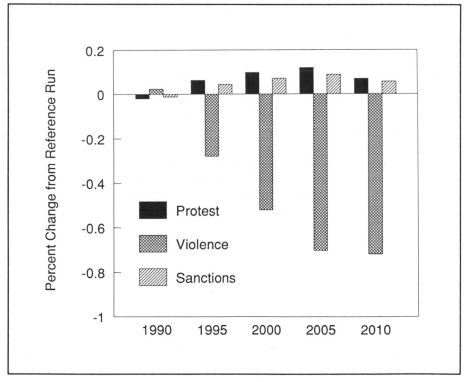

and an even greater portion of the South's. How might the total package of policies analyzed here affect economic performance and political stability in China?

To begin with, is there reason to believe that China, which receives no aid and in which we made no external changes in arms spending, will respond to the complete packet of changes? There is indeed. The world faced by China with the arms reduction of the North, the doubling of foreign aid by the West, and the introduction by all Southern countries of fiscal and exchange rate reforms, is substantially different from the world of the reference case. Consider, for instance, the competition China faces in the world economy. It faces a North that has a somewhat stronger economy after the reduction in arms spending and a South that is aggressively maintaining real exchange rates and seeking to export as one part of an overall growth package.

Figure 6-7 shows how much lower world prices are in the six economic sectors of GLOBUS in 2010 with the package of changes than they are in the reference run. The minimum difference is 5 percent; many are nearly 10 percent lower.[8] The most significant change occurs in the armaments sector, where prices are 26 percent lower, because of the very high level of overcapacity in the North after reductions in arms spending. The world of the reform package suggests one characteristic of a world in which many countries undertake export-promotion policies simultaneously; namely, the common pursuit of expanded exports by many countries in a limited global market would tend to depress world prices.

The scenario being considered here introduces the same pattern of reforms into China as into the aid recipients. That was done in part because of the more intense global competition described earlier. The Chinese economic performance thus bears considerable similarities to those of the aid-recipient economies when undertaking reforms without aid (as discussed in Chapter 5). Figure 6-8 verifies that GDP growth does improve relative to the reference run. Specifically, it reaches a level more than 6 percent higher than in the reference run. Much of that is accomplished by a higher level of investment, as also shown in the figure.

But consumers pay a considerable price for this outcome. Personal consumption levels are nearly 3 percent below the reference run by 2010. Although we saw a decline in consumption as a *portion of GDP* for aid recipients, the *absolute level* of consumption in those countries

---

[8] How, some will ask, can world prices be lower with the package of policy changes when Figure 6-1 showed inflation to be higher? The domestic inflation shown in Figure 6-1 for aid recipients occurs in association with lower exchange rates and higher exports. The countries trading with the export-promoting South face an abundance of goods on the world market and lower prices in their own currencies.

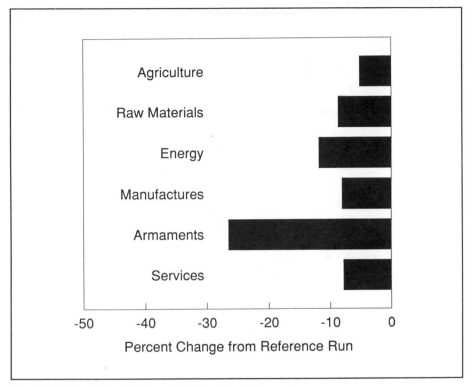

FIGURE 6–7 Price Declines in 2010 with Policy Package

grew substantially. Thus, the absolute losses in China are a sharp contrast. In the aid-recipient countries, aid inflows provide the additional investment needed for a higher growth rate; in China or other aid nonrecipients, consumption must be sacrificed for higher growth.

Under these circumstances, it would not be surprising if the implications for political stability of the overall package were also different in China from what they are in the aid-recipient South. Figure 6-9 shows this conclusion to be true. Relative to the reference run, the total package produces less protest and lower levels of sanctions, but greater violence. Because the underlying driving forces of social mobilization and basic needs provision are so closely tied to consumption, the lower consumption levels result in a reversal of these longer-term developments in political stability relative to what we saw in Figure 6-6 for the aid recipients.

We should be wary of making strong statements about the probable impact of the total policy package on any single country. The discussion at the beginning of this chapter stressed how multifaceted political stability issues are and how contradictory the theory and analysis in the

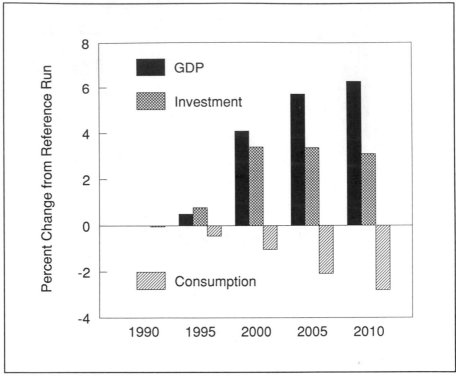

FIGURE 6–8   Aggregate Economic Performance in China with Policy Package

area have been. Even if a particular set of political leaders and a specific country like China escaped that pattern, the logic would likely hold for a number of nonaid-recipient Third World nations.

CONCLUSION

The analysis of this chapter suggests several conclusions concerning the implications of aid and reform for economic advance and political stability. But first we must repeat the point made in the introduction: Given the complex factors and the pluralistic environments that determine stability or instability, we must be very careful about any conclusions drawn. There are so many unknowns concerning the manner in which individuals will perceive their interests, in which alternative groups or classes will be affected by change, and in which the interaction among elements of society might develop that conclusions must be proffered with skepticism.

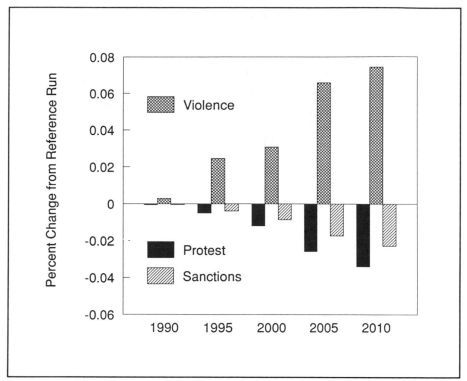

FIGURE 6–9 Protest, Violence, and Sanctions in China with Policy Package

First, the aggregate economic implications of the total policy package for aid recipients are mixed. Although GDP, disposable income, social expenditures, and consumption are up, higher inflation, higher interest rates, and a decline in consumption as a share of GDP somewhat offset those benefits.

Second, since growth inevitably causes some groups or sectors of society to lose their relative, if not absolute, positions, accelerated growth is likely to increase the rate of relative loss. We saw that to be marginally true in the agricultural sector of aid recipients. In addition, the policy package itself led to a relative decline in military spending and, by implication, the military establishment's support for the government.

Third, both aid recipients and nonaid recipients suffered from an increase in misery and a decrease in approval as a result of the proposed policy changes. That implies an immediate decline in support for political authorities.

Fourth, in aid-recipient countries, the combined economic impact is such that, in the longer run, basic needs satisfaction and social mobilization increase. That, in turn, would be likely to lower levels of political violence but to increase both protest and sanctions. In contrast, the package of changes affected China's long-term political stability in almost exactly the opposite way. In that, we see evidence of an important difference in the implications of the proposals for aid-recipient and nonaid-recipient LDCs. In combination with the differential economic impact discussed in more detail in Chapter 5, this finding reinforces the difficulties of undertaking growth-enhancing reforms in the absence of foreign aid increases.

Fifth, and derivative from the foregoing conclusions, it appears that decisions concerning increased aid should not be based on expectations concerning its positive impact on political stability. It is almost certain that, at least in the short run, aid has negative implications for stability that are as large as or larger than its positive ones.

A United World?

CHAPTER 7

We opened this volume by arguing that the East-West and the North-South cleavages demarcate the fundamental and enduring conflicts of the present and of the foreseeable future. We suggested that the reports of the Palme and Brandt commissions together contain a blueprint for how the world could be made more peaceful and prosperous, and throughout this volume, we have implemented and tested key elements of that design step-by-step to see if the predicted results were obtained. In this chapter, we consider what may be the most important question to be addressed in this book: Does this design for the future hold the key to a more peaceful world, or, more specifically, does the package of policy changes we have introduced reduce global tension?

GLOBAL TENSION

Figures 7-1 and 7-2 show the total flows of hostility and cooperation, respectively, among the twenty-five nations at five-year intervals over the period 1990–2010 for the reference and policy package runs. When looking at these figures, the reader should note that the range of the vertical axis in each has been made quite narrow so that the differences between the two runs are more obvious. This necessity reminds us that, as radical as our policy changes might be, they have not fundamentally changed global levels of conflict and cooperation.

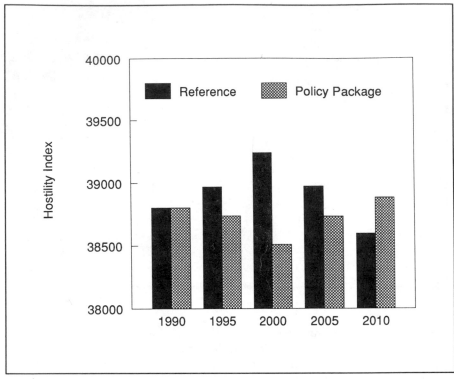

FIGURE 7–1 World Hostility with and without Policy Package

Be that as it may, it is still useful to see what impact our reform measures have had, and we will begin with world hostility. As we see in Figure 7-1, the package of policies does produce a lowering of world hostility in the decade or so following the end of the implementation period, but by the year 2010 world hostility is higher with the reforms in place. This suggests that the medium-term effect of reduced arms, increased aid, and reforms in the South is to improve global relations but that in the long-term the opposite may be so.

An examination of Figure 7-2 suggests that we should revise that conclusion, however. There we see that world cooperation is lower during the 1990–2000 period under the policy package but higher in the years following that. In other words, in the medium term, both world hostility and world cooperation are lower as a consequence of the policy changes, but both are higher by the end of the period under study. If we compare the two pairs of series by computing the ratio of world hostility to world cooperation to derive "diplomatic climate" indicators for each simulation run, we find that the ratio is very slightly lower in the policy package run throughout the twenty-year period following the onset of reforms. Based on that, one might conclude that a slight reduction in global tension might be a consequence of arms reduction, aid increases, and growth-promoting policies in the South. Whether that is true for all regions is the question we will next address.

REGIONAL TENSION

The global level results reported in the preceding section suggest that we need to distinguish between the medium- and the long-term effects of the policy package. Consequently, when we examine the impact of the policy package upon regional diplomatic behavior, we will implement that distinction by focusing on the years 2000 and 2010 separately.

Table 7-1 shows the percent changes in hostility and cooperation sent and received by the four regions in the medium term (the year 2000) and in the long term (the year 2010) that are produced by reduced

FIGURE 7–2 World Cooperation with and without Policy Package

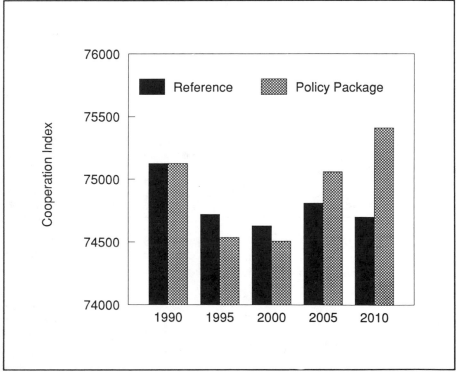

arms, increased aid, and reforms in the South. We see that in three of the regions, the amount of hostility sent and received in the medium term is lower with the policy reforms in place, while the opposite is true for the *Opec* region. Cooperation is also generally lower, but the reductions are proportionately smaller than those found for hostility. The most notable medium-term changes are the reduction in hostility received by the *East* and the reduction in hostility sent by the *South*.

Table 7-1 also contains the comparable percent changes from the year 2010, and the pattern of change is quite different from that found in the medium term. Hostility sent and hostility received are up for all regions except the *South*, which continues to send less hostility with the policy package in force. Relatively speaking, the increase in hostility sent by the *East* is the most pronounced of those to be found here, suggesting that in the long term, the reformed international order is not wholly satisfactory to the nations of the *East*. That may be true for the *Opec* nations as well.

The long-term changes in regional cooperation are more mixed. Cooperation sent and received increases in the *West* and the *East* with the policy package in place, while the opposite is true for the *Opec* region. Mixed changes are evident in the *South;* cooperation received is slightly higher, but cooperation sent is a little lower.

In sum, the strongest effects of the policy package apparent at the regional level are (1) a marked medium-term decrease in hostility generated by the *South* and (2) a significant increase in hostility sent by the *East* in the long term. The regional direction of these flows should begin to tell us something about what is causing these changes, and that is the topic to which we now turn.

TABLE 7–1　Changes in Regional Diplomatic Behavior Resulting from Policy Package (Percent Difference from Reference Run)

	Medium Term		Long Term	
DIRECTION	HOSTILITY	COOPERATION	HOSTILITY	COOPERATION
From *West*	−1.9	−0.1	+0.4	+2.0
To *West*	−1.7	+0.5	+0.9	+2.8
From *East*	−3.0	+1.7	+7.1	+1.8
To *East*	−6.6	−0.5	+2.8	+1.8
From *South*	−5.0	−1.7	−1.0	+0.4
To *South*	−2.4	−0.7	+0.1	+0.4
From *Opec*	+0.7	−1.0	+3.7	−0.8
To *Opec*	+2.2	−0.9	+3.2	−1.2

DIPLOMATIC FLOWS
WITHIN AND BETWEEN REGIONS

Table 7-2 shows the medium- and the long-term changes in the flows of hostility and cooperation sent between and within regions. In principle, this should entail the analysis of sixteen flows (four regions times four regions), but our task is somewhat simplified by the fact that in this initialization of the model, the reactivities of the *South* and the *Opec* nations with respect to one another do not change.[1] Consequently, we need not be concerned with changes in *South-South, South-Opec,* and *Opec-Opec* relations.

Viewed as a whole, Table 7-2 shows clearly that the pattern of changes is not uniform but, rather, that the impact of the policy package differs quite significantly across regional pairs. By way of summarizing this table, we offer the following conclusions. With reduced arms, more aid, and growth-promoting reforms in the South:

TABLE 7–2   Changes in Diplomatic Flows within and between Regions Resulting from Policy Package (Percent Difference from Reference Run)

	Medium Term		Long Term	
DIRECTION	HOSTILITY	COOPERATION	HOSTILITY	COOPERATION
West to *West*	−16.1	+ 4.8	−17.3	+11.4
East to *East*	− 2.7	− 0.2	+ 5.2	0.0
West to *East*	+ 5.2	− 1.9	+12.1	+ 4.6
East to *West*	+ 7.2	+ 7.5	+17.7	+15.2
West to *South*	− 0.3	− 7.1	+ 7.1	− 5.2
South to *West*	− 6.3	−10.0	− 0.6	− 8.7
West to *Opec*	+13.3	− 6.6	+21.2	− 8.6
Opec to *West*	+ 1.8	− 9.7	+12.0	− 6.2
East to *South*	−24.2	+ 4.0	− 7.6	+13.0
South to *East*	−41.2	− 1.2	−14.3	+ 8.9
East to *Opec*	+ 8.5	+ 1.1	+ 9.3	− 1.4
Opec to *East*	+ 3.6	+ 1.8	+ 6.5	− 1.6

[1] As explained by Smith (1987), the recorded frequency of interaction between the developing nations is so low that it is almost impossible to estimate how their reactivities toward one another change using statistical methods. No doubt, that is in part due to the limited coverage of the COPDAB data set with respect to these countries, but it also reflects the fact that these nations by and large interact infrequently with one another. If one is willing to make assumptions about the relative importance of the factors that lead to changes in reactivity, it is possible to calculate consistent parameter values for pairs of developing nations. Smith has done this to a limited extent, but we did not follow that strategy here.

West-West relations are much better in both the medium and the long terms.

East-East relations are slightly better in the medium term but slightly worse in the long term.

East-West relations are slightly worse in both the medium and the long terms.

West-South relations are not easily summarized. In the medium term, hostility is down in both directions but cooperation is even more reduced. In the long term, however, the result seems clearer; that is, relations are worse.

West-Opec relations are worse in both the medium and the long terms.

East-South relations are better in both the medium and the long terms.

East-Opec relations are worse in both the medium and the long terms.

In Chapter 3, we analyzed the changes in *East-West* relations, and we will not repeat that analysis here. Since our primary concern in this chapter is with the postulated improvement in North-South relations that should follow from the I/I measures, we will focus upon *West-South* and *East-South* relations.

WEST-SOUTH RELATIONS:
THE CASE OF BRAZIL AND THE UNITED STATES

To see more clearly how the I/I measures alter *West-South* relations, we will here examine in some detail how diplomatic exchanges between Brazil and the United States change when those measures are in effect. In many ways, this dyad is typical of *West-South* relations, but in some ways, it is not. For example, as with most *West-South* pairs, the United States underreacts to hostility it receives from Brazil, whereas Brazil overreacts to hostility it receives from the United States. That is, as postulated by the compensatory theory discussed in Chapter 3, the larger, richer, and stronger nation tends to discount or tolerate hostility from a smaller, poorer, and weaker nation, whereas the smaller, poorer, and weaker nation tends to be very sensitive and reactive to hostility it receives from the larger, richer, and stronger nation (Ashley 1980). On the other hand, Brazil is not a typical developing nation in that it is far larger, more developed, and more powerful than most of the developing nations. But those very characteristics make Brazil a particularly important Third World nation and make its relations with the United States worthy of special attention.

Changes in Hostile and Cooperative Behavior

Figures 7-3 and 7-4 show the amount of hostility and cooperation exchanged between Brazil and the United States from 1990 to 2010 in the reference and policy package runs. It is readily apparent that the

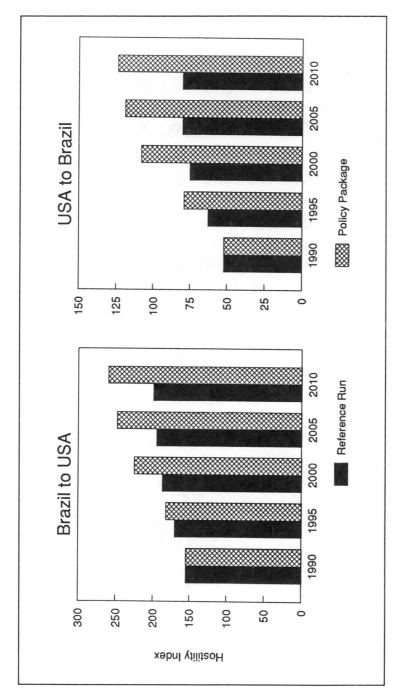

FIGURE 7-3 Hostility Exchanged between Brazil and the United States

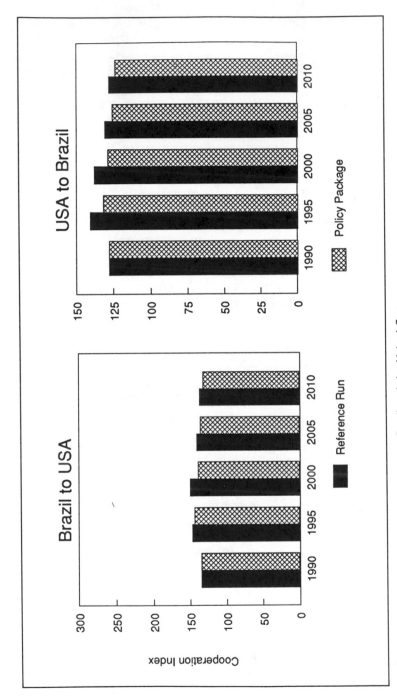

FIGURE 7-4 Cooperation Exchanged between Brazil and the United States

policy package increases hostile flows and decreases cooperative flows in both directions already within the 1990–1995 implementation period. By the end of the simulation period, Brazil is sending about one-third more hostility to the United States and about 4 percent less cooperation. The United States, in turn, is directing over 50 percent more hostility toward Brazil and about 4 percent less cooperation. The result is, of course, significantly worse relations between the two with the imposition of arms reduction, aid increase, and reforms in the South.

Hostile and Cooperative Reactivities

To begin to see how these changes in behavior come about, we must move one step back in the causal chain to see how the basic foreign policies of Brazil and the United States toward one another are changing as a consequence of our policy interventions.

Figure 7-5 displays the United States reactivity to Brazilian hostility and cooperation at five-year intervals with and without all policy changes in effect. The upward and downward shifts in the American hostile reactivities, respectively, are clearly evident in 1995. One way to understand this difference is to think in terms of a one-unit change in hostility or cooperation directed by Brazil to the United States. In the reference run in 1995, the United States would react to a unit of Brazilian hostility with 0.6 units of hostility, whereas in the policy package run, that would rise to 0.7 units. In essence, the United States becomes less tolerant of Brazilian hostility as a consequence of the policies introduced. With respect to cooperation, the opposite is true. In the reference run, a unit of Brazilian cooperation would elicit 0.75 units of cooperation in return from the United States in 1995 but only 0.65 units with the package of policies in effect. In other words, the United States becomes less responsive to Brazilian cooperative acts as a consequence of reduced arms, increased aid, and growth-promoting reforms in the South.

Figure 7-6 shows the comparable reactivities of Brazil toward American hostility and cooperation in the two simulation runs. Here we see that in 1995, the policy package leads to a lower hostile reactivity and a higher cooperative reactivity, precisely the opposite of the effect the measures have on the United States. The changes are not as large (1.15 to 1.12 for hostility and 1.14 to 1.18 for cooperation) as for the United States, but they are in the direction of improved relations. By the year 2000, however, the Brazilian hostile reactivity is higher in the policy package run than in the reference run, and by 2010 Brazil's reaction to United States hostility is stronger with the policies in place than without, while its reactivity to American cooperation is about the same.

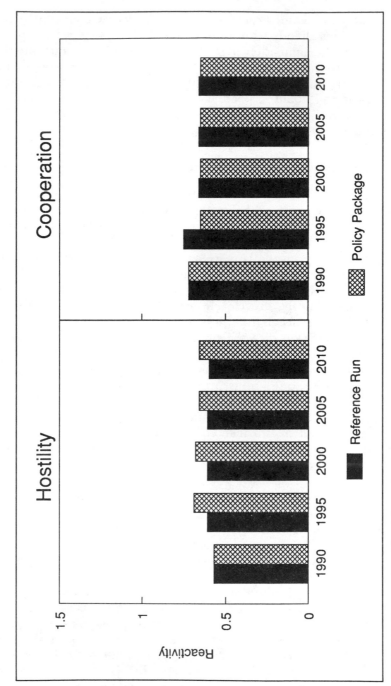

FIGURE 7–5 American Reactivity to Brazilian Actions

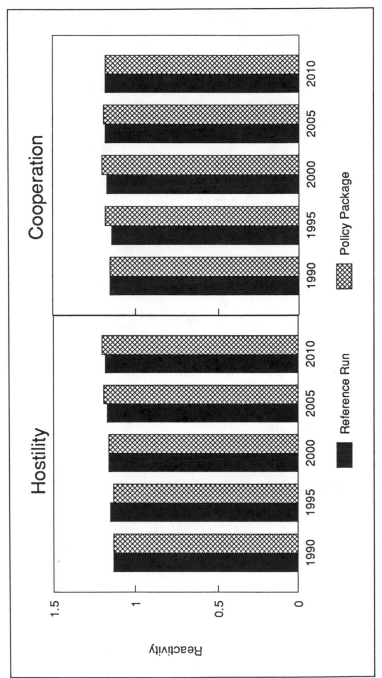

FIGURE 7–6 Brazilian Reactivity to American Actions

Causes of Change in Foreign Policy

Sorting out causes and effects in coupled, dynamic reaction processes such as we are dealing with here is difficult, but the fact that United States policy toward Brazil becomes less tolerant of hostility at least five years before Brazilian policy toward the United States becomes more hostile suggests that at least the initial deterioration in relations between the two is due primarily to changes in American policy.

In Chapter 3, we discussed the factors that can lead to a change in a simulated nation's reactivity to hostility. These were

An alteration in the balance of military power relative to another nation

A shift in the bilateral trade balance with another nation

A significant change in the mix of cooperation and hostility exchanged between the two nations involved

A change in the international (that is, *East-West*) climate

An examination of the empirically estimated parameter values that govern how United States reactivity to Brazilian hostility changes in response to these four factors shows that only the first two are of great importance in this dyad. Thus, the question we must address is how the package of policies we have introduced affects relative power and bilateral trade such that the United States hardens its foreign policy toward Brazil as a consequence.

Turning first to the relative power factor, it is probably unnecessary to remind the reader that the arms reduction component of the policy package brings substantial cuts in conventional military power in the *East* and the *West*. In some developing countries, however, *increases* in conventional military power are produced by the policy package, presumably because of higher economic growth and lower global prices for armaments. This is true with respect to Brazil. Hence, while the United States is rather dramatically reducing its conventional capabilities, Brazil is slightly increasing its capabilities, and the result is that the balance of power between the two nations changes significantly. In the reference run, the ratio of United States to Brazilian capabilities drops from about 7:1 to about 4:1 over the 1990–2010 period, whereas in the policy package run, the decline is more pronounced and ends up at about 2.5:1 by 2010.

As with most countries, the historical evidence (as reflected in the empirically estimated parameters) suggests that the United States reacts to such a lessening of military dominance by becoming less tolerant of hostility that it receives from weaker nations, and this is precisely what occurs in regard to Brazil. This is in accordance with the compensatory model, where military capabilities and hostile diplomacy tend to be substitutes for one another, but here we see a manifestation of the logical consequence of this model that is not often noted. That is, asymmetrical reductions in power that narrow the gap between nations can lead to a worsening of relations if the dominant nation is particularly sensitive to changes in its power status relative to a weaker nation.

This effect is related in some ways to Organski's so-called rear-end collision theory (Organski 1968). Under that theory, relations between two interacting nations should become worse as the faster-growing, weaker nation approaches the dominant nation in power. This deduction can also be derived from the compensatory model if certain conditions hold. Assume that nation A is losing power relative to nation B. According to the compensatory model, nation A would become more hostile toward B, but B would become less hostile toward A. That could result in no change or in an overall decline in the hostility of the relationship if nation B's reduction in hostility is greater than or equal to A's increases. If, on the other hand, A's increases are greater than B's decreases, which would follow if nation A were more sensitive to its loss of status than B was to its gain in status, then the overall relationship would become more hostile and tensions between the two nations would mount. It may be that even if nation B's decreases in hostility outweigh A's increases initially, nation B will not be willing or able to sustain its more accommodating policy in the face of A's increased hostility, and eventually B's policy toward A tends to become more hostile. If that occurs, then tensions between the two nations will mount and the likelihood of a "rear-end collision" increases. To a limited extent, that is what we see in the United States–Brazilian case, except that the circumstances for a possible collision are not being created by the weaker nation "passing" the stronger but by the stronger nation "backing-up" in the direction of the weaker.

Trade relations can also be a source of friction, and some of the policies included in the package tested do have an impact on trade between the more and the less developed nations. When we examine this aspect of United States–Brazilian relations, we discover that, from the American perspective, trade relations with Brazil are less satisfactory with the package of policies in place than without. In the reference run, the United States maintains a favorable trade balance with Brazil throughout the 1990–2010 period. Brazilian imports from the United States are about 7 percent higher than American imports from Brazil over the twenty-year span in this run. The introduction of the policy package has two effects that alter this. First, the exchange reform in Brazil leads to approximately a 10 percent reduction in its nominal imports from the United States, predominately because of the higher relative prices of imported goods that this entails. This tips the trade balance such that American imports from Brazil exceed Brazilian imports from the United States, and under these conditions, ceteris paribus, the United States becomes more hostile toward Brazil. A secondary effect, which appears some time later and partially offsets the Brazilian reduction, is a reduction in United States imports from Brazil. This stems from the fact that import decisions are affected by political tensions in the longer term, and the deterioration in Brazil-American political relations eventually leads the United States to shift some of its import demands toward friendlier nations. Although this does alleviate the trade imbalance problem, the net result of this retaliatory action is a weakening of economic ties between the United States and Brazil.

Although our analysis has focused up to this point on the United States side of the Brazilian-American relationship, that should not be taken to mean that Brazil's foreign policy toward the United States is unaffected by the reforms. As we showed in Figure 7-6, Brazil is less reactive to United States hostility and more reactive to United States cooperation in the decade following the onset of the policy reforms. Together, these changes amount to an attempt on the part of Brazil to establish friendlier relations with the United States. This initiative stems from the same conditions that the United States views so unfavorably— that is, a shift in relative military power from the United States toward Brazil and an alteration in bilateral trade. Both of these developments are favorable, at least initially, from Brazil's perspective, and presumably Brazil feels less threatened by American military power and less exploited by trade ties with the United States when the policy package is in effect. As a consequence, Brazil's policy toward the United States becomes more amicable.

After five to ten years, however, Brazil abandons part of this initiative. While Brazil continues to reciprocate United States cooperation at a higher level after the year 2000 with the policy package in place than without, their reaction to United States hostility changes such that it reacts more strongly to American hostility during the period with reforms. Two factors contribute to this development. First, the reduction in United States imports of Brazilian goods discussed previously leaves the Brazilians much less satisfied with economic relations with the United States, and, second, the United States fails to respond significantly to Brazil's efforts to improve overall relations with the United States.

All relations between aid givers and aid receivers do not follow the pattern found in the American-Brazil case, but this example shows quite clearly that some relationships between "have" and "have-not" nations may deteriorate with the implementation of the I/I theory. Our results suggest that shifts in the balance of power from the former to the latter and the emergence of more symmetrical trade relations between the two will probably exacerbate some relationships between more and less developed nations, such as between the United States and Brazil, while improving others. That is not to say that the policy prescriptions put forth by the proponents of the I/I "world view" should not be adopted but, rather, to point out that policy changes seldom have unidirectional effects and to suggest that advocates of such changes should be aware of and attempt to anticipate the possible undesirable side effects that they may generate.

EAST-SOUTH RELATIONS: THE CASE OF CHINA AND THE SOVIET UNION

The evidence presented in Table 7-2 showed a rather dramatic improvement in *East-South* relations. In fact, the largest proportionate reduction in hostility brought about by the combination of reduced arms, increased aid, and growth-promoting reforms is to be found in *East-South* relations. That is not something that we really expected, since the changes we found in *West-South* relations were of the opposite nature. An examination of the dyads that make up this set of interregional flows shows quite clearly that most of the improvement in *East-South* relations is due to dramatic changes in Sino-Soviet affairs. Consequently, we will focus our attention on this nation-pair and see how their behavior toward one another changes in response to the experimental policy package we have introduced.

Changes in Hostile and Cooperative Behavior

Figures 7-7 and 7-8 show the amount of hostility and cooperation exchanged between China and the Soviet Union from 1990 to 2010 in the reference and policy package runs. Looking first at Figure 7-7, we see dramatic reductions in hostility sent by each party to the other almost immediately after the introduction of the policy package. Soviet hostility toward China is reduced by roughly one-third, while Chinese hostility toward the Soviet Union declines so much that the level of hostility in 2010 is all but invisible on this graph. Even in the reference run, however, a significant reduction in hostility is evident after the year 2000.

Figure 7-8 shows that the exchange of cooperation also declines, however, with the package of policies in effect. The effect of these policies on cooperation is not as strong as their effect on hostility, so the net result is a significant improvement in overall Sino-Soviet relations. For the Soviets, the policies seem to accelerate a decline in cooperation, since in the year 2010 the amount of cooperative behavior it is directing toward China is about the same in both simulation runs. For the Chinese,

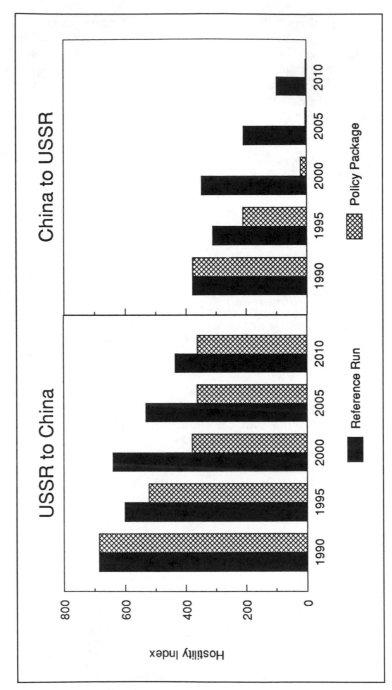

FIGURE 7–7 Hostility Exchanged between China and the Soviet Union

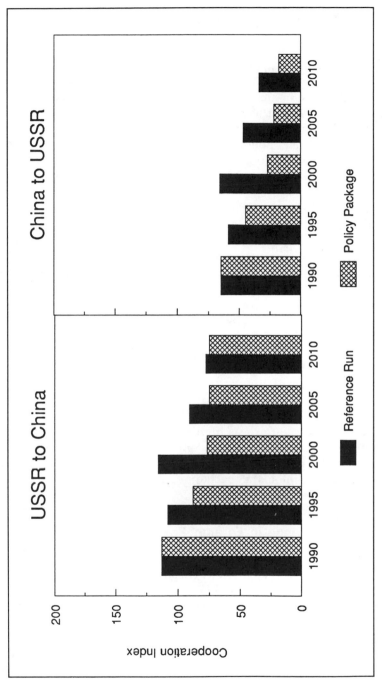

FIGURE 7–8 Cooperation Exchanged between China and the Soviet Union

however, the reduction is more substantial, constituting as it does a 50 percent decrease.

Hostile and Cooperative Reactivities

As we did in our analysis of Brazilian-American relations, we will move one step back in the causal chain to see how the basic foreign policies of China and the Soviet Union change toward one another as a consequence of our policy interventions. To do this, we need to compare the hostile and cooperative reactivities of China and the Soviet Union toward one another in the reference and policy package simulation runs.

Figure 7-9 displays the Soviet reactivity to Chinese hostility and cooperation at five-year intervals with and without all policy changes in effect. The effects of the policy package are quite clear; the Soviets are about one-third less responsive to Chinese behavior, be it hostile or cooperative, with reduced arms, increased aid, and reforms in the South. What we see here is more like movement toward a policy of "disengagement" rather than a concerted effort to improve relations. Cooperative reactivity is very low by the year 2010, but that is true also in the reference run.

Figure 7-10 shows the comparable reactivities of China toward Soviet hostility and cooperation in the two simulation runs. Here we see the same pattern of dramatically reduced reactivities in the policy package run as we did on the Soviet side. China's reactivity to hostility from the Soviet Union in the year 2010 with the policy package in place is only about one-third as high as it is in the reference run, while its cooperative reactivity is between one-third and one-half lower under these conditions. In effect, this dyad is spiraling downward toward a very low level of diplomatic exchange, a development that surprised and, at first, puzzled us.

Causes of Change in Foreign Policy

In principle, changes in Soviet and Chinese reactivity to each other's actions are a function of changes in the four factors listed on page 156. However, an examination of the empirically estimated parameter values for both sides of this dyad reveals that the military balance factor is by far the dominant one. That is, the foreign policy of each nation toward the other seems to be strongly affected by their relative conventional military capability. Because of the importance of this factor, we should examine how the military balance between the two shifts over time, and Figure 7-11 allows us to do that.

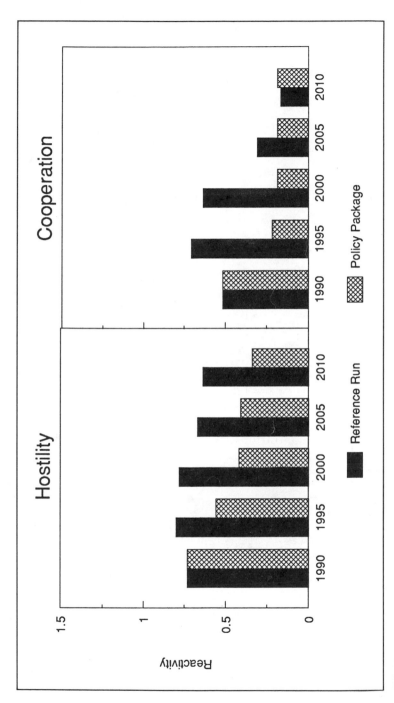

FIGURE 7–9 Soviet Reactivity to Chinese Actions

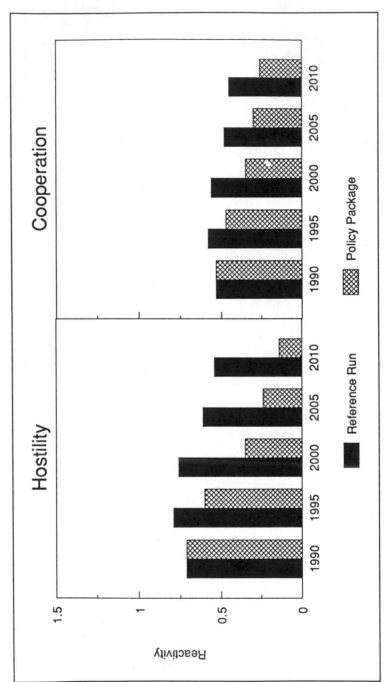

FIGURE 7–10 Chinese Reactivity to Soviet Actions

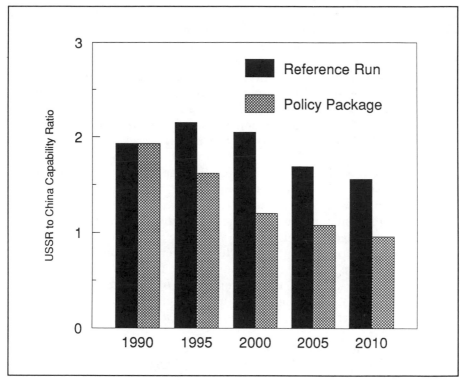

FIGURE 7–11 Sino-Soviet Military Balance with and without Policy Package

In the reference run, Soviet conventional capability peaks about 1995 and begins to decline somewhat thereafter,[2] while Chinese capabilities grow more or less steadily throughout the period. The arms reduction component of the policy package produces about a one-third decrease in Soviet capabilities while not significantly affecting Chinese capabilities. The result is as shown in Figure 7-11; in both simulation runs, the ratio of Soviet to Chinese conventional capability declines significantly, but for obvious reasons this decline is substantially accelerated by arms reduction. How do the two nations respond to this development?

Turning first to the Chinese side of the dyad, we find that they respond in accordance with the compensatory model; that is, as the balance of power moves in a more favorable direction, they reduce their hostile reactivity toward the Soviet Union. For the same reason, they reduce their cooperative reactivity as well. This is the same type of

[2] This is not due to a reduction in Soviet defense expenditures but, rather, to a shift of resources from conventional to strategic-nuclear capabilities.

change we observed occurring in Brazil's policy toward the United States as the gap in conventional capabilities was narrowed by arms reduction.

When viewed from the Soviet side, this loss of dominance should, according to the compensatory model, lead the Soviets to be less tolerant of and more reactive to hostility it receives from the Chinese, as the United States became with respect to Brazil, but that is not what we see happening. On the contrary, as the gap between Soviet and Chinese power shrinks, the Soviets become more tolerant of Chinese hostility. This paradoxical result stems from the fact that, according to Smith's empirical estimates, the Soviets have not conformed to the logic of the compensatory model in their relations with the Chinese. That is, in the past the Soviets have tended to react in a more hostile manner to Chinese hostility when the military balance was more in their favor and in a less hostile manner when it was less in their favor. This is equivalent to a "bully" model of foreign policy behavior, which is, of course, the opposite of the compensatory model. Rather than using diplomatic hostility and military capability as substitutes for one another in their dealings with the Chinese, the Soviets seem to use them in a complementary fashion. As we pointed out in Chapter 3, this type of behavior is the exception rather than the rule but nevertheless is present in many dyads.

The amelioration of the Sino-Soviet split was not one of the predicted consequences of arms reduction, increased aid, and growth-promoting reforms in the South, and we are not sure how far we can interpret the results. The impact of arms reduction on the Sino-Soviet balance is a good deal more extreme than it is on other bilateral balances, since it causes a dramatic change in their power positions relative to one another. It may be that our results exaggerate the degree of change that we would observe in the real world in this instance but that the direction of change is correct. Hence, significant improvements in Sino-Soviet relations (albeit through disengagement) may be an unexpected side benefit of the set of policies we have been investigating.

WEST-WEST RELATIONS

According to the I/I theory, relations between the West and the East and between the North and the South should improve with reduced arms, increased aid, and accelerated growth in the South, but the theory predicts little about what the impact of these measures should be on relations among the advanced market economies. If one were to apply the conventional wisdom concerning the inverse relationship between intragroup and intergroup conflict, one might conclude that poorer West-East relations may lead to better West-West relations. And, as we saw in Table 7-2, our results do suggest that *West-West* relations as a whole would become significantly less hostile and substantially more cooperative with reduced arms, more aid, and faster growth in the South, and in this section we will examine the question of why the model generates that result.

When we examine the forty-two flows of hostility that make up the *West*'s intraregional relations, we find that a large portion of the reduction in hostility brought about by the policy package is located in the United Kingdom–France dyad. A similar analysis of the cooperative flows reveals that much of the change in intraregional behavior is due to substantially more cooperation being exchanged between the United Kingdom and the United States. In what follows, we will consider these two bilateral relationships separately.

The Case of Anglo-French Relations

Figure 7-12 shows the amount of hostility sent by Britain to France on the left and that sent by France to Britain on the right in both the reference and the policy package simulation runs. The reductions brought about by the policy package are quite dramatic in both cases, even though the immediate impact of the policies (as evidenced by the 1995 values) is a slight increase. By the year 2010, however, Britain's hostility toward France in the policy package run is only about one-sixth of what it is in the reference run, while the amount of hostility that France directs toward Britain in that year with the policy package in effect is only about one-eighth of what it is in the reference run.

The next step in our analysis of Anglo-French relations involves looking at how their hostile reactivities change toward one another as a consequence of the policy measures introduced, and these are shown in Figure 7-13. The British reactivity to French hostility is cut approximately in half by the policy package, and by the end of the period, Britain is very tolerant of French hostility. The drop in French reactivity to British hostility is even more dramatic, especially in light of the fact that in the reference run their coefficient of reactivity is substantially above one, the hypothetical point where the French would exactly reciprocate British hostility. That means that France is rather powerfully amplifying hostility it receives from Britain in the reference run. The combination of reduced arms, increased aid, and growth-promoting reforms in the South eliminates this tendency and renders the French very tolerant of British hostility.

The reasons for these changes lie principally in the changes in relative power brought about by arms reduction. In the reference run, British conventional capability is only slightly less than that of the French throughout the 1990–2010 period in spite of the fact that the French

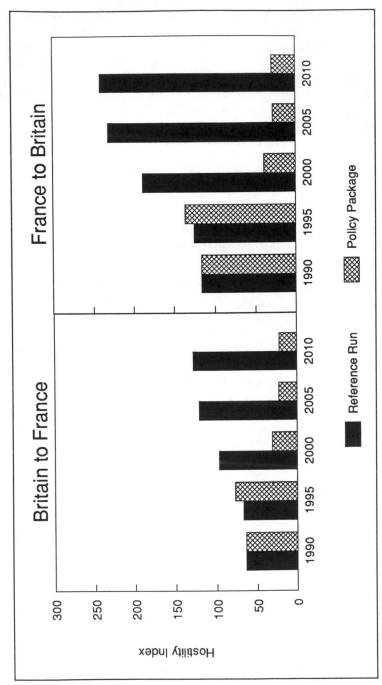

FIGURE 7–12 Hostility Exchanged between Britain and France

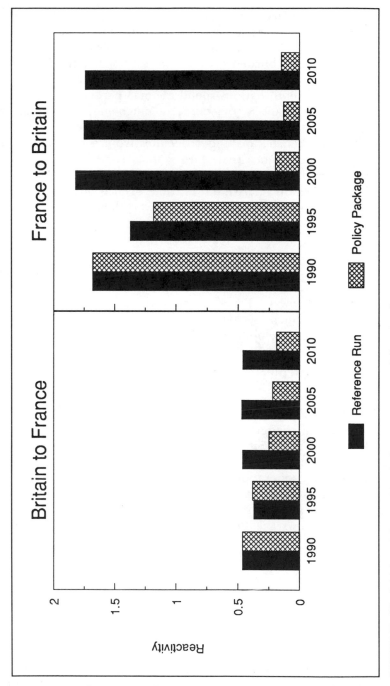

FIGURE 7–13 British and French Hostile Reactivities toward One Another

GDP is about twice as large as that of the British. The British are able to maintain approximate parity with the French only by spending proportionately more on defense than the French, and in the reference run, the British defense burden grows from a little less than 5 percent in 1990 to a little less than 7 percent in 2010. Under the terms of our arms reduction plan, both nations spend about 3 percent of their GDPs on defense, and the result is, of course, a much more dramatic drop in British capabilities than in French capabilities. As a consequence, the ratio of British to French capabilities declines from a little less than 1 to 1 in 1995 to a little more than 1 to 2 in 2010.

The British and the French react in an opposite but complementary manner to this change in relative power. The French operate in accordance with the compensatory model and lower their hostile reactivity toward Britain as the military balance moves in their favor. It is as if the French perceive less rivalry for leadership from the British and become, therefore, more willing to "turn the other cheek." The British, on the other hand, do the opposite of what is ordained by the compensatory model; that is, as they become weaker in relation to France, their foreign policy toward France becomes less hostile. It is as if the British, sensing their increased vulnerability, attempt to draw nearer to France to offset this development.

The Case of Anglo-American Relations

Having accounted for the significant drop in *West-West* hostility produced by the policy package, we now turn to the question of why there is a substantial change in cooperation among these nations under these conditions. As already indicated, the dyad with the United Kingdom on one side and the United States on the other exhibits the most dramatic change in cooperation found among the *West-West* group, and, therefore, we will focus here on how cooperative relations differ between this pair of nations as a consequence of the policy changes.

Figure 7-14 shows the flows of cooperation generated by Britain toward the United States and vice versa in the reference and policy package runs. What is immediately striking about this figure is that in the reference run, cooperative behavior exchanged between the two nations steadily declines throughout the twenty-year period, whereas it increases quite noticeably in the policy package run over the same period. This suggests that we are dealing with two questions rather than one. Why does the "special relationship" deteriorate in the reference run, and what it is about the policy package that reverses the process?

Figure 7-15 shows the cooperative reactivities of Britain and the United States toward one another in the two simulation runs, and the pattern we saw earlier is repeated here. That is, a decline in the

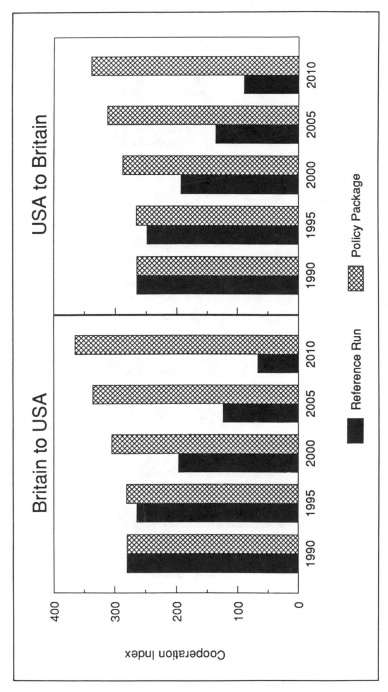

FIGURE 7–14 Cooperation Exchanged between Britain and the United States

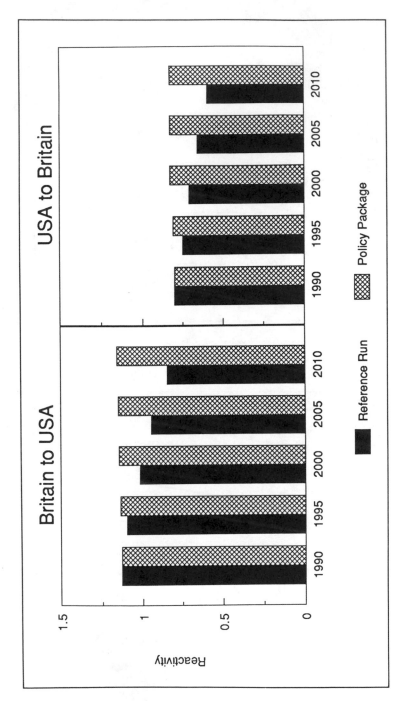

FIGURE 7–15 British and American Cooperative Reactivities toward One Another

propensity of both sides to respond in kind to cooperative acts that they direct toward one another is clear in the reference run, whereas this propensity rises slightly in the policy package run.

Although all four of the factors enumerated earlier—relative power, trade relations, dyadic climate, and international climate—have an effect on this relationship, the strongest determinant on both sides is relative power. According to the empirically estimated parameters, a narrowing of the conventional capability gap between Britain and the United States leads Britain to be less cooperative toward the United States, whereas a widening of the gap has the opposite effect. In other words, the greater the difference in conventional capability between the United Kingdom and the United States, the more responsive Britain is to American cooperative acts. Since the same is true for the United States—that is, the stronger it is in conventional capability relative to Britain, the more cooperative it is toward that nation—a shift in the balance of capability between the United States and the United Kingdom in either direction will cause their cooperative relations with one another to change as well. If the balance moves in favor of the United States, cooperative exchanges will increase, but if it moves in the opposite direction, co-operative exchanges between the two nations will decrease.

In the reference run, American conventional capability declines by about 15 percent during the 1990–2010 period, while British capability grows by about 25 percent during the same period. This decline on the part of the United States is a result of a shift of resources from conventional to strategic-nuclear forces rather than a decrease in military expenditures. Be that as it may, the net result of all this is that the conventional balance shifts toward the United Kingdom, and, for the reasons given earlier, cooperative behavior declines in the reference run.

The arms reduction component of the policy package fundamentally alters this change in the conventional balance. As a consequence of arms reduction, American conventional capability is reduced by 40 percent by the year 2010, but British capability drops by about 60 percent by that year. Under these circumstances, the balance shifts toward the United States and the widening of the capability gap between the two brings increased cooperation on both sides.

CONCLUSION

We began this chapter by asking whether the package of policy changes we have introduced reduces global tension, and the answer we have arrived at is ambiguous. Some nations have better relations with other nations as a consequence of reduced arms, more aid, and more growth in the South. Notably, relations among the advanced market economies and between the centrally planned economies and the Third World are better under these conditions, but relations between the West and the Third World are not improved overall by the measures. Nor did we find East-West relations uniformly better with arms reduction, more aid, and more growth in the South.

In sum, reduced arms, increased aid, and growth-promoting reforms in the South have not led so much to a *reduction* in global tension as to a *redistribution* of global tension. As with most policies, the I/I measures help some nations and hurt others, and when gains and losses are viewed primarily in relative terms, the game of international politics takes on a zero-sum nature. We remain convinced that there exists a package of policies that will ameliorate many (but not all) long-term global conflicts, but our work suggests that finding the optimal combination of policies will not be an easy task.

Global Momentum
and
Policy Leverage

MOMENTUM AND LEVERAGE

The policy package developed and tested in this volume has had considerably less impact on the global political economy than many proponents of the Idealist/Internationalist theory may have anticipated that it would. One reason became obvious as we explored the scenario: There is a great deal of momentum in the present world political economy, comprising as it does approximately 5 billion people, 170 states, and a $25 trillion GDP. It is appropriate that we consider some of that momentum and review the leverage that our scenario has shown policymakers can apply to it, before turning to a final evaluation of the I/I theory.

Aggregate Economic Performance

The global economy is in some ways like a large ship under full steam. It has tremendous momentum. Even in periods of dramatically slower growth, like that beginning in the mid-1970s, global growth can be surprisingly robust. In the decade following the onset of the 1973–1974 energy shock and associated global recession, the global economy grew at an average annual rate of about 2.7 percent, and global per capita GDP rose about 1 percent per annum on the average (Sivard 1986:32). That decade of considerable growth encompassed the two worst global economic downturns since the 1930s. Historic growth has been of tremendous benefit to the average global citizen, even in the bad times. In the exceptionally good decade of the 1960s, the world economy grew at an average rate of about 5 percent per year, and per capita GDP rose by about 3 percent per year.

In principle, the captain has complete control over the steaming vessel's course and speed, but his ability to alter them is very limited in the short run because of the momentum of the ship. Similarly, international policymakers have remarkably limited ability to steer the global economy over even fairly lengthy periods. Figure 8-1 traces the global GDP per capita of the reference run and of the I/I policy package run. A return after 1990 to something near the historic long-term pattern of global economic growth could produce a two-thirds increase in the average GDP per capita worldwide by 2010; in contrast, the incremental benefit of the I/I package is less than 4 percent. For the *South*, the respective figures are 123 percent and 4 percent. Although policymakers do have leverage, it appears limited in comparison with the growth processes at work.

FIGURE 8–1   Global GDP per Capita with and without Policy Package

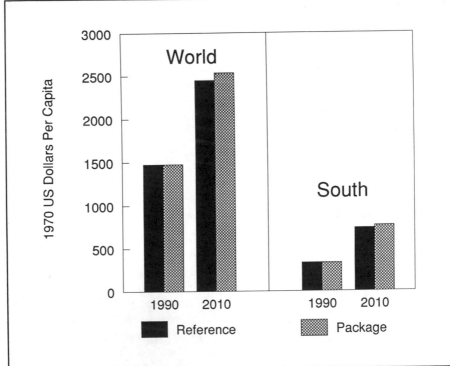

We must be careful to emphasize again that the reference run does not provide a forecast of global economic development but, rather, our current "best guess," using the full GLOBUS model, of future behavior.[1] That is, of course, true for all variables of the reference run. Although the model reproduces growth patterns of the 1970–1990 period reasonably well, that by no means guarantees future accuracy. For instance, the GLOBUS model does not represent availability of nonrenewable resources or damage by human systems to the biological and physical environment. Should these or other factors slow economic growth considerably in the future, real world growth would fall short of the reference run.[2] In such circumstances, the importance of the I/I package would increase somewhat relative to the momentum of economic growth.

Structure of the Global Economy

The structure of the world economy is undergoing steady and very considerable change. Among the most important elements of this is the growing economic role of the South. For instance, the Southern share in the world economy is steadily increasing. Table 8-1 indicates the division of the GLOBUS world economy among the four regions in 1990, 2000, and 2010 in the reference and policy package runs. Whereas the *South* share in the reference run is only 14 percent in 1990, the *South* constitutes nearly 20 percent of the total by 2010.[3] *Opec*'s share, part of a broader definition of the South, grows from under 3 percent to over 4 percent. The Eastern share also grows slightly. The only decline is in the *West*, with a share of the world's economy that erodes from 61.2 percent to 52.5 percent.

The I/I package of policy changes only marginally affects this division of the global economy in 2010. The most significant impact is on the *Opec* share, which it boosts from 4.1 percent to 4.5 percent.

---

[1] This may appear to the reader as a distinction without a difference, but for us there is an important, albeit subtle, differentiation involved. As the GLOBUS model has evolved, changes have been constantly introduced to improve its theoretical content and empirical validity, and if, as we hope, it continues to grow and develop, more such changes will be made. Hence, the reference run is quite mutable. Perhaps the difference between a forecast and a "best guess" is that the former is assumed to have a *high* probability of occurring attached to it, whereas the latter is only assumed to have the *highest* probability of occurring, even though that probability might be quite low in absolute terms. Be that as it may, since our experimental design focuses on the *changes* that a policy intervention makes, rather than the absolute *levels* reached, a change in the model and the reference run does not necessarily invalidate the conclusions reached in this study.

[2] On the other hand, given the substantial contribution that technological change makes to long-term growth and the substantial uncertainty that surrounds developments in this area, faster growth is also possible.

[3] It should always be remembered that the percentages here apply only to the GLOBUS world of twenty-five countries. Although those countries do constitute 80 percent of the total world economy, they do not represent the entire world.

TABLE 8–1 Regional Shares of the Global Economy

	North			
	West		East	
YEAR	REFERENCE	PACKAGE	REFERENCE	PACKAGE
1990	61.2	61.6	21.7	21.7
2000	56.4	55.5	23.3	23.7
2010	52.5	51.1	23.9	24.9

	South			
	South		Opec	
YEAR	REFERENCE	PACKAGE	REFERENCE	PACKAGE
1990	14.4	14.4	2.7	2.7
2000	17.0	17.3	3.4	3.5
2010	19.5	19.6	4.1	4.5

Even that is considerably less than the increase in the *Opec* share that occurs in the reference case, and no other regional grouping changes proportionally as much in response to the policy package. Again we must conclude that policy interventions are likely to have considerably less effect on the world economy than more fundamental economic forces.

Some readers may be wondering about the implications for the North-South gap of this increase in Southern share of global GDP. Because the North-South gap is measured in per capita terms and the population of the South is growing at least 1 percent per year faster than that in the North, the gap could remain unchanged even in the face of increasing Southern GDP share. But the GLOBUS model does, in fact, suggest that the per capita gap, measured as ratios of GDP per capita in the North and the South, will begin to decline. Chapter 1 showed that the gap, using this GDP per capita ratio measurement, was in reality quite stable from 1960 to 1985. The GLOBUS analysis from 1970 through the early 1980s fundamentally reproduces that historic pattern. Thereafter, however, the model indicates substantial erosion in the gap. As shown in Figure 8-2, for the GLOBUS countries it declines from 15.9 in 1970 to 11.2 in 2010 of the reference run.

After a century and a half of steady widening and several decades of stability, why might this narrowing of the gap begin? There are two mechanisms that account for most of the explanation. First, population growth rates in the South have now begun to decline and, according to most forecasts, will continue to fall into the next century. Declining

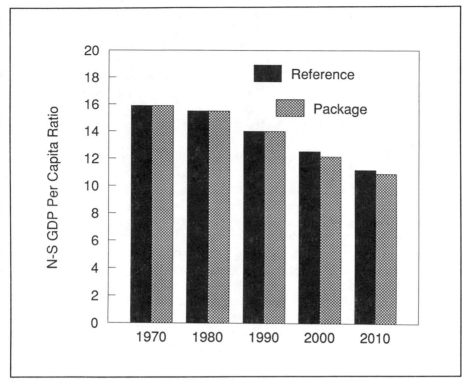

FIGURE 8–2   The North-South Gap with and without Policy Package

population growth rates will for many years result in a greater slowing of growth in young, dependent populations than in the growth of the work force. The same phenomenon, although less dramatic, has helped the Northern labor force grow relative to total population for much of this century. At this point, however, the population distributions in the North have reached a stage where continued low birth rates and declining death rates leads to the aging of population and the relative increase in another group of dependent population, retirees. Demographic factors are thus beginning to work in favor of Southern economic growth per capita and against that of the North.

The second factor is technological. Much of the advanced technology of the North can be adapted in the South, and the transfer of technology is well under way. Moreover, the South is establishing an increasingly strong base for adaptation of Northern technology. For instance, continued growth in the manufacturing sector of the South, advances in educational levels, and creation of infrastructure are among the factors that facilitate the transfer of technology. The GLOBUS economic submodel translates such factors into a slow acceleration of technological transfer and thus of Southern growth.

In comparison with the very minor variations in the North-South gap indicated across all scenarios in Figure 5-9, this significant decline in the gap after 1990 is of considerable importance. Again, we see a relatively small ability of the I/I policies to alter or accelerate a process that has a great deal of momentum inherent to it. The I/I package does reduce the gap, but only from 11.2 in the reference run to 10.9 by 2010.

Moving beyond changes in the structure of the world economy across regions, large-scale changes are also taking place within the economies of the world, especially those of the South. Figure 8-3 indicates the sectoral division of the *South* economy in both 1990 and 2010 of the reference run. Most dramatically, the agricultural value added share of GDP declines from nearly 25 percent to only 18 percent. This relative reduction in the share of economic resources devoted to agriculture does not mean that hunger will have been eliminated in the South by 2010, a development that is not likely even in the North. But conservatives and radicals agree that the problem is fundamentally one of insufficient income, not one of the physical ability to produce food. Thus, increasing per capita GDP levels, like those suggested in Figure 8-1, should result in a reduction in the percentage of global population suffering from hunger.

Also notable are rises in both the manufacturing and the service sectors of the Southern economy. The manufacturing sector increases its share by nearly 2 percent (to 22 percent) and the service sector gains 3.5 percent. Although the I/I policy package does marginally affect this breakdown, the impact of it is again nearly insignificant when considered in relation to the fundamental pattern of change.

Government Spending

One of the best forecasts in social science history is Wagner's Law, which was formulated in the late nineteenth century. Wagner (1890) argued that the share of the economy taxed and spent by government was on a steady upward curve. He based his argument on the need for governments to ameliorate the negative effects of the industrial revolution and the propensity for greater shares of income to be spent on educational, cultural, and other public-supported activities as incomes increase. Whatever the reasons, and wherever the upper boundary of government's share lies, Wagner's Law has been obeyed for a century. It has described the longitudinal pattern within almost all countries, and it is easily shown to be true across countries at different economic development levels today. The I/I policies have not altered the global

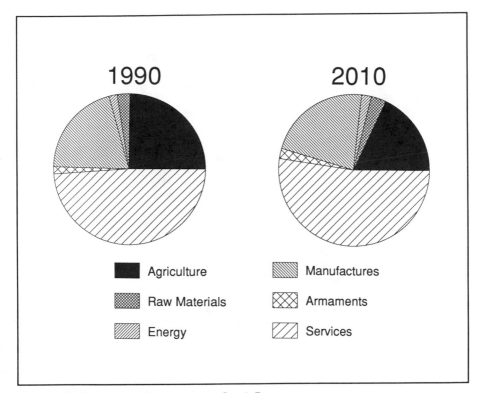

FIGURE 8–3 Sectoral Division of the *South* Economy

pattern of development foreseen by Wagner. Figure 8-4 shows the growth of governmental share in both the reference and the I/I package scenarios. In both instances, the government share rises from 36 percent in 1990 to over 44 percent in 2010.

Totals often conceal much, and in this case the comparable growth of total government spending in the two analyses conceals very significant changes in the nature of that spending. Since the I/I package specifically required a one-third reduction in military spending, the global balance of military and other government spending is quite different in the two cases. Table 8-2 shows that worldwide per capita defense expenditures fall from $174 in the reference run to $124 with the I/I package. In fact, the 2010 level in the combined scenario does not greatly exceed that of 1990. The quite dramatic $50 per capita saving is divided in the following ways: Education gains $9; health spending rises $6; welfare takes $30; and the other $5 is distributed in other categories. As we have said many times, although the aggregate impact of the policies may be low, the implications for some individuals or groups can be dramatic.

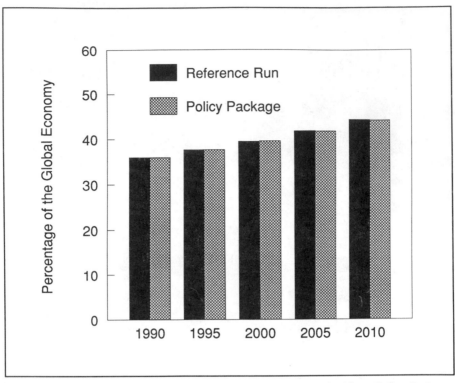

FIGURE 8–4   Government Expenditure Share of GDP with and without Policy Package

TABLE 8–2   Global Per Capita Government Expenditures (1970 Dollars)

YEAR	Defense		Education	
	REFERENCE	PACKAGE	REFERENCE	PACKAGE
1990	103.3	102.7	63.6	63.8
2000	133.9	90.1	87.2	92.6
2010	173.6	123.7	116.9	125.5

YEAR	Health		Welfare	
	REFERENCE	PACKAGE	REFERENCE	PACKAGE
1990	21.3	21.3	137.4	123.7
2000	31.7	34.2	207.8	221.6
2010	53.6	59.6	312.9	341.9

International Politics

An important expectation of many in the Idealist/Internationalist tradition is that joint actions such as significant arms reductions and substantial foreign aid programs will better relationships within the family of nations. Figure 8-5 shows that world levels of cooperation and conflict are remarkably stable over time in the reference run and even more remarkably unaffected by the package of policies.

Chapters 3 and 7 demonstrated that the absence of change at the global levels can conceal substantial variations in regional and bilateral relationships, however. For instance, in Chapter 3, we saw that even though general *East-West* relationships were affected little by the very substantial reductions in arms spending, interactions between East Germany and West Germany and between other pairs of countries changed significantly, in a largely offsetting fashion. Similarly, in Chapter 7, we saw substantial transformations of specific dyadic relationships, such as United States–Brazil and United Kingdom–France. Those findings in combination with Figure 8-5 indicate that patterns of relationships among

FIGURE 8–5 World Cooperation and Conflict with and without Policy Package

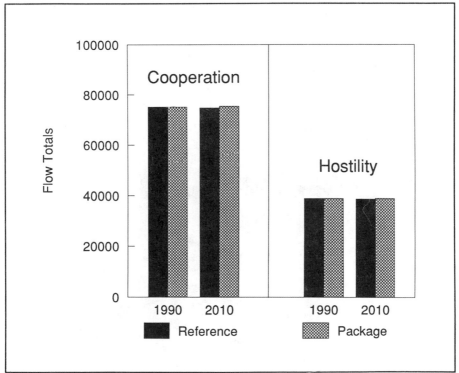

states shift but that the overall system of interacting states has a strong dynamic of its own.

Although the I/I package provided little leverage with respect to aggregate international relations, we saw in Figure 3-10 that global power distributions underwent substantial change as a result of the reduction in North arms spending. The Southern share of total global conventional power rises sharply. In addition, the arms reduction bears primary responsibility for an overall reduction in world conventional power relative to the reference run (see Figure 8-6).

Although the reduction in power by itself does not eliminate the sources of conflict and the tensions among states, it does reduce the level of threat that each state poses to the other. That is no mean accomplishment for the I/I policy package.

Domestic Stability

Chapter 6 sketched the complexity of measuring domestic stability and the difficulty of theoretical analysis in that area. We introduced there two longer-term measures of political stability that are of interest

FIGURE 8–6 World Conventional Power with and without Policy Package

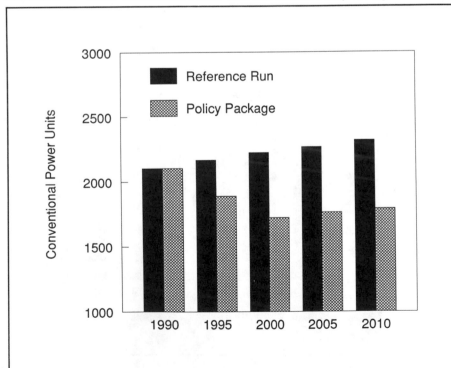

at the global level—namely, protest and violence. Both protest and violence tend to increase with social mobilization. One of the most important trends of the twentieth century has been a global increase in social mobilization, largely as a result of advances in communication and transportation technology and increasing education and literacy.

Such a secular trend in mobilization would by itself increase instability, but counteracting it are at least two other factors. The first is the growing ability of governments to impose sanctions upon their populations—that is, to repress violence. That growth in capabilities is by no means independent of the growth in governmental control of the economy that we saw earlier. The second countervailing factor is the inverse long-term relationship between the provision of basic human needs and both types of instability (although provision of basic human needs more strongly dampens violence). There, too, the growing expenditures of governments have helped contain instability, and the burgeoning world economy has also generally contributed to stabilization through provision of basic needs.

Figure 8-7 traces the global total of protest and violence across all twenty-five countries[4] and shows values for the entire 1970–2010 period. Although violence in the reference run grows substantially in the 1970–1990 period, it stabilizes and even declines after 1990. In contrast, the growth in protest actually accelerates after 1990. It appears that a kind of global threshold may be near, at which point the satisfaction of basic needs in many countries shifts stability from violent to nonviolent action. If true, that is certainly a hopeful global development. Once again, however, we must warn against too great a reliance on any analysis of political stability.

Also of interest in Figure 8-7 is the failure of the I/I package to significantly alter the long-term global pattern of the reference case. A small absolute and relative increase in violence and a small decrease in protest actually follow the introduction of the policy changes in 1990. As Chapter 6 documented, the consumption costs of the reforms needed to translate aid into additional growth, and especially of such reforms when undertaken by aid nonrecipients (for example, China), can lead to more violence and less protest.

EVALUATION OF THE I/I THEORY

This book has been an extended discussion of six propositions constituting what we called the Idealist/Internationalist theory and portrayed in Figure 2-1. In light of that examination and of the discussion in this

---

[4] To avoid confusion, the reader should bear in mind that the results reported in Chapter 6 pertained only to the developing nations, whereas those discussed here are based on all twenty-five nations.

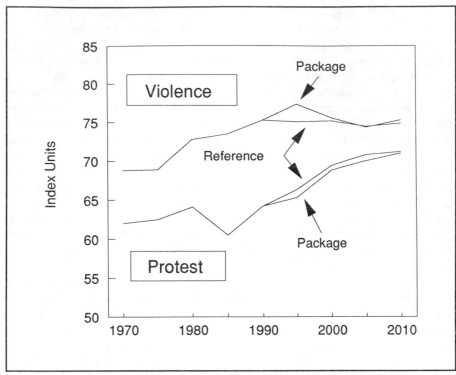

FIGURE 8–7   World Domestic Stability with and without Policy Package

chapter of the I/I policy impact relative to global momentum, let us move to a general review of the I/I theory and of our findings with respect to it. We chose to examine it in detail because the theory influences strongly, perhaps even dominates, the thinking of those presenting proposals for reduced arms spending and greater levels of international transfers. Those making policy in the North frequently take a very skeptical view of this theory; many others around the world tend to unquestioningly accept its validity. What can our analysis tell us about these critical international linkages?

1. Will reductions in arms spending improve economic performance in the North?

According to the GLOBUS results, the economic gains from reduced arms spending are positive overall, but small. Governments do have alternative opportunities to employ the funds spent on armaments, and we have found that some defense savings are allocated to investment, which enhances growth, and to social expenditures, which raise welfare levels. In both the East and the West, citizens' welfare improves more than GDP performance when arms spending is cut. It appears that the East would benefit considerably more than the West from reduced arms spending in terms of economic growth, but the final disposition of any defense savings would be a major political decision; we do not expect that all affected nations would adopt the same reallocation strategy.

---

2. Will reductions in arms spending improve East-West relations and decrease the threat of war?

Our results with respect to this question have been very mixed. The particular scenario we tested, which entailed comparable reductions in defense spending in the West and the East blocs, had very little effect on the overall climate of relationships between those states. Relations between the United States and the Soviet Union become relatively more cooperative, which would be an important contribution to world peace, since these two nations combined possess most of the world's destructive capability. Relations between each of these superpowers and the allies of the other and between the members of the opposing blocs do not necessarily become less hostile with arms reduction, however. In particular, the relations between the two Germanys deteriorate significantly with arms control because of alterations in the balance of military power between the two and increased economic dependence of East Germany upon West Germany.

Alternative scenarios, with reductions of different magnitudes and with variations in the symmetry of reductions, might produce significantly different results, but there are elements of a dilemma within Central European relations, and inter-German relations in particular; that is, arms reduction promotes increased East-West trade, which, in turn, results in a greater East European economic dependence upon the West. Since some East European governments react negatively to this economic "penetration," the price of better overall East-West relations may be the worsening of some bilateral relations. Balanced reductions, the only feasible option in the current international system, are not likely, therefore, to eliminate all East-West tensions.

---

3. Will reductions in arms spending facilitate increases in development assistance?

Reductions in arms spending would not automatically lead to significant increases in North-South transfers. The budgetary pressure for the expansion of domestic programs is very strong, and, according to our results, these programs would absorb nearly all defense savings brought by arms reduction. Although savings from even a moderate arms spending reduction scenario would be more than adequate to financially allow donors to meet the NIEO aid target of 0.7 percent of GDP, an act of substantial political will would be required to actually meet that target.

---

4. Will increased foreign aid improve economic performance in the South?

If the flow of aid were substantially increased, the response in terms of Southern economic performance might well prove disappointing. Reduced domestic savings and higher currency valuations are two likely results, and these could channel most, if not all, aid into consumption and imports, thereby providing little impulse to domestic investment and production growth. Significant improvements in the South's standard of living would result from increased aid, but the maintenance of that standard of living would require continued high levels of aid. Hence, aid recipients would become more dependent upon the largess of wealthier nations.

Yet, such an outcome of increased assistance is not foreordained. In particular, changes in the fiscal and exchange rate policies of aid recipients could channel much of the assistance into savings and investment, and thereby promote the growth of productive capacity. These policies also produce large welfare gains in the long run, and, from an economic viewpoint, there is much to recommend them. Relative to the income levels of many in the South, the improvements can be substantial. These policy reforms have costs for the countries adopting them, including higher inflation and interest rates in combination with a reduction in the share of the GDP available for consumption. It appears that an important potential benefit of aid lies in reducing those costs or in compensating for them by facilitating faster growth.

Proposals for increases in foreign aid sometimes suggest that an effort comparable to the Marshall Plan is needed if real progress is to be made in reducing the economic disparity between the North and the South. By this reference, proponents most often are alluding to the amount of political will required of the aid donors. The Marshall Plan did involve a considerably higher commitment of resources than we have examined or than is envisioned by various NIEO proposals, but in our view potential aid donors could afford such an effort with (and perhaps without) moderate, growth-enhancing reductions in arms spending. One of the most overlooked features of the Marshall Plan was the political burden it placed on aid *recipients* for coordinated and effective use of the aid. The policy changes induced by that feature of the plan were critical to its success. So, too, would they be in this case.

---

5. Will improved economic performance in the South increase domestic stability of those countries?

According to our analysis, the answer to this question is both yes and no, depending upon one's definition of political stability. In general, we found that improved economic performance in the South led to slightly *less violence* but somewhat *more protest*. In our view, a shift from violent to nonviolent expressions of opposition to government signals an increase in political stability, but others may see that as representing no net change in the stability of the political system.

---

6. Will the entire package of proposals improve North-South relations?

While, on average, West-South relations deteriorate, the East-South climate improves. The United States–Brazil interaction illustrates the West-South pattern. In response to a narrowing of the conventional power balance between the two as a result of the I/I package, the United States becomes more sensitive to its political and commercial relationship with the colossus of the South. Less sensitivity by Brazil to stimuli from the colossus of the North only partially compensates. Brazilian progress in exports provides a spark for increased United States hostility and a general deterioration of ties. The U.S.S.R.-Chinese relationship is important in understanding the East-South linkage. Accelerated movement toward conventional power parity in that dyad reduces Soviet intransigence while improving the Chinese disposition. In short, the United States and the Soviet Union react quite differently to the increased relative power of two important South states.

More generally, however, the conclusion must be that within the North-South context, specific dyads (involving either East or West) react quite differently to changed power and economic status. Thus, overall it is not possible to conclude that the I/I package would improve North-South relationships.

Figure 8-8 shows the revised version of the I/I theory shown in Figure 2-1, which takes into account these six findings, and a number of additions have been made. A black arrow denotes a relatively strong positive relationship, while a white arrow indicates a relatively weak positive effect. Cross-hatched arrows, on the other hand, mark those

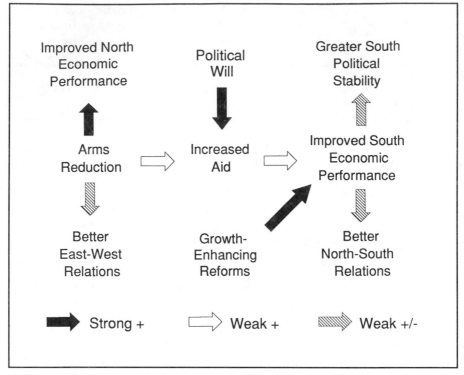

FIGURE 8–8   The Revised Disarmament-Development Argument

relationships that we found to be ambiguous; that is, both positive and negative outcomes were evident. Two factors, political will and growth-enhancing reforms, have been added to the diagram, since they were found to be important.

A comparison of this figure with Figure 2-1 suggests that (1) more policy changes than those envisioned by the proponents of the I/I theory are necessary if global conditions are to be improved and (2) while those policy changes improve some global conditions, others are made worse. Together, these observations support the often cited but just as often forgotten conclusion that complex problems do not have simple solutions.

CONCLUDING COMMENTS

Some may consider this chapter's discussion of global momentum and the quite limited leverage of the I/I policy package a statement of pessimism. It should not be so read for three reasons. First, many of the aforementioned long-term trends are quite encouraging. Certainly, the economic growth, rise in per capita incomes, narrowing of the North-South gap, and increased expenditures on education, health, and human welfare fall into that category. However, there is usually a "downside" in any prospective future, and the continuing increase in conventional military capabilities that we found in the reference run is not a development likely to reduce global tensions and threat.

Second, the impact that the I/I package does have seems most often to be desirable. For instance, as limited as the economic growth benefits of the entire package are, GDPs around the world are increased, not harmed. Moreover, much of that increase would accrue to those countries most in need. An exception to this conclusion lies in the apparent short- and mid-range increase in domestic violence that results from the reforms.

Third, perhaps the most substantial impact of the entire package is also one of the most important. The reductions in arms spending do result in a world with at least 20 percent less conventional armament power than the reference run and proportionally less total threat to states by each other. That the arms reductions did not result in a net decrease in international hostility is somewhat discouraging, but most important, they cause no net increase.

In policy analysis, little is black or white. Seldom do winners and winning strategies appear with no losers. Infrequently does improvement in the human condition come without cost. We hope that this analysis has contributed to a better understanding of the complexity of these issues of international political economy and that it has provided some suggestions as to how we might collectively design a better global future.

The Use
of Simulation

In this study, we have used computer simulation as our primary method, and since this methodology is relatively new and quite sophisticated, we expect that not many of our readers are familiar with it. In this short appendix, we will attempt to explain in relatively simple terms the "basics" of computer simulation. Naturally, in the limited space available to us, we must treat some very important questions rather superficially, and we regret having to do this very much. The alternative would have been to skip over some basic points, but we felt that some discussion of important issues, however inadequate, is better than no discussion at all. The reader should bear in mind that our desire here is to convey only a "feel" for what computer simulation is all about, and in many ways computer simulation is a great deal more complicated than we will make it sound.

In a nutshell, computer simulation is a special form of deductive analysis in which a theory is represented in the form of a computer program and a computer is used to derive (that is, deduce) the logical consequences (that is, deductions) of that theory. There are a number of elements to this definition that must be further explained, and we will begin with deductive analysis.

Deductive analysis involves using reason to obtain knowledge about the specific from the general. The simplest form of deductive analysis is called the syllogism, which looks something like this:

Major premise: Great powers spend much on defense.

Minor premise: The United States is a great power.
Conclusion: The United States spends much on defense.

There are three aspects of this example of deduction that we should discuss. First, the argument proceeds from the general to the specific, so that the conclusion is more specific than the premise. That is what we mean by reasoning from the general to the specific, or deduction. Second, the truth of the conclusion depends upon the validity of the assumptions *and* upon the correctness of our logic in drawing the conclusion from those assumptions. It is important not to forget the latter, for it is a principal reason why computer simulation is used in deductive analysis. Since it is relatively easy to construct theoretical systems that are beyond the capabilities of unassisted human logic, we usually find it necessary to use intellectual tools to help us with deduction. As we shall see, all these tools entail what is called formalization, or the reexpression of the theoretical system in a different language.

Many, perhaps most, philosophers of science believe that deductive analysis is the only way by which we can arrive at true knowledge, but some believe that it is possible to generate knowledge by working in the other direction—that is, from the specific to the general. This is usually referred to as inductive analysis, and in its purest form it involves gathering observations about specific instances of some general behavior and trying to discover some general laws based on observed regularities using intuition and even trial and error.

Deductivists frequently assert that Inductivists waste their time mindlessly gathering and analyzing data, while Inductivists counterattack that Deductivists waste their time playing around with useless abstractions. Deductivists allege that the Inductivists must use deduction to decide how and what to measure, while Inductivists charge that Deductivists must use induction to arrive at their holy first principles. And so the debate rages. Our position is that although induction and deduction may be logical opposites, in real research they are complementary activities rather than competing ones. Hence, all research is a mixture of deductive and inductive analysis.

To develop a computer simulation model, four types of activities need to be carried out: theorizing, formalizing, simulating, and evaluating, each of which we will discuss in some detail. Theorizing involves the development of a complete and consistent set of assumptions about how something works. Formalizing is a process by which this theory is translated into a language that a computer understands to produce a computer model. Simulating requires one to give specific, concrete values to selected unknowns contained within the computer model and execute the computer model to solve for (or deduce) other unknowns. To judge the quality of our computer model, we compare the results obtained in the simulation run(s) with our expectations, and this is, of course, evaluating the model.

Theorizing

Theory is one of those words that we use frequently but that is difficult to define in a concrete way. Webster's New World Dictionary offers us many possibilities:

1. A mental viewing; contemplation
2. A speculative idea or plan as to how something might be done
3. A systematic statement of principles involved (for example, the theory of something)
4. A formulation of apparent relationships or underlying principles of certain observed phenomena which has been verified to some degree
5. That branch of an art or science consisting in a knowledge of its principles and methods rather than its practice; pure, as opposed to applied, science, etc.
6. Popularly, a mere conjecture or guess

For our purposes, "theorizing" means "contemplation" (definition 1) in order to achieve "a formulation of apparent relationship or underlying principles of certain observed phenomena which has been verified to some degree" (definition 4). That formulation, one hopes, would lead to "a systematic statement of principles" (definition 3) about how the world works, which can be used to develop a plan as to how it might be improved (definition 2). We concede that much theorizing activity is by necessity "mere conjecture or guess" (definition 6).

The central problem with our definition lies with the phrase "verified to some degree." Some scientists interpret that to mean that the would-be theory has been subjected to extensive testing and no single instance of contradictory evidence has been found. Under such a very strict view, very few would-be theories throughout science would graduate to the status of "theory." Others would interpret the condition much more loosely and grant the status of "theory" to formulations that do not violate common sense and certain logical principles such as internal consistency. We lean toward the latter view, and to us, theories are like horses engaged in an endless race. As evidence accumulates in favor of one theory as opposed to others, it pulls ahead of the pack (and the betting shifts accordingly), but "dark horses" (that is, crazy ideas) given no chance of winning early in the race may suddenly move to the front as a result of a single significant discovery. The race is further complicated by the fact that horses may enter and leave the race continuously, depending upon the determination of their sponsors and the distribution of wagers. Unlike a normal horse race, however, there is never any winner, for ultimate truth, the finish line, is never achieved. That should not be surprising, however, since science is based on the assumption that the application of its methods will bring us closer to, but not completely to, the truth.

One important criterion that is used to evaluate theories is the degree to which they conform to reality, and we will have more to say about that later. But other criteria are also relevant. A theory should be complete (that is, no extra, ad hoc assumptions are needed later to derive a particular deduction), consistent (that is, no assumption should logically contradict another), and parsimonious (that is, the set of assumptions should be as small and simple as possible). Moreover, we expect theories to be at a reasonably high level of generality. By that we mean that they should allow us to make statements about whole classes of objects rather than about only a single case. In other words, if each observed phenomenon requires a different explanation, each of which is derived from different assumptions, then those assumptions taken together do not constitute a general theory.

The need for theories to be general stems from the reason we construct theories in the first place. Good theories (that is, useful but not necessarily true theories) are those that enable us to understand novel or unexpected developments with a minimum of mental effort. Just as levers allow us to lift large weights with a small effort, good theories enable us to understand a great variety of things by knowing a small number of basic principles. To see how important this principle of generality is, let us consider the following statements:

1. The United States spends much on defense.
2. Panama spends little on defense.

Most would consider those descriptive or empirical statements rather than theoretical ones, and virtually no one would suggest they constitute a theory because, assuming they are true, no amount of logical manipulation can generate any additional knowledge.

Suppose the statements were changed as follows:

1. The United States spends much on defense because it is rich.
2. Panama spends little on defense because it is poor.

Those statements taken together begin to look more theoretical, since there is some indication of causality, but they are still not general enough for use in other cases. For example, they don't allow us to answer the question of how much a medium-rich or an extremely poor nation will spend on defense.

We can solve this problem conceptually by combining the statements and raising them to a higher level of abstraction.

> The richer a nation is, the more it will spend on defense.

We now have a general theoretical statement that covers all entities that are nations, not just the United States and Panama, and once we have operationalized (that is, given empirical meaning to) concepts, such as "richness," that the statement contains, we can use it to make predictions about how much each nation will spend on defense.

Some would argue that our statement constitutes not a theory but a hypothesis. For the purposes of this example, it is not important whether it is a minitheory or merely a hypothesis, but we would note that a great deal of empirical research and policy advice has been based on theories no more complicated than this. In any event, our theoretical statement is simple enough that we can deduce the conclusions that flow from it without the aid of a computer, and we would not resort to computer simulation to study such a small set of assumptions.

In the course of theorizing about a problem, one usually discovers that the matter is a great deal more complicated than first thought and that many more assumptions are required to derive an intuitively satisfying explanation. Consider our example for a moment. Why should rich nations spend more on defense? Pondering that question might lead us to speculate that rich nations spend more on defense because they have more enemies and their governments have more access to resources. That might lead us to extend our minitheory thus:

> The richer a nation is, the more resources its government will have access to, and the more it will spend on defense.
> The richer a nation is, the more enemies it will have, and the more it will spend on defense.

Each of those statements spawns more questions. Why do governments in rich nations have access to more resources? Is it simply because their tax base is larger, or is it also due to their ability to extract more with less effort than poor nations can? Similarly, why should rich nations have more enemies. Is it because they exploit other nations to become rich, or is it merely that their power causes other nations to fear them?

You can see that once one begins to ask "why" in search of basic principles, there would appear to be no end to the process, and logically that is so. The chains of causality become longer and longer and more and more intertwined, and very quickly the set of statements becomes so complex that the unassisted human mind is no longer capable of dealing with them as a whole or of seeing what their implications are. It is for that reason that we formalize theories, the next step in the development of a computer simulation.

Formalizing

In reality, theories are purely mental constructs, and when we express a theory in symbols that can be communicated and manipulated, we are formalizing it. The expression of a theory may be done in a variety of languages. English, German, Boolean algebra, differential calculus, FORTRAN, and PASCAL are all examples of languages in which theories may be expressed. The language used will affect the meaning of the theory, but, equally important, it will also determine the way in which the elements of the theory may be manipulated. That is because every language has a grammar or calculus that defines a set of permissible operations that may be performed on the terms expressed in that language. Let us take a simple example to clarify this point.

When we theorized that "the richer a nation is, the more it will spend on defense," we expressed that thought in what is sometimes called ordinary (or natural) language, which is a representational system that most of us understand best. That characteristic, along with its valuable ability to cope with ambiguous and vague ideas, makes ordinary language the most frequently used means of expressing theories. But the deductions that can be derived from ordinary language theories are quite limited because of the simplicity of the available operators. For example, we can combine (concatenate) words, but we cannot meaningfully add them together. Thus, the term "rich-poor" would suggest to a reader that the thing being referred to is in some ways rich and in some ways poor, while the term "rich+poor" has no intrinsic meaning in ordinary language. The calculus of ordinary language is composed of qualitative or categorical operators, such as concatenation, and the strength of this type of calculus is that it allows one to deal better with vague or ill-defined concepts. However, this strength becomes a weakness when we wish to derive more precise deductions. In the example under discussion, we cannot deduce how much *more* a rich nation will spend on defense than a poor nation because the concepts and relationships involved are not stated in quantitative terms.

If a theory can be translated into quantitative concepts and relationships, then the language of mathematics may be used to manipulate the terms of the theory, and more precise deductions may thereby be derived. For example, if we were to restate our minitheory in ordinary mathematics, it would look like this:

$$DEX = PAR \times GDP$$

where *DEX* and *GDP* are the short names for defense expenditure and wealth, respectively, both of which are assumed to be measured in comparable units (for example, 1985 U.S. dollars).

PAR is a constant, or parameter, whose exact value will be later specified, but the range of sensible values can be deduced already. By definition, both *DEX* and *GDP* must be greater than or equal to 0; hence, *PAR* must also be greater than or equal to 0. How do we know that? We know that because by the rules of ordinary mathematics, the product of a negative number and a positive number is a negative number. *PAR* must not be negative, therefore, because if it were, then either *DEX* or *GDP* would need to be negative, too, and we have defined that as theoretically impossible.

We have succeeded in setting a lower bound of 0 for the parameter *PAR;* we can also establish an upper bound through mathematical reasoning. If *PAR* had a value equal to 1.0, then the nation would be devoting all of its resources to defense preparations. Although that is possible (but extremely unlikely), it is not possible for a nation to spend more resources than it has; hence, *PAR* may be equal to but not greater than 1.0. We can now make our first deductive statement:

$$0 \leq PAR \leq 1.0$$

which simply states in mathematical notation that the parameter *PAR* must be greater than or equal to 0 but less than or equal to 1. That is not a terribly profound or precise deduction, but, as we shall see, when we start to assign the parameter *PAR* real values, then we will be able to make some very precise statements about defense spending, all of which are possible only because the theory is now in a mathematical form.

Mathematics is a language that is rich in powerful operators, and expressing a theory in this language allows one to deal with fairly complex theoretical systems with relatively little effort.[1] Moreover, it is an economical, even terse, language in which it is easy to add elements to a theoretical system. For example, when we theorized that external threat was also a factor in the determination of defense spending, we were saying in mathematical terms the following:

$$DEX = (PAR1 \times GDP) + (PAR2 \times THREAT)$$

That is, high defense spending is a result of either high *GDP* or high *THREAT* or both.

At the risk of making things more complicated than they need be here, we will point out that we could have chosen to express the relationship differently; that is,

---

[1] Not counting, of course, the years of study that virtually everyone invests in learning mathematics.

$$DEX = (PAR1 \times GDP) \times (PAR2 \times THREAT).$$

Our use of the multiplication operator ($\times$) rather than the addition operator ($+$) has theoretical significance, for in this second case, defense spending will be high only when both *GDP* and *THREAT* are high. What that demonstrates is that in the process of formalizing a theory, one often finds that what appears to be an unambiguous relationship in ordinary language can be translated into several different mathematical statements. That is not an indication that therefore mathematics is an inferior language but, rather, that in ordinary language, it is easy to conceal ambiguity. The result of this is that the formalization of a theory in mathematical language often forces one back to theorizing because ambiguities become apparent that can be resolved only by conceptual changes. Some of these may be so serious as to require a fundamental rethinking of the entire theory.

A theory may become so complex that the language of mathematics (but not necessarily the logic of mathematics) is inefficient for representing it.[2] Under those conditions, the theory is often expressed in a computer language and the deductive reasoning left to the computer. Computer languages also contain operators, including those found in ordinary language and mathematics but other operators as well. For example, in computer language it is perfectly reasonable to state

$$A = A + B$$

whereas in mathematics, such a statement makes sense only if B is 0, in which case it is superfluous. The reason for this difference is that in most computer languages the equal sign is an *assignment* operator rather than an *equivalence* operator. That is, our example does not mean "A equals A plus B" but, rather, "replace the value of A with the sum of the values of A and B." We point this out not to teach elements of computer programming but to show that computer languages have distinctive operators, too.

A large number of computer languages exist today, and which one is used depends upon the nature of the theory being represented combined with more practical concerns, such as familiarity and portability. The choice of computer language is not without importance, however, since some concepts and relationships are much more easily expressed in one language than in another. We will continue the development of

[2] This is not to suggest that mathematical models and computer models are inherently interchangeable. The true power of mathematics as a representational language can be realized only when it allows one to derive an analytic or general solution to a set of equations. Since it is fairly easy to construct systems of equations that do not have such solutions, one is forced in these instances to construct computer models and generate computed or specific solutions. In those cases where mathematics can provide a general solution, a mathematical model should be used rather than a computer model.

our example by using BASIC, a widely known and relatively simple computer language.

In BASIC, the core equation of our first model might be

$$DEX = (PAR1 * GDP) + (PAR2 * THREAT)$$

which looks a great deal like its mathematical counterpart.

Before this one-line program would run, we would have to assign values to PAR1, PAR2, GDP, and THREAT. To do that, we need either to set them equal to some numbers or to specify a relationship by which they can be determined.

With respect to GDP, we might take what in economics is called a Cobb-Douglas production function as the GDP defining relationship. In BASIC, it would look like this:

$$GDP = PAR3 * (KAP \char`^ PAR4) * (LAB \char`^ (1-PAR4))$$

This simply says the GDP is the product of a constant, PAR3, and two variables, capital (KAP) and labor (LAB). The " $\char`^$ " indicates that the variables are raised to the PAR4 and 1-PAR4 power, respectively, before they are multiplied. By adding this relationship, we have added complexity to our model, and our minitheory now incorporates a standard formulation frequently used in economics. What can we do about the THREAT term?

Many international relations scholars say one nation will view another as threatening when the other nation possesses a good deal of military capability and it displays hostile intent toward the nation. That is:

$$Threat = Capability * Intent$$

We can incorporate this theoretical relationship into our emerging computer model as follows:

$$THREAT = DEXO * HOST$$

where DEXO is the other nation's defense spending and HOST is the amount of hostility that the other expresses to the nation deciding how much to spend on defense.

Combining the three elements we have formalized and adding a statement to print out the end result would produce the following minimodel.

$$GDP = PAR3 * (KAP \char`^ PAR4) * (LAB \char`^ (1-PAR4))$$
$$THREAT = DEXO * HOST$$

```
DEX = (PAR1 • GDP) + (PAR2 • THREAT)
PRINT DEX
```

With this program, we could solve (deduce) values of defense expenditure (DEX), given different values of capital stock (KAP), labor force (LAB), and the other nation's defense expenditure (DEXO) and hostile behavior (HOST). We could also experiment, of course, with different values for the parameters PAR1, PAR2, PAR3, and PAR4.

This four-line model is simple enough that one could easily solve it with nothing more than a pocket calculator. However, we quickly move beyond the capabilities of a pocket calculator when we start to make the minimodel more complex. To do that, we will need to introduce a few more aspects of BASIC, but it is important only that you understand the logic of what we are doing, not the technical details.

Up to this point, we have been assuming that we are dealing with a two-nation world: the nation deciding how much to spend on defense and its potential enemy. That is clearly not a very realistic assumption, since almost all nations perceive more than one potential enemy in their environments. And since the logic of our theory would imply that the other nation's defense spending is also affected by threat, a component of which is what the deciding nation has spent on defense, we must conclude that our model should represent a set of interdependent nations rather than a single nation. To show how we might do that, let us assume that we are dealing with a five-nation world.

To differentiate between the five nations, we will *dimension* our variables. When we dimension a variable, we make it possible to refer to several different values of a variable by adding an identifier (in mathematics, a subscript) to the variable name. In BASIC, such identifiers are surrounded by parentheses, so the defense expenditure of nation 1 would be

DEX(1)

and the defense expenditures of the other five nations would be

DEX(2), DEX(3), DEX(4), DEX(5)

Using this notation, we could rewrite our original DEX statement as follows:

DEX(1) = (PAR1 • GDP(1)) + (PAR2 • THREAT(1))

which would compute the defense expenditure for nation 1 only. To calculate the defense expenditures of all five nations, we could take advantage of one of the most powerful features of computer languages: the loop.

A loop tells the computer to perform a certain set of operations a specified number of times, making stated substitutions during each pass through the loop. In BASIC, these are called FOR..NEXT loops because the statement that begins the loop starts with FOR and the statement that ends the loop begins with NEXT.

Placing our dimensioned DEX statement within such a loop would produce the following:

```
FOR N% = 1 TO 5 STEP 1
    DEX(N%) = (PAR1 * GDP(N%) ) + (PAR2 * THREAT(N%) )
NEXT N%
```

This would cause the computer to perform the following operations. The index variable, N%,[3] would first be set equal to 1 and this value substituted for all the references to N% that precede the NEXT N% statement. After solving the equations contained in the loop for N% equal to 1, the NEXT N% statement would direct the computer back to the FOR statement, where N% would be incremented by 1 (the value specified by STEP 1) and set equal to 2. The statements within the loop would then be executed again, and the whole process repeated until the defense expenditures of all five nations had been computed. The power of the loop becomes obvious when you consider that extending this equation to twenty-five or one hundred nations only requires changing the 5 in the FOR statement to 25 or 100.

Bringing the GDP equation into the loop would require us to change that statement as follows:

```
GDP(N%) = PAR3 * (KAP(N%) ^ PAR4) * (LAB(N%) ^ (1-PAR4) )
```

where once again N% is an index variable defined by the FOR..NEXT loop.

Bringing the THREAT equation into the loop is more complicated because our HOST variable should now differentiate between, for example, the hostility that nation 1 sends to nation 2 and that which nation 2 sends to nation 1. We can handle this quite easily, however, by assigning two dimensions to the HOST variable, the first indicating

[3] An index variable must be an integer (that is, a whole number), and in BASIC a percent sign (%) on the end of a variable tells the computer that it should treat that variable as an integer. Unless otherwise specified, in BASIC variables are considered to be real (that is, decimal numbers); hence, we need to add the percent sign to the index variable N.

the identity of the sending nation, the actor, and the second the identity of the receiving nation, the target. Thus,

HOST(1,2)

would refer to the hostility sent by nation 1 to nation 2, and

HOST(2,1)

would refer to the flow of hostility from nation 2 to nation 1.

With that revision, our basic THREAT equation should now be

THREAT(N%) = DEX(O%) * HOST(O%,N%)

This says that the threat that nation N% perceives from nation O% (for Other) is the product of nation O%'s defense expenditure and the hostility that O% directs toward N%.

We are not quite finished, however, because we stated that each nation considers all the other nations potential enemies. We need to add another loop that will sum up the amount of total threat nation N% perceives from all the others. Such a loop could look like this:

```
THREAT(N%) = 0
FOR O% = 1 TO 5
        THREAT(N%) = THREAT(N%) + (DEX(O%) * HOST(O%,N%) )
NEXT O%
```

By setting THREAT(N%) equal to 0 before we enter the loop, we can use it as the place to accumulate the threat from others. One of those "others" covered by the loop will be the nation itself, so we may want to make one further modification as follows:

```
THREAT(N%) = 0
FOR O% = 1 TO 5
    IF N% <> O% THEN
            THREAT(N%) = THREAT(N%) + (DEX(O%) * HOST(O%,N%) )
        END IF
NEXT O%
```

The IF statement tests that N% and O% are not the same nation, since the "<>" operator means "not equal to" in BASIC and it guarantees that nation N%'s threat calculation will not include itself.

We could go on and on elaborating this model, and after quite a while, we would begin to approach the complexity of GLOBUS. The

GLOBUS computer model contains many thousands of statements like those shown in this appendix (except in FORTRAN) and somewhere around 40,000 variables and parameters. Our intention in developing this minimodel was to show you how one in principle constructs such a model, and we think what we have up to this point is sufficient to enable us to discuss the next step in computer simulation. Before doing that, however, let us put together all the pieces we have developed and add some internal documentation to the program with REM statements. The computer ignores these, but they REMind us of what is being done in different parts of the program.

```
REM Repeat for each nation
FOR N% = 1 TO 5 STEP 1

REM          Compute GDP
     GDP(N%) = PAR3 * (KAP(N%) ^ PAR4)) * (LAB(N%) ^ (1-PAR4) )

REM          Compute Threat
     THREAT(N%) = 0
     FOR O% = 1 TO 5 STEP 1
          IF N% <> O% THEN
                    THREAT(N%) = THREAT(N%) + (DEX(O%) * HOST(O%,N%) )
          END IF
     NEXT O%

REM          Compute Defense Expenditure
     DEX(N%) = (PAR1 * GDP(N%) ) + (PAR2 * THREAT(N%) )

REM          Print Defense Expenditure
     PRINT DEX(N%)

REM     Continue with next nation
NEXT N%

REM  Quit
END
```

Simulation

Before our minimodel would actually run on a computer, several things would need to be done. First, the computer program would have to compile successfully, a process whereby the computer instructions we have written are translated by the computer into the language that it really understands (sometimes called machine language). A program that compiles without errors may not run, however, since the compiler checks mostly for logical and syntactical errors and only in part for consistency and completeness of the model and theory. More to the point, our program will not run because we have not assigned values to the parameters and initial conditions that the program contains, and unless we give values to these "unknowns," a solution is impossible.

Doing that is not really part of the formalization process because formalizations should be of a very general nature, like the theories that guide them, and it is very rare that a theory is so precisely defined that even the values of parameters are specified by it. Therefore, it is usual in modeling to differentiate between a model's structure, which is laid out during formalization, and its parameters, which are assigned values in the simulation phase. Another way to look at it is to say the changing of the structure of a model leads to a new version of the model, whereas changing a model's parameters does not. Let us return to our example and see what that means in concrete terms.

Our minisimulation contains six variables and four parameters. Three of the variables,—KAP, LAB, and HOST—are not determined by the model (that is, they do not appear anywhere on the left side of an equal sign), and variables such as these are referred to as exogenous variables. Two variables, GDP and THREAT, are endogenous variables because they are completely defined by statements in the model. One variable, DEX, is partly exogenous and partly endogenous because it is used in the calculation of THREAT but is itself redefined a few lines later. Implicitly, there is a temporal ordering indicated here where the DEX referred to in the THREAT statement is the current value and the DEX statement determines the future value. In sum, we must assign initial values to four variables: DEX, KAP, LAB, and HOST. Since the first three of these are dimensioned 5 (for five nations) and the fourth is 5×5 (for twenty-five interaction possibilities), forty variables must be initialized before our model would run.

Parameters are also externally determined but differ from exogenous variables because they are assumed not to vary during a run of the simulation. That is, they are what might be called the fundamental constants of the model. They, too, must be assigned values, and we should point out, in case it has not already been noticed, that we have made a great simplification in our model. By not adding a nation dimension (for example, PAR1(N%)), we have implicitly assumed that the parameter values are the same for all nations. For example, by not assigning nation-specific values to PAR4, we are stating that the way in which capital and labor contribute to GDP is the same for all nations, although the amount of capital and labor they have may be quite different. We did that here to keep the example simple, but a better formalization would allow for national differences. Very few parameters in GLOBUS are assumed to be the same for all nations, for example.

In spite of this simplification, we still need four values for our parameters before the model will run. Where do we get them?

Not surprisingly, the most important factor in initializing a model's variables is the referent system we are trying to simulate. That is, the model described above might be used to simulate the behavior of a few major contemporary nations (for example, the United States, the Soviet Union, China, France, and Great Britain) or a few historical nations (Germany, France, Great Britain, Russia, and Austria-Hungary in 1890) or even five mythical nations. The numerical values given to variables (and to a lesser extent parameters) define in concrete and very specific terms the reality we are trying to recreate or create. We shall assume here that we are interested in simulating the behavior of the few contemporary nations.

The first thing we would discover when we began our search for data on defense expenditure, capital stock, and labor force for these five nations is that almost no data are available for the immediate past. Because of the time required to collect, collate, publish, and distribute data that are produced by organizations such as the United Nations, there is at best a two- to three-year time lag in data availability. The second thing we would discover is that in spite of great advances in the collection of data, in many cases data are not available for all nations or the values given are inconsistent with other values and, therefore, are of questionable accuracy. In some instances, such as defense expenditure, the definition and measurement of the variable is itself a politically controversial matter. The Soviet Union's statement of what it spends on defense is substantially lower than what Western sources estimate it to be, for example. A third discovery would be either that some basic and frequently used concepts do not have generally accepted operational definitions or, as in the case of capital stock, that no standard measures have been computed for a large number of nations. The fourth discovery we would make is that there is relatively little that is known with some precision about some very important world actors. Until quite recently, for example, very little reliable statistical information was available for China, and even basic information such as labor-force size may be five to ten million people higher or lower than what most experts estimate.

We could go on and on itemizing and detailing the kinds of problems one confronts in assigning meaningful numbers to variables, but we will not. Our intention has been to point out that it is rarely the case that all the initial values needed can be gathered by simply consulting one or two standard sources and that much more is usually required to assemble accurate and comparable values. Let's assume we have been able to piece together the values shown in Table A-1 for our five nations for 1985.

One more variable, HOST, needs to be initialized, and this is even more difficult to measure than those discussed earlier. We said that this

TABLE A–1   Initial Values of DEX, KAP, and
LAB

NATION	DEX*	KAP*	LAB**
U.S.A.	266	45,000	150
Britain	24	2,500	35
France	21	3,100	34
U.S.S.R.	275	11,000	175
China	25	100	650

* Billion U.S.$ ** Million

variable is supposed to measure how hostile the nations *behave* toward one another, so our measure should be based on their observed interactions with one another. A rather substantial part of the international relations research community has devoted much time to gathering this kind of information when doing what is called events data research. What that entails is the systematic examination of sources of information on current affairs (for example, events) of one nation doing something cooperative or conflictual toward another. For example, one nation expelling the ambassador of another nation is considered a hostile act and would be perceived as such by the nation whose ambassador is being expelled. Prominent nations like the five we have selected send and receive thousands of such acts in a particular year, and they are especially active with respect to one another. After we have collected all these events data, how do we boil them all down into single numbers that measure (we hope) how hostile each of our five nations behaved toward one another in 1985?

The problem faced here is the same as that which economists confront when they try to measure aggregate economic flows like GDP. The goods and services that make up GDP are very heterogeneous, like the behavior of nations toward one another, and to add them together, economists must apply weights to the various goods and services. In economics, the weights used are prices, and apples and oranges are added together in terms of their assumed value (that is, quantity times price) rather than, for example, their physical weight.

International relations scholars have endeavored to develop scales that measure the perceived hostility or cooperation that various international acts represent. Thus, for example, the expulsion of an ambassador might represent six "units" of conflict, whereas a border incursion might correspond to thirteen "units" of conflict. Cooperative acts, like cultural exchanges, are similarly scaled, and we can use these weights, called intensities, to derive the values needed.

For each nation with respect to each other nation, we first multiply the frequency of each type of act by the intensity (either hostile or cooperative) of the act and then sum these products. Since we are dealing with directional behavior, we need to perform this operation for how nation A behaves toward nation B and how nation B behaves toward nation A.

After collecting and scaling all these data, we might end up with a matrix of hostility values for 1985 that looks like Table A-2. Since nations do not behave hostilely toward themselves, the corresponding diagonal cells are by definition 0. We now have all our initial values specified, and we can turn to the question of parameter values.

Deriving the values for parameters in any type of model is difficult because parameters tend to represent things that are not directly observable. For the most part, they indicate how variables are related to one another, and since we cannot directly observe but can only infer relationships, we must use indirect methods to determine the parameter values as well.

There are three main ways in which parameter values may be derived: statistical estimation, conventional wisdom, and educated guessing. The first of these involves collecting data on the variables contained in a relationship and performing statistical analysis on those data to derive parameter values. Most consider this the best method, but when the number of parameters is large or the available high quality data are few, then it is very difficult to use.

Conventional wisdom (the values that others believe or have found comparable parameters to have) is an important source of parameter values, since it allows one to take advantage of the work that others have done. As our rigorous scientific knowledge about how the world works continues to grow, this will increasingly be a valuable source of parameter values. Unfortunately, at this stage, precise conventional wisdom is rather scarce and much of it is inconsistent.

The third method, educated guessing, is not as frivolous as it sounds. It does not mean throwing darts at a dart board or spinning a roulette wheel to generate numbers; rather, it means the systematic evaluation of all types of direct and indirect evidence pertaining to a relationship with an eye to narrowing the range of values that a pa-

TABLE A-2 Initial Values of HOST Variable

ACTOR NATION	Target Nation				
	U.S.A.	BRITAIN	FRANCE	U.S.S.R.	CHINA
U.S.A.	0	40	60	370	110
Britain	50	0	40	140	120
France	70	60	0	100	20
U.S.S.R.	570	20	50	0	710
China	290	200	20	400	0

rameter could logically assume and then identifying one or more reasonable values that should be tried.

One might be tempted to conclude that statistically estimated parameters are always better than "guesstimated" ones, but experience has demonstrated to us that that is often not true. Because of imperfections in data or the shortcomings of statistical methods, it is not uncommon for statistically estimated parameters to produce absurd results when they are introduced into a model, and one finds it necessary to modify these values by calling upon the same techniques as are used in educated guessing.

With respect to the four parameters contained in our model, let's assume we do the following: We assemble data with respect to DEX and THREAT for the five nations and use a simple statistical procedure to derive the values for PAR1 and PAR2 that appear to fit the data best. Let's assume these turn out to be 0.02 and .005, respectively. PAR3 and PAR4, which are used in the GDP equation, are taken from conventional wisdom; that is, others have found that the value of PAR4 is approximately 0.5 and the value of PAR3 is approximately 1.5. All these values should be considered tentative and subject to change based upon the performance of the model.

Introducing the initial values and parameter values into the program either by reading them in from a file or by adding statements assigning the values at the very beginning of the program would enable us to actually run the model. It would not produce much output, since it is a very simple model, just the computed defense expenditures of the five nations. To determine whether our model is a good one (or, more accurately, to discover the ways in which it is inadequate), we would move to the next stage, evaluation.

Evaluation

The fourth phase of computer simulation is the evaluation of the model that has been constructed. In reality, of course, evaluation is something that is continuously done during the development of the model, but by necessity this continuing evaluation is partial and piecemeal. During the evaluation phase, one undertakes a comprehensive analysis of the model and its behavior in as objective a fashion as possible.

The evaluation of a complex model is by no means an easy or a trivial task.[4] We want our models to possess several characteristics: verisimilitude, usefulness, and relevance. Verisimilitude refers to the

---

[4] One of the present authors has recently written something that describes the philosophy and method that has been used to evaluate GLOBUS (Bremer 1987: 723–775). Some of the points made there will be repeated here, but those seeking to learn more about this topic should consult Bremer.

degree to which the model's behavior matches that of the referent system. Usefulness refers to the extent to which builders and users of the model gain valuable insights into the phenomena being modeled by developing and using the model. Finally, by relevance we mean the degree to which a model helps us to understand better and develop policies for dealing with real-world problems.

Strangely enough, these are quasi-independent standards. Inaccurate models (for example, Columbus's model of the globe, in which the circumference of the earth was several thousand miles smaller than it really is) can be very useful if they lead to new discoveries (for example, the Americas). Models possessing much verisimilitude may not be very policy relevant if they don't contain variables that can, in fact, be changed by decision makers. And, because of the rapidity with which issues come and go as they are added to and removed from the agenda of public concerns, a model that is deemed very relevant at one moment may be declared irrelevant in the next. Hence, when we say that evaluating a model is a complex task, we mean that there is no simple test that the model has to pass to be judged worthy.

Some scientists do not accept that and argue that the fundamental test is the degree to which a model reproduces reality—that is, its verisimilitude, in our terminology. With respect to our minimodel, this would entail comparing the computed (simulated) values of DEX with comparable values drawn from the referent system. We would be interested in the size and the distribution of discrepancies between the simulated and the observed values because these give us clues as to where the model may need improvement. Unfortunately, the presence or the absence of such discrepancies does not constitute conclusive proof that the theory/model is right or wrong. It is tempting to believe that one tests theories and models by comparing them with "reality," but that is impossible, since we never precisely know "reality." What we have instead is an image of reality that is based upon incomplete and imperfect observations and measurements. Since a model also generates an image of the thing being simulated, when we compare simulated and observed behavior, we are really comparing two images, both of which are distorted representations of that thing we call reality. Differences between simulated and observed behavior may, therefore, be due to errors in the simulation or errors in our observations of reality, or, most likely, both. For that reason, it is rarely true that one simple, straightforward comparison is an adequate test of a model's correspondence to "reality."

There is a deep, continuing debate between and among philosophers and practitioners of science about how to determine whether our theories are "true." The majority opinion (in our judgment) is that science can never prove that a theory is true but only that it is false. That is, advances in our knowledge occur not because we discover truth but because we eliminate falsehood. This means that at any one time, we have two types of theories: those that have been proven false and those that have not *yet* been proven false. If one takes the strict position that one false deduction proves that an entire theory is wrong, then it seems inevitable to us that all theories are false.

We do not view models and theories as true or false but, rather, as better and poorer approximations of reality (or, more accurately, what we think is reality). Hence, the purpose of evaluating a model is not to assess whether it is "true" but, rather, to determine how it could be made better. In the case of the minimodel we have been developing through this appendix, we might find systematic differences between what the model says national defense expenditures should be and what the data say they are, and this might lead us to suspect that one or more of the parameter values (for example, PAR2) should not be the same for all nations. This would lead us to reformulate the model and, with luck, produce a better model. It is an unending process from a logical point of view, since, as with all complex structures, there is always something that should be changed or could be improved.

Putting the Pieces Together

Figure A-1 shows the four activities we have been discussing as steps in a process, and in the best of all worlds, one would progress steadily through them, one after the other, as shown by the black arrows on the left. That is, one would first finish the theoretical work before beginning formalization, with all the necessary assumptions thought out in advance. The formalization process would not introduce any errors of omission or commission in our ideal world, so that one could move on to the simulation phase relatively quickly. In this ideal world, data are abundant, so the assignment of values to some unknowns proceeds without problems, and simulation results are quickly obtained. And in this best of all possible simulator's worlds, the model's behavior is found to be accurate, useful, and relevant, and the entire simulation effort may be declared resoundingly successful.

Needless to say, in the real research world, things seldom, if ever, go so smoothly. For all but the simplest theories, formalization usually reveals ambiguities or missing links in the theoretical structure that require rethinking parts (or all) of the theory and making conceptual changes. Or one may find by formalization that some assumptions are inconsistent with one another, a condition that the human mind can tolerate to an amazing degree but one with which the computer has great difficulty. For that and other reasons, the process of formalizing a theory usually entails at least a partial respecification of the theory,

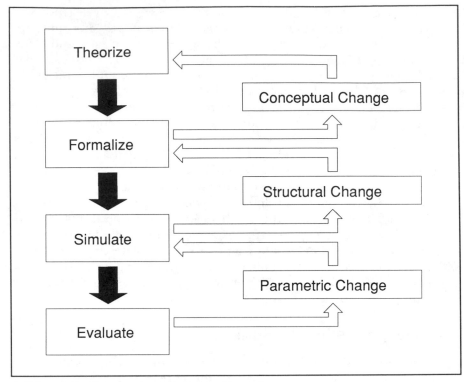

FIGURE A–1   Constructing a Computer Simulation

and it is not unusual for one to have to iterate several times through the conceptual change loop shown in the top right of Figure A-1.

Problems can arise in the simulation phase that make it necessary to move back a step and revise the computer model. One may discover that data needed to estimate a particular parameter do not exist and that to be able to use the inadequate but available data, a structural change is required. Or a run of the computer model may reveal that some condition that should never occur, can occur, and something that should be defined for all cases is not, in fact, defined for all cases. A simple example of this is when we take the ratio of two numbers and do not take into account that the result of this operation is undefined when the second number is 0. In this and many other ways, running a computer model reveals problems in the theory's formalization that dictate structural changes. Deeper analysis of the problem may reveal that the problem lies at the theoretical level rather than in the way it is formalized, in which case one must move back two steps rather than only one.

   Comparing the behavior of a computer model with one's expectations usually reveals ways in which the model deviates from what is expected. Some of these turn out to be genuine discoveries of unanticipated consequences of our original theory, and the generation of these is one of the principal reasons one uses simulation. These "good" anomalies are new knowledge. Unfortunately, close inspection of the surprising results will also reveal that some are due to errors. Eliminating these "bad" anomalies may be achieved by moving back one step and changing the values of one or more parameters, a process sometimes called tuning a model, but it may also turn out that the problem goes deeper. If so, then two or three backward steps may be necessary to deal with the problem.

   If all this leads you to conclude that developing a computer simulation is a great deal of work, you are certainly correct. To do so successfully, one must draw upon the skills of a philosopher, a logician, a mathematician, a statistician, a computer scientist, and an engineer, and combine these with, of course, extensive substantive knowledge of that which is being simulated.

The GLOBUS Model

APPENDIX B

GLOBUS is a computer simulation model of many important macro-political and macroeconomic relationships within and among twenty-five prominent contemporary nations plus a rest-of-world entity. It was designed and is being used to explore alternative solutions to long-term global problems of a political-economic nature. The developers of the model do not consider it a forecasting device per se, since there remain too many important unknowns about the future to permit its unequivocal prediction; rather, they view the model as a laboratory in which experiments about the future can be conducted that, they hope, shed light upon that future. The model is very complex, and in this appendix we can do little more than sketch some of its more salient features; a complete description of the model is to be found in Bremer (1987).

THE GENERAL APPROACH

Since GLOBUS was designed to deal with a variety of problems, including such diverse subjects as East-West political and economic relations, the North-South gap, arms races, domestic political stability, economic growth, demographic developments, and alternative international economic orders, to name just a few, the theory upon which the model rests must also encompass a wide range of phenomena. Since no such theory was at hand, GLOBUS was constructed by synthesizing existing partial theories, and an eclectic strategy of theory construction was followed. Hence, to build GLOBUS, the developers borrowed bits and pieces of theory, chiefly from political science and economics, and integrated them into a comprehensive and coherent whole.

In spite of what may appear to be a patchwork approach, there is a basic theoretical "backbone" in the model, which, like a theme repeated with variations throughout a symphony, is evident in all parts of the model. This is sometimes called the cybernetic theory of behavior. In its most primitive form, this theory states that systems are steered by regulators, and a change in behavior occurs when the system regulator detects an unacceptable deviation between the desired and the actual states of the system. The desired state of the system is either fixed or exogenously determined, whereas the actual state of the system is influenced by exogenous disturbances and the behavior of the regulator itself. Variations are sensed by the regulator through feedback signals that trigger corrective actions. It should be made clear that *exogenous* in this context often does not mean outside of the GLOBUS model but, rather, outside of the local system and with origins elsewhere in the model. In addition, *regulator* does not always imply a regulatory entity but, rather, a regulating mechanism, such as freely varying prices regulate a market economy.

By assembling and linking many servomechanisms, one can construct very complex control systems that exhibit a wide variety of behaviors. Servomechanisms are feedback systems in which a regulator (like an ordinary household thermostat) operates to maintain stability or equilibrium. If, for example, two or more regulators with divergent desires attempt to control the same aspect of system performance, then what appear to be "power struggles" are likely to emerge. Or if such mechanisms are hierarchically linked and the desired states of lower-level regulators are altered by higher-level regulators in the pursuit of higher-level goals, the kind of apparently inconsistent behavior that organizations exhibit can be represented. And, of course, in all but the simplest systems, the regulator attempts to achieve more than one goal, monitors many aspects of system behavior, and has a variety of responses that it can apply when it detects deviations. Combining all those characteristics would produce a system whose behavior would begin to approximate that which we observe in the real world.

In the classic servomechanism, environmental influences may positively or negatively affect the state of the system being regulated. The regulator assesses the gap between current and desired states and initiates corrective action to bring the future state of the system closer to the desired state. In GLOBUS, however, the goals of the system are not fixed but change in response to environmental factors external to a specific system and the historical development of the system itself. Thus, goals may be raised or lowered by outside forces such as higher regulatory mechanisms, or goals may be internally altered through learning,—for example, the persistent failure to achieve a goal creates pressure to lower that goal, whereas success exerts upward pressure on goals. When a time dimension is explicitly introduced, a number of additional features of the GLOBUS version of this mechanism become important—that is, the role of expectations and adjustment speeds. In many places in GLOBUS, the problem that the regulator faces is not where the system is in relation to some goal but knowing in which direction the system is moving and how fast. This information is necessary if the regulator is to anticipate where the system is likely to be in the future and adjust its responses accordingly. Thus, in many parts of GLOBUS, expectations play an essential role, and much behavior is future-oriented rather than merely reactive.

The existence of delays or lags in the processes by which the regulator senses the state of the system, selects responses, and finally brings about a change in the system means that corrective action is not instantaneous. The rate at which the gap between the current (or anticipated) and the desired states of the system is closed is the adjustment speed. As a general rule, an adjustment speed that is too slow tends to produce responses that fail to narrow the gap between desired and actual conditions, while an adjustment speed that is too fast can produce overreaction and cyclical behavior. The GLOBUS model contains many adjustment speeds, and their values are important determinants of the dynamic behavior of the model.

Regulatory processes of this type are to be found throughout GLOBUS. In the domestic economic area, such a mechanism determines the way by which a balance between supply and demand is sought (but rarely achieved) by price adjustments. In the domestic political area, a nation's population is assumed to give or withhold support for a government in response to how well that government meets their changing expectations. In the budget model, one finds many goal-seeking processes; for example, a central element in the setting of desired defense expenditures is the attempt to balance expected threat and support by means of increases or decreases in military spending. In the international economic portion of the model, changes in the level and the direction of trade are assumed to be driven by the differences between nations' desired trade patterns, which change in response to economic and political conditions, and their existing trade patterns. Similarly, in the international political model, foreign policy bureaucracies are seen as setting and pursuing desired relations with other nations by incrementally adjusting current policies.

With so many control processes operating, it might be supposed that the model is normally in a state of equilibrium, but that is not the case. Since the achievement of some goals conflicts with others, actions in one area can adversely disturb equilibria elsewhere; and because feedback-controlled responses are not instantaneous, the normal state of the system is disequilibrium. In the next section, we will see how these general cybernetic principles are manifested in the model.

A GOVERNMENTAL PERSPECTIVE

One way to understand the structure of the GLOBUS model is to consider what the simulated world looks like to one of the twenty-five national governments represented. Figure B-1 offers this perspective and shows the basic control problems that GLOBUS assumes a government confronts. Toward the edges of the diagram are four environments, which are defined by the intersection of the foreign and domestic and political and economic dimensions. Each of the quadrants represents an area in which a government sets goals, monitors developments, and attempts changes. In this figure, the main concerns of a government in each area are shown, as well as the principal policy instrument available to it for steering developments in the relevant area. In general, the goals of government may be summarized as a growing domestic economy, a stable domestic political situation, an advantageous international economic position, and a secure international political environment.

The outermost arrows are intended to show the interconnections between the environments in which a simulated government operates. These interconnections mean that problems in one area may spill over into others and that policies intended to change conditions in a particular area may have unintended and undesirable consequences in another. It is one of the basic assumptions of GLOBUS that these linkages are very important in the long run and not always obvious in the short run.

The two-headed arrows that connect the problem areas with the policy instruments are meant to convey that, as described above, there is a continuous flow of action and information between the two. The observant reader may wonder why there are no arrows linking the four clusters of policy instruments to one another. They are omitted not because the pursuit of policies in one area is completely independent of policies undertaken in other areas but to emphasize our assumption that at this level policies are, at best, only weakly coordinated. In our view, a government is not a unitary, rational actor guided by a single objective function, but a complex organization pursuing a multiplicity of only partly compatible goals by means of routine, but not necessarily optimal, procedures. In such organizations, problem solving tends to be myopic, incremental, and sporadic, and the overall behavior of the organization is only loosely coordinated.

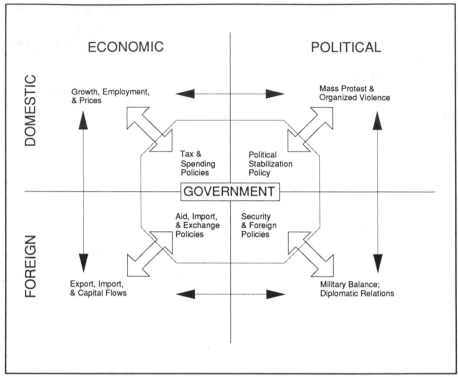

FIGURE B–1   The GLOBUS Structure

The upper left-hand quadrant in Figure B-1 represents the domestic economic area. From a government's perspective, the national economy is part of its environment, and developments there with respect to growth, prices, employment, and so on, directly affect its resource base. Hence, governments attempt to steer, with varying degrees of exactitude and success, these developments by means of their domestic economic policies. In GLOBUS, this principally takes the form of manipulating expenditures and rates of taxation.

The government's domestic political environment is located in the upper right-hand quadrant. The level of support and opposition directed toward the constitutional order and the governing elite changes in response to how satisfied a nation's population is with respect to their living conditions. Intense dissatisfaction may manifest itself in one or both of two ways: mass protest or organized violence. Governments attempt to increase support and reduce opposition indirectly by improving the conditions that are the source of dissatisfaction, but, in addition, they may seek to directly control opposition by repression.

Moving clockwise, the next quadrant represents the government's international political environment. In its quest for security, a government must constantly assess the intentions and the capabilities of other nations and formulate defense and foreign policies aimed at safeguarding and, if possible, extending its influence in the international system. In particular, governments are concerned with threat and hostile military power and seek security by building and maintaining their own military forces.

The lower left-hand quadrant represents a government's international economic environment. Since the national economies are linked to one another in a variety of ways, all governments must monitor and attempt to regulate this interdependence in order to steer their domestic economies. As an example, one could cite the way governments closely watch the national balance-of-payments position and adjust their trade and exchange policies accordingly.

OVERVIEW OF MODEL PARTS

In this section, we will briefly discuss each of the six main parts of GLOBUS, sketching their internal structures and indicating their main interconnections with one another.

Demographic Conditions

The part of the model that determines how nations' populations change through time is very simple. Exogenously set growth rates for total population, labor force, urban population, and various age groups are used to generate changes in the size and the composition of the populations of the twenty-five GLOBUS nations. Since these growth rates are taken from the United Nations' estimates and projections, the "theory" that is embedded in this portion of the model is that which was used by them in preparing these values (United Nations 1982).

Although the demographic part of the model does have an impact on other parts, its own behavior is not conditioned by what occurs in those other areas. The reasons for this are discussed elsewhere (Bremer 1987); here we will merely point out that our relatively short time horizon, to 2010, severely limits the impact that political-economic factors can have on demographic conditions.

Domestic Economic Conditions

The national economies are portrayed as producing, consuming, and exchanging six goods: agricultural goods, primary energy, raw materials, manufactures, armaments, and services. The balancing of supply and demand in each of those six markets is the core mechanism in all twenty-five economies. In contrast to most macroeconomic models, it is not assumed that supply and demand are in equilibrium but, rather, that they *seek* equilibrium. Hence, the theoretical underpinnings of the domestic economic model stem as much from development and disequilibrium economics as from general equilibrium economics.

Three types of economies are distinguished: advanced market, centrally planned, and less developed. These differ from one another structurally and parametrically, with most of the differences represented by very different parameter values for each of the three types. An example of structural differentiation is that active labor and capital markets are to be found in the advanced market economies but not in the centrally planned economies.

In addition to a very complex set of processes internal to the domestic economic area, domestic economic conditions are influenced by developments in three other parts of the model. The demographic model specifies population and labor force, which are partial determinants of consumption and production. The international economic area determines national exports and imports and the feedback effects of domestic prices and exchange rates on the nations' balance-of-payments positions. The government budget portion of the model exerts a strong influence on the domestic economy, chiefly through the size and the nature of government expenditures and taxes. A fourth factor influencing domestic economic conditions would be reductions in economic output by strikes, slowdowns, or sabotage resulting from low political support. This link between domestic political and economic conditions remains to be implemented.

Government Budget

Four main classes of expenditure are distinguished: consumption, which is composed of military and civilian outlays, welfare benefits of several types, investment, and debt management payments. Five revenue streams are identified: indirect taxes, business taxes, personal taxes, welfare contributions, and government profits. The theoretical orientation of this part of the model was greatly influenced by organization theory, and accordingly government is portrayed as being composed of bureaucracies with different goals and interests that compete with one another for resources. The processes by which these divergent demands are reconciled and a desired revenue-expenditure balance achieved form the core of this part of the model.

The decisions concerning spending and taxing are influenced by developments in many other areas of the model. The size and the composition of population affect, for example, the demand for educational outlays. Domestic economic conditions constrain revenues and generate demands for expenditure as, for example, when increasing unemployment requires higher welfare expenditures. International economic relations influence the budgetary behavior of less developed nations through foreign aid receipts, and the balance-of-payments positions of these nations and the centrally planned economies directly influence their degree of fiscal restraint. The amount of hostility and cooperation received from other nations, generated in the international political relations area, affects a government's perception of external threat and military needs. Although our conceptual framework clearly calls for a direct influence of domestic political conditions on government budget decisions, this link is not now operative. However, an indirect link is present, since many of the domestic economic factors that affect political support and opposition are monitored by government.

Domestic Political Conditions

The focus of the domestic political portion of GLOBUS is on how support for and opposition to government varies in response to changing political-economic conditions. Three types of political systems are distinguished: liberal democratic polities, centrist (Eastern European) polities, and traditional or less developed polities. The processes by which support and opposition are generated differ from type to type. Since much of the content of this area was derived from diverse empirical studies, the theoretical foundation of this area is also diverse.

Demographic conditions affect domestic political conditions as the size and the composition of a nation's population place certain demands upon the political system and define the pool of dissidents. Domestic economic conditions influence both support and opposition in direct ways, for a central assumption of this part of the model is that people will withhold support from, and sometimes actually oppose, governments if their economic expectations are not fulfilled. And government expenditures can have a direct effect on support and opposition as people come to expect a certain level of public goods and services. If these expectations are not fulfilled, then support for a government will tend to fall.

International Economic Relations

As we have indicated, the twenty-five GLOBUS nations trade with one another in six commodities. Since trade is also bilateral, the number of economic flows between nations is very large. These are modeled according to a theory first outlined by Armington (1969) whereby goods are distinguished not only by type but also by national origin; thus, agricultural goods from one nation, for example, are not assumed to be a perfect substitute for agricultural goods from another. Since we believe that political considerations and not only price enter into trade decisions, this formulation provided us with an attractive starting point.

The key decisions in this part of the model are how much and from which nations to import, while the flows of exports emerge as a consequence of these import decisions. In both of these decisions, relative prices play a key role such that, for example, nations experiencing rapid inflation find imported goods more attractive than domestically produced goods. In addition, other domestic economic conditions, such as the level of domestic demand, are important determinants of total import demand. The direction of trade is influenced by political factors and supply constraints, in addition to relative prices. By assuming that, ceteris paribus, nations would prefer to import goods from nations with which they have relatively cooperative political relations rather than from those with which they have hostile relations, international political relations are given a direct influence on international economic relations. Foreign aid flows are also represented, and in deciding how much and to which nation to give aid, some governments in GLOBUS directly influence international economic flows as a consequence of budgetary decisions.

International Political Relations

The last main element of GLOBUS is concerned with how nations behave diplomatically toward one another. Bilateral flows of cooperation are distinguished from bilateral flows of hostility, and different determinants are seen as affecting each. The assumption that foreign policy behavior is best viewed as a reaction to the behavior of other nations lies at the core of this part of the model. However, unlike other models of this genre, the degree to which a nation reacts to another's actions is not constant but changes in response to the context of the actions.

The factors that affect the reactivity of one nation to the actions of another are (1) their relative military power, (2) their international economic relations, (3) the overall state of their past relations, and (4) the level of East-West tension. The first two are the means by which the government budget area (through defense expenditure) and international economic area (through bilateral trade flows) influence international political relations.

THE COMPUTER MODEL

Many hard choices are faced in designing and building a computer model that are not directly confronted in other, less rigorous means of representing and manipulating theory. In developing GLOBUS, many design decisions that entailed difficult trade-offs had to be made. Since those have been discussed elsewhere (Bremer 1986), the reasoning behind the major design decisions will not be reviewed here. A detailed description of the structure and functioning of the computer model is to be found in Gruhn (1987).

Although GLOBUS does contain "if-then-else" elements, it relies fundamentally upon numerical calculus rather than logical calculus. The central factors in deciding whether a model should be primarily numerical or primarily logical are the type of questions that the model is supposed to answer and the level of abstraction at which the referent system is represented. Since GLOBUS is intended to investigate long-term developments at a relatively high level of abstraction, the numerical approach is most suitable. If the focus of the model were more short term and much more micro, then an alternative design might have been called for.

More specifically, GLOBUS is dynamic, continuous, and recursive. Taken together, that means that (1) the basic relationships contained in the model describe how the system changes over time, (2) time is assumed to advance continuously rather than in discrete chunks, and (3) the state of the system is dependent upon its past state (that is, simultaneity is not present). System dynamics models are also of this type, and the design of GLOBUS incorporates many of the basic assumptions of this modeling approach, but it should not be considered a system dynamics model per se.[1]

GLOBUS is programmed in FORTRAN V (sometimes referred to as FORTRAN 77), a venerable and widely used computer language. Newer languages such as PASCAL and C incorporate some very desirable features that FORTRAN lacks, although for "number-crunching," FORTRAN is still a very powerful and efficient language. The compelling argument for FORTRAN was its universality and standardization, for whatever its weaknesses, FORTRAN is the closest thing we have to a world computer language.

The simulation runs upon which the analyses reported in this book are based were done using the microcomputer version of the model, *Micro GLOBUS* (Bremer and Gruhn, 1988). This adaptation of the model is designed for DOS, IBM-compatible machines, and it is available to all interested researchers.[2]

---

[1] A discussion of the mathematical aspects of the GLOBUS model is to be found in Rindfuβ (1987).

[2] Those interested in acquiring the model should write to *edition sigma*, Mittenwalder Str. 48, 1000 Berlin 61, Federal Republic of Germany. The cost of the model and user's manual is $125 U.S. (or DM 199) plus shipping and handling charges.

GLOBUS STUDIES TO DATE

A significant number of studies have been completed using the GLOBUS model, and some of the questions these investigations have addressed are as follows:

> Under what conditions can foreign aid accelerate development in the Third World? (Hughes 1987)

> What might be the political effects of "fiscal responsibility" in Western nations? (Eberwein 1987)

> What are the socioeconomic implications of alternative assumptions about long-term population growth? (Bremer 1987)

> How might efforts on the part of Western governments to balance their budgets affect the long-term growth of government in those nations? (Cusack 1987)

> Would the granting of special trade concessions by nations of the West to nations of the South facilitate development, and who would bear the cost of these? (Pollins and Brecke 1987)

> What might be the implications of the adoption of a "hard-line" foreign policy by the United States toward the Soviet Union over the long run? (Smith 1987a)

> Can a combination of arms reduction measures in the North and increased aid flows to the South reduce both East-West tension and the North-South gap? (Bremer and Hughes 1987)

> Does the global market economy operate in such a way that the terms of trade for developing nations almost inevitably decline over time? (Pollins 1987)

> What could be the impact of different long-range patterns of taxation and defense spending in major Western industrialized nations? (Cusack and Hughes 1986)

> How beneficial would be the adoption of a policy by the West to give special preference to imports from the South? (Pollins 1986)

> Who is likely to gain and who is likely to lose from the imposition of protectionist measures by nations of the West? (Brecke 1985)

> What are the possible national and international long-term consequences of alternative Western defense postures? (Cusack 1984)

References

ADELMAN, IRMA, and HOLLIS B. CHENERY. 1966. Foreign Aid and Economic Development: The Case of Greece. *Review of Economics and Statistics* 48 (February): 1–19.

ADELMAN, IRMA, and SHERMAN ROBINSON. 1978. *Income Distribution Policy in Developing Countries*. Oxford: Oxford University Press.

ALKER, HAYWARD R., JR., and BRUCE M. RUSSETT. 1964. Multifactor Explanations of Social Change. In *World Handbook of Political and Social Indicators*, ed. Bruce M. Russett et al. New Haven: Yale University Press, pp. 311–321.

ALLAN, PIERRE, and URS LUTERBACHER. 1983. The Future of East-West Relations: A Computer Simulation of Five Scenarios. In *East-West Relations*, vol. 2, ed. Daniel Frei and Dieter Ruloff. Cambridge, Mass.: Oelgeschlager, Gunn, and Hain Publishers, pp. 285–318.

ARMINGTON, PAUL S. 1969. A Theory for the Demand for Products Distinguished by Place of Production. *International Monetary Fund Staff Papers* 16 (1): 159–176.

ARMS CONTROL AND DISARMAMENT AGENCY [ACDA]. 1987. *World Military Expenditures and Arms Transfers 1986*. Washington, D.C.: USGPO.

ARMS CONTROL AND DISARMAMENT AGENCY [ACDA]. 1988. *World Military Expenditures and Arms Transfers 1987*. Washington, D.C.: USGPO.

ASHLEY, RICHARD K. 1980. *The Political Economy of War and Peace*. London and New York: Frances Pinter and Nichols Publishing.

BALL, NICOLE. 1983. Defense and Development: A Critique of the Benoit Study. *Economic Development and Cultural Change* 31 (3): 507–524.

BARAN, PAUL A., and PAUL M. SWEEZY. 1968. *Monopoly Capital: An Essay on the American Economy and Social Order*. New York: Modern Reader Paperbacks.

BAUER, PETER, and BASIL YAMEY. 1984. Adverse Repercussions of Aid. In *Leading Issues in Economic Development*, 4th ed., ed. Gerald M. Meier. New York: Oxford University Press, pp. 293–297

BECKER, ABRAHAM S. 1981. *The Burden of Soviet Defense: A Political-Economic Essay*. Santa Monica, Calif.: Rand Corporation (October), R-2752-AF.

BECKER, ABRAHAM S. 1982. *Guns, Butter and Tools: Tradeoffs in Soviet Resource Allocation*. Santa Monica, Calif.: Rand Corporation (October), P-6816.

BECKER, ABRAHAM S. 1983. *Sitting on Bayonets? The Soviet Defense Burden and Moscow's Economic Dilemma*. Santa Monica, Calif.: Rand Corporation (September), P-6908.

BEER, FRANCIS A. 1981. *Peace Against War.* San Francisco: W. H. Freeman & Company Publishers.

BENOIT, EMILE. 1973. *Defense and Economic Growth in Developing Countries.* Lexington, Mass.: Lexington Books.

BIRD, GRAHAM. 1984. Balance of Payments Policy. In The Quest for Economic Stabilisation, ed. Tony Killick. London: Heinemann Educational Books, pp. 86–127.

BLAKE, DAVID H., and ROBERT S. WALTERS. 1987. *The Politics of Global Economic Relations,* 3rd ed. Englewood Cliffs, N.J.: Prentice-Hall.

BOULDING, KENNETH, ed. 1970. *Peace and the War Industry.* Chicago: Aldine.

BRANDT, WILLY. 1986. *World Armament and World Hunger.* London: Victor Gollancz.

BRANDT COMMISSION (Independent Commission on International Development). 1980. *North-South: A Program for Survival.* Cambridge, Mass.: MIT Press.

BRANDT COMMISSION (Independent Commission on International Development). 1981. *The Brandt Commission Papers.* Geneva: Independent Bureau for International Development Issues.

BRANDT COMMISSION (Independent Commission on International Development). 1983. *Common Crisis.* Cambridge, Mass.: MIT Press.

BRAUDEL, FERMAND. 1979. *The Perspective of the World.* New York: Harper & Row, Pub.

BRECKE, PETER K. 1985. Who Wins and Who Loses from Protectionism. Wissenschaftszentrum Berlin, IIVG/dp 85–103.

BREMER, STUART A. 1980. National Capabilities and War Proneness. In *The Correlates of War, II,* ed. J. David Singer. New York: Free Press, pp. 57–82.

BREMER, STUART A. 1986. Ten "Global" Modeling Issues: Experiences Gained from GLOBUS. In *Im Spannungsfeld von Wirtschaft, Technik, und Politik,* ed. Rolf Kappel. Munich: Guenter Olzog Verlag, pp. 17–31.

BREMER, STUART A., ed. 1987. *The GLOBUS Model: Computer Simulation of Worldwide Political and Economic Developments.* Frankfurt am Main and Boulder, Colo.: Campus Verlag and Westview Press.

BREMER, STUART A., and WALTER L. GRUHN. 1988. *Micro GLOBUS.* Berlin: Edition Sigma.

BREMER, STUART A., and BARRY B. HUGHES. 1987. Reducing East-West Conflict and the North-South Gap. Paper presented at the 1987 American Political Science Association meetings, September, in Chicago.

BROWN, SEYOM. 1988. *New Forces, Old Forces, and the Future of World Politics.* Glenview, Ill.: Scott, Foresman.

BUENO DE MESQUITA, BRUCE. 1980. Theories of Conflict: An Analysis and an Appraisal. In *Handbook of Political Conflict,* ed. Ted Robert Gurr. New York: Free Press, pp. 361–398.

CAMPBELL, DONALD T. 1969. Reforms as Experiments. *American Psychologist* 24 (April): 409–429.

CAPUTO, DAVID A. 1975. New Perspectives on the Public Policy Implications of Defense and Welfare Expenditures in Four Modern Democracies: 1950–1970. *Policy Sciences* 6:423–446.

CASSEN, ROBERT, and ASSOCIATES. 1986. *Does Aid Work?* Oxford: Clarendon Press.

CHAN, STEVE. 1985. The Impact of Defense Spending on Economic Performance: A Survey of Evidence and Problems. *Orbis* 29 (2): 403–434.

CHAN, STEVE. 1987. Military Expenditures and Economic Performance, in the United States Disarmament Agency. *World Military Expenditures and Arms Transfers 1986* (April), pp. 29–47.

CHOUCRI, NAZLI, and ROBERT C. NORTH. 1975. *Nations in Conflict: National Growth and International Violence.* San Francisco: W. H. Freeman & Company Publishers.

CLAYTON, JAMES L., ed. 1970. *The Economic Impact of the Cold War: Sources and Readings.* New York: Harcourt Brace Jovanovich.

CNUDDE, CHARLES, and DEANE E. NEUBAUER, eds. 1969. *Empirical Democratic Theory.* Chicago: Markham Publishing.

COLLINS, JOHN M. 1985. *U.S.-Soviet Military Balance 1980–1985.* Washington, D.C.: Pergamon-Brassey's.

CUSACK, THOMAS R. 1987. Government Budget Processes. In *The GLOBUS Model,* ed. Stuart A. Bremer, pp. 325–458.

CUSACK, THOMAS R. 1984. One Problem, Three Solutions: A Simulation Analysis of Alternative Western Defense Policy Options. IIVG discussion paper, IIVG/dp 84–109, Wissenschaftszentrum Berlin.

CUSACK, THOMAS R. 1982. The Sinews of Power: Labor and Capital in the Production of National Military Force Capability. IIVG discussion paper, IIVG/dp 82–106, Wissenschaftszentrum Berlin.

CUSACK, THOMAS R., and BARRY B. HUGHES. 1986. Using GLOBUS to Explore Alternative Taxation and Security Policies in the West. In *Persistent Patterns and Emergent Structures in a Waning Century*, ed. Margaret P. Karns. New York: Praeger, pp. 237–272.

DACY, DOUGLAS C. 1975. Foreign Aid, Government Consumption, Saving and Growth in Less-Developed Countries. *Economic Journal* 7 (339): 548–561.

DAVIES, JAMES C. 1962. Toward a Theory of Revolution. *American Sociological Review* 27 (February): 5–19.

DAVIES, JAMES C. 1969. The J-Curve of Rising and Declining Satisfactions as a Cause of Some Great Revolutions and a Contained Rebellion. In *Violence in America: Historical and Comparative Perspectives*, vol. 1, A Staff Report to the National Commission on the Causes and Prevention of Violence, June 1969, ed. Hugh Davis Graham and Ted Robert Gurr. New York: Praeger, pp. 547–575.

DAVIES, JAMES C., ed. 1971. *When Men Revolt and Why*. New York: Free Press.

DEGER, SAADET, and RONALD P. SMITH. 1983. Military Expenditure and Growth in Less Developed Countries. *Journal of Conflict Resolution* 27 (June): 335–353.

DERVIS, KEMAL, JAIME DE MELO, and SHERMAN ROBINSON. 1982. *General Equilibrium Models for Development Policy*. Cambridge: Cambridge University Press.

DE TOCQUEVILLE, ALEXIS. 1945. *Democracy in America*. New York: Vintage Books.

DEVELOPMENT COMMITTEE. 1986. *Aid for Development: The Key Issues*. Washington, D.C.: The World Bank and IMF.

DIEHL, PAUL F. 1983. Arms Races and the Outbreak of War, 1816–1980. Ph.D. diss., Political Science, University of Michigan.

DUCHIN, FAYE. 1983. Economic Consequences of Military Spending. *Journal of Economic Issues* 17 (2): 543–553.

EASTON, DAVID. 1975. A Re-Assessment of the Concept of Political Support. *British Journal of Political Science* 5 (3): 435–457.

EBERWEIN, WOLF-DIETER. 1982. The Seduction of Power: Serious International Disputes and the Power Status of Nations, 1900–1976. *International Interactions* 9 (1): 57–74.

EBERWEIN, WOLF-DIETER. 1987. Domestic Political Processes. In *The GLOBUS Model*, ed. Stuart A. Bremer, pp. 159–282.

FEIERABEND, IVO K., ROSALIND L. FEIERABEND, and BETTY A. NESVOLD. 1969. Social Change and Political Violence: Cross National Patterns. In *Violence in America: Historical and Comparative Perspectives*, ed. Hugh Davis Graham and Ted Robert Gurr. New York: Praeger, pp. 107–124.

FEIS, HERBERT. 1970. *From Trust to Terror: The Onset of the Cold War 1945–1950*. New York: W. W. Norton & Co., Inc.

FISCHER, GREGORY W., and MARK S. KAMLET. 1984. Exploring Presidential Priorities: The Competing Aspiration Levels Model of Macrobudgetary Decision-Making. *American Political Science Review* 78:356–371.

FLANIGAN, WILLIAM H., and EDWIN FOGELMAN. 1970. Patterns of Political Violence in Comparative Historical Perspective. *Comparative Politics* 3 (1): 1–20.

FREEMAN, CHRISTOPHER, JOHN CLARK, and LUC SVETE. 1982. *Unemployment and Technical Innovation*. Westport, Conn.: Greenwood Press.

GHOSH, PRADIP K., ed. 1984. *Foreign Aid and Third World Development*. Westport, Conn.: Greenwood Press.

GILPIN, ROBERT. 1981. *War and Change in World Politics*. Cambridge: Cambridge University Press.

GRIFFIN, K. B., and J. L. ENOS. 1970. Foreign Assistance: Objectives and Consequences. *Economic Development and Cultural Change* 18:313–337.

GRUHN, WALTER L. 1987. The GLOBUS Simulation Package. In *The GLOBUS Model*, ed. Stuart A. Bremer, pp. 777–802.

GUPTA, DIPAK K., and YIANNIS P. VENIERIS. 1981. Introducing New Dimensions in Macro Models: The Sociopolitical and Institutional Environments. *Economic Development and Cultural Change* 29:31–58.

GURR, TED ROBERT. 1970. *Why Men Rebel*. Princeton: Princeton University Press.

HANSEN, ROGER D. 1982. Power, Purpose, and Proportion: U.S. Foreign Policy in the 1980s. In *U.S. Foreign Policy and the Third World: Agenda 1982*, ed. Roger D. Hansen. New York: Praeger, pp. 3–46.

HANSEN, ROGER D., and CONTRIBUTORS. 1982. *U.S. Foreign Policy and the Third World: Agenda 1982*. New York: Praeger.

HAYTER, TERESA, and CATHARINE WATSON. 1985. *Aid: Rhetoric and Reality*. London: Pluto Press.

HIBBS, DOUGLAS A. 1973. *Mass Political Violence*. New York: Wiley-Interscience.

HICKMAN, BERT G. 1983. Exchange Rates in Project LINK. In *Exchange Rates in Multicountry Economic Models*, ed. Paul De Gauwe and Theo Peeters. London: Macmillan, pp. 103–133.

HIRSCH, FRED. 1977. *Social Limits to Growth*. London: Routledge & Kegan Paul.

HOLDREN, JOHN P. 1986. The Dynamics of the Nuclear Arms Race: History, Status and Prospects. In *Nuclear Weapons and the Future of Humanity*, ed. Avner Cohen and Steven Lee. Totowa, N.J.: Rowman and Allanheld, pp. 41–84.

HOLSTI, K. J. 1975. Underdevelopment and the "Gap" Theory of International Conflict. *American Political Science Review* 69 (3): 827–839.

HOROWITZ, DAVID. 1971. *The Free World Colossus*. New York: Hill & Wang.

HUGHES, BARRY B. 1980. *World Modeling: The Mesarovic-Pestel World Model in the Context of Its Contemporaries*. Lexington, Mass.: Lexington Books.

HUGHES, BARRY B. 1985a. *World Futures*. Baltimore: Johns Hopkins University Press.

HUGHES, BARRY B. 1985b. The Impact of the First Oil Shock on Domestic and International Conflict. In *Rhythms in Politics and Economics*, ed. Paul M. Johnson and William R. Thompson. New York: Praeger, pp. 128–151.

HUGHES, BARRY B. 1985c. World Models: The Bases of Difference. *International Studies Quarterly* 29 (1): 77–101.

HUGHES, BARRY B. 1987. Domestic Economic Processes. In *The GLOBUS Model*, ed. Stuart A. Bremer, pp. 39–158.

HUNTINGTON, SAMUEL P. 1985. Will More Countries Become Democratic? In *Global Dilemmas*, ed. Samuel P. Huntington and Joseph S. Nye. New York: University Press of America, pp. 253–279.

IKRAM, KHALID. 1980. *Egypt: Economic Management in a Period of Transition*. Baltimore: Johns Hopkins University Press.

INTER-AMERICAN DEVELOPMENT BANK [IDB]. 1987. *Economic and Social Progress in Latin America*. Washington, D.C.: IDB.

INTERNATIONAL INSTITUTE FOR STRATEGIC STUDIES [IISS]. 1987. *The Military Balance 1987–1988*. London: IIES.

INTERNATIONAL INSTITUTE FOR STRATEGIC STUDIES [IISS]. 1988. *The Military Balance 1988–1989*. London: IIES.

INTRILIGATOR, MICHAEL D., and DAGOBERT L. BRITO. 1984. Can Arms Races Lead to the Outbreak of War? *Journal of Conflict Resolution* 28 (1): 63–84.

INTRILIGATOR, MICHAEL D., and DAGOBERT L. BRITO. 1986. Mayer's Alternative to the I-B Model. *Journal of Conflict Resolution* 30 (1): 29–31.

KALDOR, MARY. 1986. The Military in Third World Development. In *Disarmament and World Development*, 2nd ed., ed. MacGraham, Richard Jolly, and Chris Smith. Oxford: Pergamon Press, pp. 71–100.

KENNEDY, PAUL. 1983. *Strategy and Diplomacy 1870–1945*. London: George Allen and Unwin.

KENNEDY, PAUL. 1988. *The Rise and Fall of Great Powers: Economic Change and Military Conflict from 1500 to 2000*. New York: Random House.

KINDLEBERGER, CHARLES. 1973. *The World in Depression 1929–1939*. Berkeley and Los Angeles: University of California Press.

KINDLEBERGER, CHARLES P., and BRUCE HERRICK, eds. 1977. *Economic Development*, 3rd ed. Tokyo: McGraw-Hill Kogakusha.

KOLKO, GABRIEL. 1972. *The Limits of Power*. New York: Harper & Row, Pub.

KRASNER, STEPHEN D. 1976. State Power and the Structure of International Trade. *World Politics* 28 (3): 317–347.

KRUEGER, ANNE O. 1979. *The Development Role of the Foreign Sector and Aid.* Cambridge: Harvard University Press.

LAIDLER, DAVID. 1984. The Buffer Stock Notion in Monetary Economics. *Economic Journal* (Suppl) 94: 17–34.

LAKE, DAVID A. 1983. International Economic Structures and American Foreign Economic Policy, 1887–1934. *World Politics* 35 (4): 517–543.

LANDAU, DANIEL L. 1986. Government and Economic Growth in the Less Developed Countries: An Empirical Study for 1960–1980. *Economic Development and Cultural Change* 35 (1): 35–76.

LEBEDEV, N. I. 1976. *A New Stage in International Relations.* Elmsford, N.Y.: Pergamon Press.

LEONTIEF, WASSILY, and FAYE DUCHIN. 1983. *Military Spending: Facts and Figures, Worldwide Implications and Future Outlook.* New York: Oxford University Press.

LEONTIEF, WASSILY, ALISON MORGAN, KAREN POLENSKE, DAVID SIMPSON, and EDWARD TOWER. 1965. The Economic Impact—Industrial and Regional—of an Arms Cut. *Review of Economics and Statistics* 47 (3): 217–240.

LEWIN, LEONARD C., ed. 1967. *Report from Iron Mountain on the Possibility and Desirability of Peace.* New York: Dell Pub. Co., Inc.

LEWIS, JOHN P. 1983. Can We Escape the Path of Mutual Injury? In *U.S. Foreign Policy and the Third World: Agenda 1983,* ed. John P. Lewis and Valeriana Kallab. New York: Praeger, pp. 7–48.

LIPSET, SEYMOUR MARTIN. 1959. Some Social Requisites of Democracy: Economic Development and Political Legitimacy. *American Political Science Review* 53 (March): 69–105.

MACGRAHAM, RICHARD JOLLY, and CHRIS SMITH, eds. 1986. *Disarmament and World Development,* 2nd ed. Oxford: Pergamon Press.

MCNEILL, WILLIAM H. 1982. *The Pursuit of Power.* Chicago: University of Chicago Press.

MADDISON, ANGUS. 1987. Growth and Slowdown in Advanced Capitalist Economies. *Journal of Economic Literature* 25 (June): 649–698.

MAGDOFF, HARRY. 1969. *The Age of Imperialism: The Economics of U.S. Foreign Policy.* New York: Monthly Review.

MARSDEN, KEITH, and ALAN ROE. 1983. The Political Economy of Foreign Aid: A World Bank Perspective. *Labour and Society* 8 (1): 3–12.

MAYER, THOMAS F. 1986. Arms Races and War Initiation: Some Alternatives to the Intriligator-Brito Model. *Journal of Conflict Resolution* 30 (1): 3–28.

MAXWELL, S. J., and H. W. SINGER. 1979. Food Aid to Developing Countries: A Survey. *World Development* 7:225–247.

MEADOWS, DONNELA H., JOHN M. RICHARDSON, JR., and GERHART BRUCKMANN. 1982. *Groping in the Dark.* New York: John Wiley.

MERCENIER, JEAN, and JEAN WAELBROECK. 1984. The Sensitivity of Developing Countries to External Shocks in an Interdependent World. *Journal of Policy Modeling* 6 (2): 209–235.

MIKESELL, RAYMOND F. 1983. *The Economics of Foreign Aid and Self-Sustaining Development.* Boulder, Colo.: Westview Press.

MODELSKI, GEORGE. 1978. The Long-Cycle of Global Politics and the Nation-State. *Comparative Studies in Society and History* 20 (2): 214–235.

MOON, BRUCE. 1987. Political Economy and Political Change in the Evolution of North-South Relations. In *Political Change and Foreign Policies,* ed. Gavin Boyd and Gerald W. Hopple. London: Frances Pinter, pp. 225–250.

MOSLEY, HUGH G. 1985. *The Arms Race: Economic and Social Consequences.* Lexington, Mass.: Lexington Books.

NADIRI, M. ISHAQ. 1972. International Studies of Factor Inputs and Total Factor Productivity: A Brief Survey. *Income and Wealth* (Series H) 2: 129–154.

NINCIC, MIROSLAV, and THOMAS R. CUSACK. 1979. The Political Economy of U.S. Military Spending. *Journal of Peace Research* 16 (2): 101–115.

NOEL-BAKER, PHILIP. 1958. *The Arms Race: A Programme for World Disarmament.* London: John Calder.

OLSON, MANCUR. 1971. Rapid Growth as a Destabilizing Force. In *When Men Revolt and Why*, ed. James C. Davies. New York: Free Press, pp. 215–227. Originally published in *Journal of Economic History* 23 (December 1963): 529–552.

OLSON, MANCUR, and RICHARD ZECKHAUSER. 1966. An Economic Theory of Alliances. *Review of Economics and Statistics* 46:266–279.

ORGANIZATION FOR ECONOMIC COOPERATION AND DEVELOPMENT [OECD]. 1983. *OECD INTERLINK System*. Paris: OECD.

ORGANSKI, A.F.K. 1968. *World Politics*. New York: Knopf.

PALME COMMISSION (The Independent Commission on Disarmament and Security Issues). 1982. *Common Security*. New York: Simon & Schuster.

PAPANEK, G. F. 1972. The Effects of Aid and Other Resource Transfers on Savings and Growth in Less Developed Countries. *Economic Journal* 82:934–951.

PAPANAK, G. F. 1973. Aid, Foreign Private Investment, Saving and Growth in Less Developed Countries. *Journal of Political Economy* 81:120–130.

PAPANEK, G. F. 1983. Aid, Growth and Equity in Southern Asia. In *Poverty and Aid*, ed. John R. Parkinson. New York: St. Martin's Press, pp. 169–182.

PARKINSON, JOHN RICHARD, ed. 1983. *Poverty and Aid*. New York: St. Martin's Press.

PARVIN, MANOUCHER, 1973. Economic Determinants of Political Unrest. *Journal of Conflict Resolution* 17 (June): 271–296.

PEARSON, LESTER B. 1969. *Partners for Development: Report of the Commission on International Development*. New York: Praeger.

POLLINS, BRIAN M. 1986. Assessing the Political and Economic Effects of Protection against Third World Exports. Wissenschaftszentrum Berlin: FGG/dp 86-1.

POLLINS, BRIAN M. 1987. International Power and Unequal Exchange. Mershon Center, Ohio State University, Informal papers.

POLLINS, BRIAN M., and PETER K. BRECKE. 1987. International Economic Processes. In *The GLOBUS Model*, ed. Stuart A. Bremer, pp. 459–567.

PORTER, RICHARD C., and SUSAN I. RANNEY. 1982. An Eclectic Model of Recent LDC Macroeconomic Policy Analysis. *World Development* 10 (9): 751–766.

PYE, LUCIEN W. 1964. Armies in the Process of Political Modernization. In *The Military and Society in Latin America*, ed. J. J. Johnson. Stanford: Stanford University Press.

RICHARDSON, JOHN M., JR. 1987. Modeling Domestic Violence: Mexico and Argentina. Paper presented at the annual meeting of the American Political Science Association, September, in Chicago.

RICHARDSON, LEWIS F. 1960. *Arms and Insecurity: A Mathematical Study of the Causes and Origins of War*. New York: Quadrangle/ The N.Y. Times.

RIKER, WILLIAM H. 1962. *The Theory of Political Coalitions*. New Haven: Yale University Press.

RINDFUβ, PETER. 1987. Mathematical Aspects of GLOBUS. In *The GLOBUS Model*, ed. Stuart A. Bremer, pp. 803–819.

RUMMEL, RUDOLPH J. 1963. The Dimensions of Conflict Behavior within and between Nations. *General Systems Yearbook* 8:1–50.

RUSSETT, BRUCE M. 1970. *What Price Vigilance?* New Haven: Yale University Press.

RUSSETT, BRUCE M. 1982. Defense Expenditures and National Well-Being. *American Political Science Review* 73 (4): 767–778.

RUSSETT, BRUCE M. 1983a. *The Prisoners of Insecurity*. San Francisco: W. H. Freeman & Company Publishers.

RUSSETT, BRUCE M. 1983b. Prosperity and Peace. *International Studies Quarterly* 27 (December): 381–387.

SALMON, MARK. 1982. Error Correction Mechanisms. *Economic Journal* 92:615–629.

SIEGMANN, HEINRICH. 1987. *World Modeling*. Paris: Bureau of Studies and Programing, UNESCO.

SINGER, J. DAVID, and ASSOCIATES. 1979. *Explaining War: Selected Papers from the Correlates of War Project*. Beverly Hills, Calif.: Sage Publications, Inc.

SINGER, J. DAVID, ed. 1980. *The Correlates of War: II*. New York: Free Press.

SIVARD, RUTH LEGER. 1985. *World Military and Social Expenditures 1985*. Washington, D.C.: World Priorities (Box 25140).

SIVARD, RUTH LEGER. 1986. *World Military and Social Expenditures 1986*. Washington, D.C.: World Priorities (Box 25140).

SIVARD, RUTH LEGER. 1987. *World Military and Social Expenditures 1987.* Washington, D.C.: World Priorities (Box 25140).

SMITH, DALE L. 1987a. International Political Processes. In *The GLOBUS Model,* ed. Stuart A. Bremer, pp. 569–721.

SMITH, DALE L. 1987b. Linking the Foreign Policy Process to International Action: A Formal and Empirical Analysis of Policy Dynamics. Ph.D. diss., Political Science, MIT.

SMITH, RONALD P. 1977. Military Expenditure and Capitalism. *Cambridge Journal of Economics* (1):61–76.

SMITH, RONALD P. 1980. Military Expenditure and Investment in OECD Countries, 1954–1973. *Journal of Comparative Economics* 4:19–32.

SMITH, THERESA CLAIR. 1980. Arms Race Instability and War. *Journal of Conflict Resolution* 24 (2): 253–284.

SMITH, THERESA CLAIR. 1982. Trojan Peace: Some Deterrence Propositions Tested. *Monograph Series in World Affairs,* vol. 19, book 2. Denver: Graduate School of International Studies.

SPERO, JOAN. 1985. *The Politics of International Economic Relations,* 3rd. ed. New York: St. Martin's Press.

TANTER, RAYMOND, and MANUS MIDLARSKY. 1967. A Theory of Revolution. *Journal of Conflict Resolution* 11 (3): 264–280.

TAYLOR, LANCE. 1979. *Macro Models for Developing Countries.* New York: McGraw-Hill.

THORSSON, INGA. 1976. Arms Reduction. In *Reshaping the International Order,* Jan Tinbergen, coordinator. New York: Dutton, pp. 295–304.

UNITED NATIONS [U.N.]. 1985. *The United Nations and Disarmament: 1945–1985.* New York: United Nations.

WAGNER, A. 1890. Finanzwissenschaft. Partly reproduced in *Classics in the Theory of Public Finance* (1953), ed. R. A. Musgrave and A. T. Peacock. London: Macmillan, pp. 1–15.

WALLACE, MICHAEL D. 1979. Arms Races and Escalation: Some New Evidence. *Journal of Conflict Resolution* 23 (1): 3–16.

WALLACE, MICHAEL D. 1980. Some Persisting Findings: A Reply to Professor Weede. *Journal of Conflict Resolution* 24 (2): 289–292.

WALLACE, MICHAEL D. 1982. Armaments and Escalation: Two Competing Hypotheses. *International Studies Quarterly* 26 (1): 37–56.

WALLENSTEEN, PETER, JOHAN GALTUNG, and CARLOS PORTALES, eds. 1985. *Global Militarization.* Boulder, Colo.: Westview Press.

WALTZ, KENNETH. 1959. *Man, the State and War.* New York: Columbia University Press.

WARD, MICHAEL DON, and HAROLD GUETZKOW. 1979. Toward Integrated Global Models: From Economic Engineering to Social Science Methodology. *Journal of Policy Modeling* 1 (3): 445–464.

WEEDE, ERICH. 1970. Conflict Behavior of Nation States. *Journal of Peace Research* 7:229–235.

WEEDE, ERICH. 1980. Arms Races and Escalation: Some Persisting Doubts. *Journal of Conflict Resolution* 24 (2): 285–287.

WEISSKOPF, THOMAS E. 1972. The Impact of Foreign Capital Inflow on Domestic Savings in Underdeveloped Countries. *Journal of International Economics* 2:25–38.

WEISSKOPF, THOMAS E. 1978. Imperialism and the Economic Development of the Third World. In *The Capitalist System,* ed. Richard C. Edwards, Michael Reich, and Thomas E. Weisskopf. Englewood Cliffs, N.J.: Prentice-Hall, pp. 499–514.

WEISSMAN, STEPHEN R., ed. 1975. *The Trojan Horse: A Radical Look at Foreign Aid.* Palo Alto, Calif.: Ramparts Press.

WHALLEY, JOHN. 1984. The North-South Debate and the Terms of Trade: An Applied Equilibrium Approach. *Review of Economics and Statistics* 66 (2): 224–234.

WIJNBERGEN, S. V. 1986. Macroeconomic Aspects of the Effectiveness of Foreign Aid: On the Two-Gap Model, Home Goods Disequilibrium and Real Exchange Rate Misalignment. *Journal of International Economics* 21:123–136.

WILLIAMS, WILLIAM APPLEMAN. 1959. *The Tragedy of American Diplomacy.* New York: Dell Pub. Co., Inc.

ZIMMERMANN, EKKART. 1983. *Political Violence, Crises and Revolutions: Theories and Research.* Boston: Hall.

Index